the nourished kitchen

the nourished kitchen

Farm-to-Table

recipes for the

Traditional Foods Lifestyle

Featuring Bone Broths, Fermented Vegetables,
Grass-Fed Meats, Wholesome Fats,
Raw Dairy, and Kombuchas

Jennifer McGruther

TEN SPEED PRESS
Berkeley

contents

introduction

"Everyone had a garden back then; you just couldn't get by without it. We fried our dinner in lard, and sauerkraut got us through the winter," Trudy explained, answering a question about how the old-timers survived in the rough-and-tumble Colorado mining community of Crested Butte long before the roads were paved and imported, packaged foods traveled up the winding mountain passes in eighteen-wheel trucks to line the shelves of our grocery store.

Trudy, you see, is an old-timer. She grew up when convenience foods and long-traveled fruit and vegetables simply couldn't be found. That time lingered in the isolated town of Crested Butte, where I make my home, longer than it did in most American communities. Here, seasonal vegetables straight from the garden filled the dinner table, along with whole milk and butter from the local creamery, and locally produced meat and lard. In the fall, plenty of sauerkraut was put up to last until late spring lest bellies go hungry.

These foods—meat loaf and liver, whole raw milk and just-gathered eggs, sourdough bread and soaked oatmeal porridge—nourished generation after generation of healthy people the world over until the global food supply began to change slowly but dramatically at the dawn of the Industrial Revolution of the nineteenth century and again after the Green Revolution of the mid-twentieth century.

A Traditional Foods Movement

Traditional foods are the foods of our great-great grandmothers—the foods of gardens and of farms. They represent a system of balance, emphasizing the value of meat and milk, grain and bean, vegetables and fruits.

There is a movement afoot to restore this way of eating. The movement honors the connection between the foods that we eat, how we prepare these foods, and where they come from. In this way, the traditional foods movement celebrates the connection between the farm that produces the food, the cook who prepares it, and the individuals who eat it. Traditional foods is a system of connection, emphasizing support for time-honored ways in farming, cooking, and eating, and finding a place for fat and lean, animal and vegetable, raw and cooked.

Where other diets and philosophies of eating emphasize good and bad, black and white, a message of balance exists within the traditional foods movement. Unlike vegan and vegetarian diets, which restrict animal foods, the traditional foods movement emphasizes their importance while encouraging the purchase of locally produced meats, milks, cheeses, and fats from grass-fed and pasture-raised animals. Where the Paleo diet restricts grain, pulses, and dairy, the traditional foods movement embraces them, focusing not only on how the food is produced, but also on how it is prepared to maximize the nutrients it contains. While the raw foods movement restricts cooked foods, the traditional foods movement embraces them, honoring the place of cooking as one of balance in partnership with raw foods, and fermented foods, too.

Emphasizing whole and minimally processed foods, the traditional foods movement calls you back to the kitchen, to real home cooking, and offers you an opportunity to weave the connections between the food on your table, the time you take to prepare it, and the farms that produce it.

Weston A. Price, DDS

Weston Price, a native of Canada, practiced dentistry in Cleveland, Ohio, during the early part of the twentieth century. There he witnessed firsthand the introduction of processed foods to the American diet and the damage they wrought upon the health of the public, and of children in particular. Committed to finding the cause of rampant tooth decay, malformations of the palate, and other health concerns he saw in his practice, Dr. Price embarked upon several journeys that led him to isolated regions of the world where people still relied on their native diets of traditionally prepared, local, unprocessed foods. He recorded the foods people consumed and how they were not only produced on the farm, but also prepared in the kitchen, taking the time to analyze them for nutrient content.

While the traditional diets of the peoples he studied differed dramatically based on the local availability of foods, they all bore striking similarities. The people who still ate their traditional foods exhibited exemplary health, while those who abandoned tradition for modern, processed foods suffered. Healthy people consumed unrefined, unprocessed foods. Their diets comprised foods from both animals and plants, including vitamin-rich animal fats, mineral-rich broths, and liver and organ meats, as well as other nutrient-dense foods. Their diets were considerably richer in fat-soluble vitamins and minerals than those people who instead relied on modern, processed foods like white sugar, white flour, refined soy products, and vegetable oils. His work, championed by the Weston A. Price Foundation and the Price-Pottenger Nutrition Foundation, emphasizes the importance of a balanced diet of traditionally prepared whole foods with special emphasis on fat-soluble vitamins and trace minerals. This diet includes consuming (not avoiding) animal fats and other animal foods in partnership with fresh, cooked, and fermented vegetables, as well as whole grain sourdough breads and other grains and pulses that have been prepared in a way that maximizes the availability of the nutrients they contain.

The Philosophy of the Nourished Kitchen

As I choose what and how to cook, I focus on a simple philosophy that combines sustainability, balance, tradition, and community involvement.

Sustainable

Sustainability is a word tossed about rather easily, and yet its concept rests at the heart of the way I nourish myself, my family, and my broader community. Sustainability provides a broad and comprehensive approach to agriculture, food, and community building. That is, not only does small-scale sustainable agriculture minimize chemical inputs, build upon soil reserves, and nurture the plants, animals, and people, but it also provides fair economic benefit for farmers. The work of small-scale farmers practicing organic and holistic methods warrants fair compensation and livable wages.

When I spend my money locally and purchase farm-direct through CSAs, farmstands, and farmers markets, I ensure that the agricultural roots of my community are well fed and that the farmers profit from the hard work they undertake nurturing the soil, sowing the seeds, harvesting crops, and raising animals with both compassion and respect. By connecting directly with food producers, I ensure that the food with which I nourish myself and my family is not only safe, but grown and raised under as close to optimal conditions as possible.

Raising animals on holistically managed pasture helps to sequester carbon in the soil and improve the variety of native flora. In this way, the plants need the animals that feed upon them as much as the animals need the plants. Moreover, foods grown locally, sustainably, and picked fresh offer their peak nutrition, flavor, and texture to the consumer.

Balanced

There's a deeply pervasive disconnect in the collective relationship with food that persists in American culture: We often view healthy eating as synonymous with restrictive eating, and we likewise view joyful eating as a guilty pleasure, something that begs for strict limits. I believe that real food allows us both the gift of nourishment, and the gift of pleasure, without unnecessary restrictions. Eating a diet of traditional foods helps us to develop a positive relationship with our food, not one born out of guilt and denial;

rather, the traditional foods movement teaches us to purchase, prepare, and enjoy our food with intention.

Real, traditionally prepared foods offer nuanced flavors, subtle differences in texture or aroma that change continuously as the seasons of the year wax and wane. Enjoy meats and fish. Relish grains, breads, and pulses. Take pleasure in good fat and take a mindful approach to sweets. The multidimensional flavors of traditionally prepared real foods bring a complexity of different notes and textures to your tongue, and even a small amount of concentrated foods like butter from the raw cream of grass-fed cows, or a lovely single varietal honey will bring deep satisfaction that is otherwise missing from industrialized foods with their single notes, cloying sweetness, or overt saltiness.

Meat from wholesome, pasture-raised animals offers concentrated sources of vitamins, minerals, and wholesome healthy fats. Vegetables, fruits, and plant foods offer antioxidants, vitamins, and minerals. Properly prepared whole grains offer minerals and energy. Whole, raw, fresh milk provides conjugated linoleic acid (CLA), vitamins, and minerals—all nutrients that have a powerful positive effect in supporting health and wellness. From all whole and minimally processed foods, seek out balance and flavor.

Unprocessed

I favor unprocessed, unrefined whole foods. Choosing to purchase single ingredient foods is one step—perhaps the most important step—to finding the joy of food again. Industrial processing strips foods of their inherent, natural nutrients and value. By consuming foods in an unprocessed state, you consume their naturally present nutrients and no additives.

Traditionally Prepared

The nourishment we receive from the foods we eat depends not only on which foods we choose to eat, but also on how we choose to prepare them. Preparing whole grains through a slow process of sourdough fermentation maximizes B vitamins, reduces glycemic load, and enhances the availability of minerals. B vitamins perform many functions, from helping to support the nervous system to preventing neural tube defects in offspring, while a reduction in glycemic load supports the body's handling of blood sugar, reducing the load on the pancreas and other organs. The fermenting of vegetables (as in sauerkraut and kimchi) was born of practicality—a way to preserve the harvest well into winter—but this process also serves a dual purpose of increasing beneficial bacteria, food enzymes, and B vitamins. By preparing foods traditionally, we maximize their nutrient density.

Involved

Much of my love for real food and farms arises from devotion to community, and from a spirit of giving. In this spirit, my husband and I started the Crested Butte Farmers Market in 2007, growing it into one of Colorado's most progressive markets. We dedicated much of our time to exploring and growing the availability of local, organic foods within our tiny mountain town. The soul of food comes not only through its farms, but through the community that supports those farms, and each other in the process. Farmers markets, CSAs, bulk buying clubs, community gardens, and farms all allow like-minded food lovers to come together, increase access to traditional foods, and develop a cooperative effort that protects and binds the interests of everyone together.

Join a CSA. Hold a community supper featuring wholesome, local foods. Celebrate the beauty of your foodshed, and support local farmers practicing sustainable agriculture. Support nutritional advocacy groups like the Weston A. Price Foundation and the Savory Institute, as well as the work of farmer and consumer rights organizations like the Farm-to-Consumer Legal Defense Fund.

Fruits and Vegetables

Fruits and vegetables prepared in their season bring joy to the table. As the days turn from dark to light as spring nears, and just when you've had enough of hearty stews and root vegetables, the brightest and lightest of vegetables appear—sprouts, herbs, tiny little strawberries, and crisp lettuces. These vegetables fade and bolt with the heat of summer that, in its turn, brings robust and juicy foods—watermelons, vivid red tomatoes, and plums that drip with juice at the first bite. The days grow dark and cold once more, and the apples, pumpkins, potatoes, and roots return. The changing seasons bring excitement and heady anticipation that cannot exist in the seasonless aisles of the supermarket.

We purchase most of our foods directly from farmers, ensuring that we enjoy them at the peak of the season, when their flavor is richest. This gives us a connection both to the land and to the person who nourishes my family, and, together, both the farmers and my family begin to reclaim that lost sense of connection and communal support.

The foods we consume are organically grown, though not all growers can afford organic certification, and others still object to certification that allows consumers to rely on government guidelines and inspections rather than interactions directly with farmers and farms to ensure their food is safe and produced without chemicals. Many of the chemicals used in industrialized food production contribute to cancers as well as endocrine and metabolic dysfunction. While the overall chemical load consumers of conventionally or industrially grown food eat may vary, what worries me is the repetitive exposure of farm workers to these potentially dangerous chemicals.

Beyond the social and economic factors that influence decisions to purchase organically grown, farm-direct, or industrially grown fruits and vegetables, there exists another benefit in favor of fresh, farm-direct foods: flavor. Industrially grown fruits and vegetables must rely on long distances of transport before they arrive at your supermarket. These fruits and vegetables are bred not for their uniqueness or their nuances of flavor, but for their ability to withstand transportation without bruising, as well as the ability to remain in near-perfect visual condition despite long times in transit and on supermarket shelves. Heirloom varietals purchased soon after picking may not last thousands of miles in transit, but they offer the benefit of flavor, nuanced by the condition of the soil in which they are grown.

Meats, Milk, and Eggs

For a long time I avoided meat, having read about the deplorable conditions of factory farms. Yet a diet devoid of meat didn't sustain my health. Meat provides essential nourishment, minerals, vitamins, and some micronutrients that are otherwise difficult to come by. Moreover, animal foods—meat, milk, and eggs—have supported human health over millennia.

Meat, milk, and eggs are only as healthy for you as the health of the animal. Sick animals produce food lacking in healthy fats, with potentially high levels of dioxins, antibiotics, and hormones that can adversely affect your family's health. While factory farming is undoubtedly troubled and warrants collective opposition, that opposition is best expressed by embracing those who practice holistic management, which honors the animals, their health, and the lands upon which they graze. For this reason, I purchase grass-fed beef, pasture-raised pork and chicken, eggs from truly free ranging hens, and milk from grass-fed cows straight from the farm just down the road. For more information on sourcing these types of foods in your own area, see Resources (page 300).

Fats and Oils

I emphasize using traditional, old-fashioned fats in my cooking and avoid new, refined, and processed oils. Fats (including saturated and monounsaturated fats) can build upon health, nourishing the body and helping it to better absorb vitamins and antioxidants in our foods.

Butter from Grass-Fed Cows

Butter is sweet, soft, and deeply comforting. It gives foods a touch of richness, maximizing and reinforcing the flavor of vegetables. Predominantly comprised of saturated fat, butter has drawn ire from the health-minded, low-fat community. Yet butter, like many traditional fats, provides our bodies with nourishment. When produced from the cream of grass-fed cows, butter is extraordinarily rich in fat-soluble vitamins A, D, E, and K_2, which perform many functions, from supporting fertility and immune system health to supporting heart and bone health; it is a rich source of the antioxidant beta carotene, which accounts for its golden color. Butter is also an excellent source of conjugated linoleic acid (CLA)—a fat with strong cancer-fighting properties that also supports metabolic health.

Formed of churned heavy cream, butter also contains a fair amount of milk solids, which imbue it with its utterly rich, creamy flavor. Milk solids reduce butter's smoke point, which hovers at around 350°F. I favor butter for light sautéing, baking, and using fresh and raw.

The process of clarifying butter removes those milk solids, leaving only the golden butterfat. Clarified butter lacks the resolute creaminess of plain butter, and its flavor is reminiscent of nuts; however, clarified butter has a smoke point of about 485°F, so it is a good choice for high-heat applications.

Lard and Bacon Fat from Pastured Pigs

While butter is slowly making a comeback, rightfully reclaiming its place from the usurper margarine, lard and bacon fat still remain relatively reviled among many health-food advocates and registered dieticians, despite the fact that they have a fatty acid composition similar to an oil lauded for its cardiovascular benefits: olive oil. The primary fatty acid in lard is monounsaturated, comprising about 40 to 45 percent of the fat content. The remaining 55 to 60 percent is a combination of saturated fat and polyunsaturated fat, all of which play a role in several biological functions and the support of systemic wellness.

Lard is also an extraordinarily rich source of vitamin D, second only to cod liver oil—that is, if it has been rendered from the fat of pasture-raised hogs. Hogs, like humans and unlike cows, are monogastric animals, and they manufacture vitamin D in their skin. As a result, lard and bacon fat from pasture-raised pigs are extraordinarily rich in vitamin D.

This is not the lard of your supermarket; rather, it is difficult to come by, though increasingly more available. You can purchase lard from ranchers and farmers who raise their pigs out on pasture, with free access to grass, water, and, most importantly, sunshine. Lard is excellent in pastries and baked goods, for frying as well as for sautéing vegetables and braising meats. Lard's smoke point hovers around 370°F.

Extra-Virgin Olive Oil

A good olive oil has flavor—it is grassy or fruity or faintly dusty; it is not, however, the flavorless and near-colorless liquid you find in most grocery stores. When olive oil became the shining star of heart-smart health due to its monounsaturated fatty acid content, it became the first choice for cooking. And while it can be used for light cooking due to its monounsaturated fatty acid content, I prefer to use it on salads or as a finishing oil, except in those dishes that truly benefit from its fruity, grassy notes. Extra-virgin olive oil is extraordinarily rich in phytonutrients and antioxidants as well as vitamin E, all of which are extremely heat-sensitive, meaning that by cooking with your olive oil you're negating many of its potential benefits. So despite the relatively high smoke point of extra-virgin olive oil (375°F), it's best to use this particular fat as a finishing oil where its complex flavors can shine, and its heat-sensitive vitamins and antioxidants can remain intact.

Nut and Seed Oils

Walnut, pumpkin seed, and hazelnut oils also bring beautiful flavors to the kitchen table. I choose cold-pressed nut and seed oils, and use them sparingly because these oils are typically high in omega-6 fatty acids, which may be difficult to balance even with a diet rich in wild-caught fish. I enjoy using them as a finishing oil or to add flavor to salad dressings. Many of these cold-pressed nut and seed oils are, like olive oil, rich in heat-sensitive antioxidants, and they are always best used unheated because heat can easily damage their fragile polyunsaturated fatty acids.

I avoid industrially produced oils like canola, soybean, corn, and vegetable. Extraction of oil from these crops often employs petroleum-based chemical solvents such as hexane, and the oils are typically refined and deodorized before bottling and transport. This type of processing damages the oils' heat-sensitive polyunsaturated fatty acids. Further, these oils lack the complex flavor found in traditionally processed fats and oils.

Sweeteners

I use a minimal amount of sweeteners in my cooking because they often disguise the subtle flavors in the dish themselves. But used with an expert hand and a mindful eye, they can enhance and not overpower other foods. Sweeteners are strong foods, and as strong and concentrated foods, they're best used as an accent, or in desserts for special occasions, not daily.

Honey

European cave paintings tell tales of gathering honey, and honey has been consumed for at least the past ten thousand years. Honey is sweet, and its flavor varies depending upon the diet of the bees. Single varietal honeys can vary wildly from one another both in flavor and in color and consistency. Honey offers a variety of antioxidants, enzymes, and trace amounts of vitamins like thiamin and niacin.

I favor raw, unfiltered honey, which retains heat-sensitive vitamins, antioxidants, and food enzymes, though I take no issue with cooking honey for custards or sweetened desserts (some cooks avoid heating honey in an effort to preserve its food enzymes and heat-sensitive vitamins).

Unrefined Cane Sugars

First domesticated in Asia about eight thousand years ago, sugarcane is one of the oldest farmed plants. Minimally processed, unrefined cane sugars have a sweetness tempered by the flavor notes of mineral-rich molasses. To produce cane sugar, juice is extracted from the sugar cane by pressing, then that juice is heated to reduce it to a thick syrup. As the syrup cools, it crystalizes. For unrefined cane sugar, the process stops here and the crystals are left lightly coated with molasses, which naturally contains many minerals, including iron, calcium, chromium, and potassium. The unrefined crystals are left to dry further, and then are ground so that the sugar pours freely and can be easily measured. But to make refined sugar, the molasses is extracted from the crystals through centrifuging and other separation measures, and the sugar is decolorized, leaving it stripped of any trace minerals. The refined sugar is then sold or reblended with molasses to make brown sugar.

Molasses

Molasses is a byproduct of processing cane juice into white sugar, and it is a good source of niacin, thiamin, magnesium, copper, and potassium. Its flavor is bittersweet and deeply rich. For that reason it should be used in small quantities so as not to impart too strong of a flavor to the end dish. I prefer blackstrap molasses, which is darker in color and deeper in flavor than light and dark molasses varieties.

Sorghum Syrup

Sorghum is an African grain, brought to the Americas with the slave trade. Sorghum syrup is prepared in autumn. The process begins by harvesting the sorghum canes, which are then stripped of their leaves and milled so as to extract the sweet juice. The juice is then heated and reduced to a thick golden-copper syrup that is nicely sweet with a unique, subtle flavor reminiscent of tropical fruit. Sorghum syrup is a good source of manganese, vitamin B6, riboflavin, magnesium, and potassium. You can use it in any recipe that calls for a liquid sweetener, such as honey or molasses. Sorghum pairs well with nuts, particularly pecans.

Maple Syrup and Maple Sugar

Produced from the sap of sugar maple trees, maple syrup and maple sugar are minimally processed sugars with a strong, sweet, complex flavor. Maple syrup's color ranges from light amber to a deep, dark brown, depending on the grade and quality. I prefer to use Grade B maple syrup in my cooking, as its dark and complex flavor brings greater richness and depth of flavor to desserts and sweet breads. Maple syrup and sugar contain the minerals zinc and manganese, and also provide trace amounts of calcium, iron, and magnesium.

chapter one

from the garden

HUMBLE LITTLE POTS OF SAVORY AND THYME rest on my porch; a patch of potatoes grows, bedded in straw, in my garden where an old bed frame makes a trellis that hangs heavy with English peas in spring and green beans in late summer. The garden provides a rhythm for my home, a sense of cyclical continuity within the revolving seasons that bring warmth and cold, light and dark. Lettuces, peas, asparagus, and little radishes arrive in spring, while tougher greens like kale and larger winter radishes wait until the weather grows colder once again. We travel not too far down the road to the farm that provides us boxes of produce each week, and we pluck the first artichokes from their prickled bushes in the mild warmth of early summer, later helping the farmers to harvest bushels of tomatoes and peppers as the days grow hotter and hotter still. Later, the daylight wanes, giving way to the looming cold of autumn and winter. Then thick purple-topped turnips, blood-red beets, and knobby celeriac poke out above the soil, having grown too large for their beds. Always late and slow to grow on their expansive, creeping vines, pumpkins and winter squash arrive, bearing their thick skins that will keep them fresh for months after the harvest until the first glimmering yellow-green sprouts of early spring appear once more. The rhythm comforts me and exhilarates me all at once, for the decline of each season brings great anticipation for the rising of the next one.

That cycle of opposing forces—warmth and cold, light and dark, growth and rest—governs the garden, and, in turn, governs the kitchen. My family eats what can be had, finding pleasure in the availability of vegetables and fruits at their peak season rather than seeking to satisfy an immediate desire for some long-traveled fruit desperately out of season. There's no joy in a tomato in January, no delight in a pumpkin in May.

My garden rests under a blanket of snow from November to May. Frost can linger into June and begin again in September—leaving me only the months of July and August. I coax what I can from the dark, rich alpine soil in those sixty days—greens and radishes, peas and turnips, supplementing what I can from nearby growers at lower altitudes where the microclimate can support the fruits and vegetables of longer growing seasons.

Little Salads of Weeds, Leaves, and Greens

Simple salads serve as a staple in our home, and no meal seems complete without one. They evolve with the rhythm of the seasons: peas and radishes in the spring give away to robust tomatoes in summer, and eventually to the sweet and bitter flavors that arrive in autumn and winter: radicchio, endive, bitter greens, pumpkin, and apples.

In spring, tender lettuces and wild herbs arrive from area farms. After months of snow and bitter cold, those little heads of brilliant red Lolla Rossa lettuce or bunches of Deer Tongue lettuce with its soft, dagger-shaped leaves seem particularly welcome. I dress them with vinegar or with the juice of the last of winter's lemons. It's about this time of year that weeds begin to arrive, too—succulent and lemony purslane, bitter dandelion. We pluck what we can from the garden bed, or find them tucked away in our CSA box—and mix them with the softer flavors of springtime vegetables like sliced young carrots, green onions, and chive blossoms.

As the weather warms, the lettuces bolt—their leaves embittered by the sun's rays. We pull them from the garden and move onto the crisp, juicy cucumbers and the robust tomatoes at the farmers market. Those will last until September, and then cold-hardy roots, tough greens, and bulbous winter squash take their place. We gorge ourselves until we've had our fill, and by that time, the season has changed and newer foods and flavors begin to arrive.

Still, I grow what I can. Every day I pluck a few leaves of lettuce from the garden, or, in the cold months, from a pot that sits on my kitchen table bathing in the light of a nearby window. I toss them together with a few herbs—basil if I have it, sometimes mint or lemon sorrel. I slice a radish, or a stray carrot, or whatever vegetables linger in the crisper of my refrigerator, and toss them together in a bowl with a splash of olive oil and a drizzle of lemon juice or aged balsamic vinegar—all sweet and viscous like honey.

The intense seasonality of salads coupled with their versatility and no-fuss preparation appeals to me. I pair them with long-simmered brothy soups, or freshly baked bread slathered with butter or liver mousse, and that provides just enough to satisfy.

While leafy greens can provide the bulk of any salad, don't limit yourself only to greens; rather, most vegetables lend themselves to salads: sweet roasted pumpkin pairs well with bitter radicchio, tomatoes with basil and mint, peas with radishes.

In making a good salad, emphasize not only pairing seasonal vegetables and aromatics with one another, but also balancing the plants with a good source of high-quality fat. Consuming vegetables with fat helps to increase the availability of antioxidants and other fat-soluble nutrients. Pairing lettuce with buttermilk, or roasted tomatoes with extra-virgin olive oil not only deepens the flavors of the dish, but also extends the nourishment your body receives.

Finding Good Olive Oil

Olive oil, ranging from a pale straw color to a vibrant green, can coax out the subtle fruitiness in vegetables. The flavor of each oil depends on the manner in which the farmer cared for the groves, where the olive trees grow, the variety of olives grown, and when farm workers picked and pressed the oil. For these reasons, the olive oil from different areas of the world, or even from different groves within the same region, can yield remarkably different oils. I keep a variety of olive oils in my cupboard, ranging from the mild and fruity mid- and late-harvest California oils that I reserve for light cooking and the making of Olive Oil Mayonnaise (page 80) to the assertive Italian oils with their grassy undertones that I prefer to use as a finishing oil over salads, roasted tomatoes, or fish.

As if flavor were not enough to steer you to a good olive oil, it's worth noting that olive oil has been, and remains to this day, one of the most frequently adulterated foods in the food supply. While olive groves dot the hills of California, less than 5 percent of the olive oil consumed in the United States is produced in the United States. Instead, growers worldwide often sell their olives to processors, who then sell it to middlemen, who then sell it to manufacturers for private labeling. With so many middlemen between grower and customer, there exists many opportunities for adulteration and mislabeling. Some unscrupulous middlemen cut extra-virgin olive oil with less expensive oils—namely soybean oil, canola oil, and corn oil—most of which are produced from genetically modified plants.

Many people suggest that transferring your olive oil to your refrigerator to see if it solidifies will help you to determine whether your olive oil is real. This hypothesis rests on the fact that monounsaturated fat comprises the bulk of the fats found in olive oil, with small portions of saturated and polyunsaturated fatty acids. Monounsaturated fats, which are also found in avocados, lard, and bacon fat, typically remain solid in cold temperatures and semisolid at room temperatures. However, whether or not an olive oil solidifies in the refrigerator or remains liquid also depends on other factors, including the type of olive from which the oil was produced. In addition to oils, olives contain natural waxes. High-wax olives typically yield oil that solidifies in cold temperatures while low-wax varieties, like Mission olives, yield oil that usually remains liquid. Not only is this method of refrigerating olive oil to determine its authenticity inaccurate; cold temperatures may affect the bloom of flavors in olive oil, dampening them.

Like most of the foods I purchase, I typically buy olive oil directly from family farms practicing sustainable farming techniques—from growers who take pride in how their olive groves are cared for and how their oil is produced (see Resources, page 300). Moreover, this allows me to purchase unfiltered and unrefined olive oils–something not typically sold in stores. These unrefined olive oils retain a greater level of antioxidants, including vitamin E, a nutrient that helps to mitigate oxidative stress and thereby reduces the risk of several chronic diseases, such as cardiovascular disease.

pea *and* radish salad *with* yogurt chive dressing ❧

The early months of spring bring sweet English peas and brilliantly colored radishes to our farmers market, and our garden also teems with the little vegetables. The two pair together nicely—the bitter crisp bite of radishes offsetting the gentle, soft sweetness of peas.

Late in the evenings, when the spring air takes a chill, I take my little boy by the hand and we walk to the community garden that houses our English peas along ramshackle trellises, haphazard rows of French breakfast radishes, as well as the little cabbages that will continue to grow until fall. We gather what we can, and I always pluck a few handfuls of pea greens for good measure. It's easy to neglect the pea greens while the pods grow fat and sweet, but they're lovely—mild and sweet and rich in color. While pea tendrils can be tough, the leaves themselves are richly sweet with a clover-like aroma. I like to toss the greens, peas, and radishes together with yogurt, chives, and olive oil for one of my favorite early season salads. SERVES 2 TO 4

SALAD

3 pounds English peas, shelled (about 3 cups)

8 medium radishes, trimmed and thinly sliced

1 cup loosely packed pea leaves

4 green onions, white and green parts, thinly sliced

DRESSING

3 tablespoons yogurt

2 tablespoons snipped chives

2 tablespoons extra-virgin olive oil

Pinch of finely ground unrefined sea salt

Bring about 4 cups of water to a boil in a saucepan. As the water begins to bubble, prepare an ice bath by filling a large bowl with a few cups of ice and enough cold water to reach halfway up the sides of the bowl.

Dump the peas into the boiling water and simmer, covered, for 3 to 5 minutes, until their color brightens and the peas can be pierced with a fork. Drain the peas using a fine-mesh sieve, then plunge the pea-filled sieve into the ice bath. Allow them to chill for 3 to 4 minutes, then pull them from the cold water.

Toss the peas with radishes, pea leaves, and green onions.

In a separate bowl, whisk the yogurt with the chives, oil, and salt until well combined. Drizzle the yogurt dressing over the pea salad and toss to coat before serving.

simple green salad *with* buttermilk herb dressing ⚗

Buttermilk, sharp and sour, provides a beautiful acidity to this simple salad. I like to whisk in fresh herbs snipped from the little pots that sit on the railing of my porch: chive, parsley, dill, and chervil. An egg yolk helps to emulsify the oil and buttermilk while also adding a luxurious creaminess to the dressing. Make sure to choose very fresh eggs from pasture-raised hens. Their eggs are also richer in vitamins and antioxidants. SERVES 4 TO 6

SALAD

8 cups loosely packed mesclun greens

6 carrots, peeled and sliced into ⅛-inch-thick rounds

6 radishes, trimmed and sliced into ⅛-inch-thick rounds

1 small red onion, sliced paper thin

1 hard-cooked egg, peeled and thinly sliced

DRESSING

1 egg yolk

1 tablespoon apple cider vinegar

¼ cup buttermilk

1 clove garlic, finely minced

2 tablespoons finely snipped chives

2 tablespoons chopped fresh flat-leaf parsley

1 teaspoon chopped fresh dill

½ teaspoon chopped fresh chervil

½ teaspoon freshly ground black pepper

¼ teaspoon finely ground unrefined sea salt

½ cup extra-virgin olive oil

Arrange the greens on a serving platter, and top them with the carrots, radishes, red onion, and egg.

Drop the egg yolk into a mixing bowl. Pour in the apple cider vinegar and buttermilk, whisking well. Drop in the garlic, herbs, pepper, and salt and continue whisking. Very slowly, drizzle the olive oil into the bowl as you continue to whisk the dressing vigorously, until the liquid thickens very slightly. Spoon over the greens and vegetables, tossing lightly to coat.

garden trimming salad *with*
lemon herb vinaigrette

In summertime I spend many afternoons hunched over the roots and shoots in our small bed at the community garden. High in the Rockies, my garden enjoys only 60 days of growth between frosts, so I cherish every little bit I can coax from the cold, dark mountain soil. Such limited time leaves me with a persistent need to use every sprig, tiny root, sprout, and leaf that my garden can produce. Here I serve all the trimmings—beet greens and carrot tops, pea tendrils and flowers—in a simple salad that leaves nothing wasted.

As you prepare this salad, keep in mind that carrot tops contain an alkaloid that can be potentially toxic when eaten in large quantities; small amounts, like the 2 tablespoons called for in this salad, aren't typically cause for concern—particularly if they're from young plants. SERVES 2 TO 4

SALAD

2 cups chopped beet greens

2 cups chopped pea leaves

2 green onions, white and green parts, thinly sliced

1/4 cup edible flowers, such as pansies, calendula, or rose

2 tablespoons chopped young carrot tops

Coarse unrefined sea salt and freshly ground black pepper

VINAIGRETTE

1 shallot, minced

2 tablespoons chopped fresh chives

1 tablespoon chopped fresh dill

1 tablespoon chopped fresh flat-leaf parsley

Juice of 1 lemon

1/2 cup extra-virgin olive oil

To make the salad, toss together the beet greens, pea leaves, green onions, flowers, and carrot tops. Sprinkle generously with the salt and pepper.

To make the dressing, in a separate bowl, whisk the shallot, chives, dill, and parsley with the lemon juice and olive oil. Drizzle the dressing over the salad, toss to coat, and serve.

roasted tomato salad *with* mint

Roasting heightens the flavor of tomatoes, allowing them to develop both their sweetness and their acidity. I tend to favor Sungold tomatoes for eating out of hand and for roasting in this salad. Upon first glance, the Sungold looks like an anemic orange version of the cherry tomato. I often see shoppers pass over them at our farmers market, unaware of their candy-like sweetness and rich tomato flavor that seems particularly magnified for such a small marble-sized bite.

In this salad, I roast them in a hot oven with olive oil and red onion. Roasting concentrates their sweet and complexly flavored juices. I toss in a handful of mint right before serving the salad, though a handful of basil works just as well. SERVES 4

2 pounds cherry or grape tomatoes, halved

1 small red onion, sliced ⅛ inch thick

1 tablespoon extra-virgin olive oil

2 teaspoons finely ground unrefined sea salt

¼ cup chopped fresh mint leaves

Preheat the oven to 425°F. Line a baking sheet with parchment paper.

Arrange the tomatoes and red onion in a single layer on the lined baked sheet. Drizzle with the olive oil and sprinkle with the salt.

Roast for 40 to 45 minutes, until the tomato juices thicken to the consistency of maple syrup and the tomatoes wrinkle. Spoon the roasted tomatoes and onions into a mixing bowl, toss in the mint, and serve immediately before the mint wilts in the residual heat of the tomatoes.

cucumber salad *with* dill *and* kefir

In July and August, our farmers market blooms with cucumbers of all kinds: sweet English cucumbers, creamy-fleshed Dragon's Egg, and squat, prickly-skinned lemon cucumbers. While any cucumber works in this salad, I tend to favor Armenian cucumbers with their twisted, serpentine coils. Armenian cucumbers can reach a yard long if you let them, but they're best plucked from the vine when about 18 inches long and still sweet.

Kefir, with its tart and milky flavor, yields a bit of richness to this salad, while a teaspoon of honey provides just enough sweetness to complement the cucumbers. SERVES 4

SALAD
1 1/2 pounds cucumbers

1 small shallot, minced

2 tablespoons chopped fresh dill

KEFIR DRESSING
1/4 cup milk kefir (page 62)

1 teaspoon honey

2 teaspoons apple cider vinegar

1/4 teaspoon finely ground unrefined sea salt

1/4 teaspoon ground white pepper

Peel the cucumbers if their skin is tough and bitter, then halve them and scoop out the seeds with a spoon. Slice them no thicker than 1/8 inch, and toss them into a mixing bowl with the shallot and dill. Stir gently to distribute the shallot and dill evenly among the cucumbers.

In a separate bowl, whisk the kefir with the honey, vinegar, salt, and white pepper until smooth and uniform. Pour the dressing over the cucumbers, stir until well coated, and serve.

warm radicchio *and* pumpkin salad ✤

The bitterness of radicchio is offset by the innate sweetness of apple and pumpkin. The prosciutto provides that lasting and pleasant saltiness characteristic of cured meats. While you can certainly serve small portions of this salad as an appetizer before a larger meal, I find that it's filling enough to stand on its own as a main course.

I typically make this using the Golden Delicious pumpkin, though any sweet pie pumpkin will work. The Golden Delicious is tear-shaped, with brilliant red-orange skin and firm, sweet flesh. SERVES 4 TO 6

---

1 small pie pumpkin (about 3 pounds)

2 tablespoons extra-virgin olive oil

$^1/_2$ teaspoon coarse unrefined sea salt

2 heads radicchio, cored and coarsely chopped

$^1/_2$ cup chopped pecans

1 apple, cored and sliced no thicker than $^1/_8$ inch

2 ounces thinly sliced prosciutto, cut into $^1/_4$-inch ribbons

Cold-pressed pumpkin seed oil or walnut oil, for drizzling

Aged balsamic vinegar, for drizzling

Preheat the oven to 425°F.

Peel the pumpkin, then cut it in half with sturdy knife, scoop out its seeds with a spoon, and chop it into chunks about $^1/_2$ inch thick. Toss it with 1 tablespoon of the olive oil and sprinkle it with $^1/_4$ teaspoon of the sea salt.

In a separate bowl, toss the chopped radicchio with the remaining 1 tablespoon of olive oil and $^1/_4$ teaspoon salt.

Spread the pumpkin on a baking sheet in a single layer and roast for about 30 minutes, until its flesh softens and its edges begin to caramelize and brown. Turn the pumpkin once as you roast it to promote even cooking. Add the radicchio to the pan and continue roasting for 12 to 15 minutes, until the edges of the radicchio leaves brown and wilt. Remove the baking sheet from the oven and allow to cool for about 5 minutes before assembling the salad.

Toss the roasted radicchio and pumpkin with the pecans, apple, and prosciutto. Drizzle with the pumpkin seed oil and balsamic vinegar before serving.

roasted beet *and* walnut salad *with* spiced kombucha vinaigrette ❧

Kombucha, a fermented tea of Asian origin, offers a flavor reminiscent of apple cider vinegar: it's sour, but also mildly sweet. Its flavor pairs well with warm spices like cinnamon, cloves, and allspice, while its acidity is strong enough to stand up against the sweet and earthy flavors of root vegetables and nuts.

Beets number among the few vegetables that my family eats year-round, fresh in spring and autumn and stored in boxes of dirt during the cold part of the year. Lacking greens in the winter, we often eat beets as a salad, sprinkled with roasted walnuts and dressed with a spiced vinaigrette. SERVES 4 TO 6

SALAD

2 pounds beets

1 tablespoon clarified butter (page 59)

3/4 cup chopped walnuts

1 small red onion, sliced into rings no thicker than 1/8 inch

VINAIGRETTE

2 tablespoons kombucha (page 286)

1/4 teaspoon finely ground unrefined sea salt

1/4 teaspoon ground allspice

1/8 teaspoon ground cloves

2 tablespoons cold-pressed walnut oil

2 tablespoons extra-virgin olive oil

Preheat the oven to 425°F.

To prepare the salad, trim the beets by removing any beet tops and the tips of their roots. Dot each beet with a touch of clarified butter, then wrap each in parchment paper and again in aluminum foil. Roast the beets for 45 to 60 minutes, until they yield under the pressure of a fork. Refrigerate the beets for at least 8 and up to 24 hours.

To prepare the vinaigrette, whisk the kombucha tea with the salt, allspice, cloves, and the walnut and olive oils. The vinaigrette will store at room temperature for up to 3 weeks, but remember to shake it vigorously before dressing the salad because the oil will separate from the tea and spices when left sitting.

Just before serving, heat a skillet over medium-high heat for 2 to 3 minutes until very hot. Toss in the walnuts and toast them for 3 to 5 minutes, stirring frequently to avoid scorching.

Remove the cold beets from the fridge, peel them, and chop into bite-sized pieces. In a large bowl, toss the beets with the sliced onion and toasted walnuts. Drizzle with the vinaigrette, toss again, and serve.

kohlrabi, apple, *and* pomegranate slaw

Kohlrabi are strange vegetables, martian-like in appearance. I like them for their strangeness, for their odd bulbous bodies that can range from deep purple to pale green. Their long stems shoot off into ruffled, dark green leaves and can serve as an excellent replacement for collard greens.

You can typically find kohlrabi at farmers markets or tucked away in farm boxes in early autumn. With a flavor like that of a young turnip, kohlrabi calls out for roasting, but I prefer to use it as a base for ferments or in salads in which a drizzle of fruity olive oil and a hint of citrus highlight its crisp, watery flesh. SERVES 6

SLAW

1 kohlrabi (about 1 pound)

2 apples (about 1 pound)

Seeds of 1 pomegranate

2 tablespoons minced fresh flat-leaf parsley

DRESSING

$1/4$ cup extra-virgin olive oil

1 tablespoon maple syrup

1 teaspoon Dijon-style mustard

$1/4$ cup orange juice

To prepare the slaw, with a sturdy paring knife, peel the tough skin and exterior stems and leaves from the kohlrabi. Using a mandoline, or by hand, slice the kohlrabi into matchsticks about $1/16$ inch thick and no longer than $1^{1}/_{2}$ inches. Core the apples, but do not peel them, and slice them into matchsticks the same length and width as the kohlrabi.

Toss the kohlrabi, apples, pomegranate seeds, and parsley together in a large bowl. Gently mix them by hand until they're so well combined that you're sure to taste a bit of each with every forkful.

To make the dressing, in a separate bowl, whisk the olive oil with the maple syrup, mustard, and orange juice. Pour over the slaw and serve.

Cooking with Seasonal Vegetables

My family's meals center around vegetables: anything that can be plucked, pulled, or dug up from the garden. I love the sweet earthiness of roots, the crispness of a just-picked snap pea, the salinity of lamb's quarters, an edible weed with dagger-like leaves that appears from time to time in my garden. Extraordinarily versatile, and ever-changing with the seasons, vegetables contribute variety—not only in flavor and appearance, but also in the nutrients they bring to the dinner plate.

I choose heirloom varietals when I can. I love their old-world charm, their whimsical colors and oddly shaped bodies. I love the conical heads of the Coeur de Boeuf cabbage, the long tapering maroon roots of the Crapaudine beet, and the rosy orange, wart-ridden skin of the Cinderella squash. Beautifully imperfect, their often marred and peculiar appearance disguises some of the most subtly nuanced flavors. Those flavors, bred by vegetable-loving gardeners and farmers generation after generation, can enhance dishes of braised, steamed, sautéed, and roasted vegetables, imbuing them with a distinct and deeply appealing strength. Unlike the limited varieties grown for grocery store shelves, heirloom vegetables are a product of collective culinary and gardening heritage, grown for flavor, color, and hardiness.

I also take care to choose vegetables that have been grown in mineral-rich soil that has not been treated with synthetic fertilizers or pesticides. What feeds the soil feeds the plant that, in turn, feeds you. Synthetic fertilizers and pesticides contribute to environmental damage and physical illness, particularly for farm workers. I purchase my family's vegetables from small, local growers with whom I've developed relationships over the years—both in my role as a farmers market manager, and by visiting and volunteering at their farms. Take the time to know your growers, and to lend a hand in a time of need.

Another Reason to Butter Your Vegetables

I always serve vegetables with fat: butter and cream in collards, bacon fat with carrots and parsnips, olive oil with tomatoes. Vegetables benefit from fat. Their potent antioxidants and plentiful array of vitamins become more available to your body when you serve them with fat, particularly monounsaturated fats like olive oil and lard as well as saturated fats like butter. The two—vegetables and fat—work synergistically together, with fat increasing the efficacy of vegetables' fat-soluble nutrients, such as carotenoids and vitamins.

blistered radishes *with* parsley ❧

In the dark days of the year, I buy winter radishes by the case. They store
well when kept cool in a root cellar, exterior closet, basement, or garage,
covered in dirt, and insulated with an old blanket. I ferment quite a few but
save others for cooking: either roasting with salt and pepper or sautéing
on the stove until they blister. Watermelon radishes, daikon, purple plum
radishes, and the long Violet de Gournay all do well. Winter radishes have
thicker skins than do spring radishes, but do not be tempted to peel them
as their color can brighten your plate with its charm.

In spring, when milder and more tender radishes begin to arrive at area
farms, I prepare this same dish from little Cherry Belle, Pink Beauty, and
elongated French Breakfast radishes. SERVES 4

---

16 radishes

1 tablespoon unsalted
butter

¹/₄ cup chopped fresh
flat-leaf parsley

Freshly ground unrefined
sea salt

Chop the radishes into ¹/₄-inch dice and set them in a bowl
while you prepare the remaining ingredients.

Melt the butter in a wide skillet over medium-high heat.
When the butter foams, decrease the heat to medium-low
and stir in the radishes. Cook the radishes in the butter,
stirring frequently, for 8 to 10 minutes, until their skins blister
slightly. Sprinkle them with the parsley and season with salt
to suit your preference. Serve warm.

buttered spinach ❧

I first came across this recipe scrawled in the pages of an old journal given to me by a close friend. Dated 1846 and yellowed with time, its fragile pages describe farm chores coupled with the details of household management, favorite poems, and recipes like the one below, which specifies the use of young spinach, freshly picked, and, like most old recipes, provides few details on quantity. I've adapted the recipe, substituting white pepper for black. I make it often in the spring, when tender baby spinach arrives in our CSA box weekly, until the weather grows too hot and stifles the tender greens. SERVES 4

2 large bunches young spinach (about 1¼ pounds)

1 tablespoon unsalted butter

½ teaspoon finely ground unrefined sea salt

¼ teaspoon ground white pepper

2 hard-cooked eggs, peeled and minced

Trim the spinach of any tough stems or veins, then coarsely chop the spinach leaves. Toss the spinach into a large, heavy stockpot. Set it on the stove over medium-low heat, cover the pot with a tight-fitting lid, and cook for 15 to 20 minutes, until completely tender.

Drain the wilted spinach in a colander, pressing it down to remove any excess liquid. Return the pot to the stove, add the butter, and melt over low heat. Toss in the spinach. Stir in the salt, white pepper, and minced egg, then serve.

new potatoes *with* chive blossoms *and* sour cream

Chives bloom in the late spring. Their long, tough stems shoot up from bundles of slender dark green, grass-like leaves and erupt in a sphere of pale violet petals. I love the blossom's faint but distinct onion-like flavor and enjoy adding them to salads, frittatas, and baked eggs. I particularly like the way they pair with young potatoes, for it's about this time of year that the first potatoes appear at farmers markets. Tender and about the size of a marble, these potatoes make a simple side dish, and their sweetness pairs well with the sharp green bite of chives and the creamy acidity of sour cream.

SERVES 4 TO 6

1½ pounds marble-sized new potatoes

½ cup sour cream

¼ cup snipped fresh chives and chive blossoms

Finely ground unrefined sea salt and freshly ground black pepper

Bring about 8 cups of water to a boil in a deep pot. Toss in the potatoes, cover, and boil until tender, about 20 minutes. Drain and let the potatoes cool for about 5 minutes.

Toss the potatoes with cultured cream and chives and chive blossoms until uniformly coated. Season with salt and pepper and serve warm.

peas *and* carrots *with* cream

Peas and carrots remind me of my elementary school lunch line, where cafeteria workers served the vegetables from industrial-sized cans. I never cared for the combination then, but I've grown to love the pairing now.

Peas and carrots, both sweet and both hallmarks of spring, make a nice marriage, particularly when gently steamed until their flavors bloom without becoming muddy from overcooking. I like to serve them with cream, mint, and parsley. SERVES 4 TO 6

1 1/2 pounds carrots, peeled and cut into 1/4-inch dice

1 pound English peas, shelled (1 cup)

2 tablespoons heavy cream, preferably raw

1/2 teaspoon finely ground unrefined sea salt

1/4 teaspoon ground white pepper

2 tablespoons chopped fresh mint

1 tablespoon chopped fresh curly parsley

Pour the carrots and peas into a steamer basket and steam them over rapidly boiling water until crisp-tender, about 10 minutes. Transfer them to a serving bowl, then stir in the cream, salt, white pepper, mint, and parsley. Serve warm.

braised beets *with* their greens

This is one of my favorite ways to prepare beets. The dish comes together in about 15 minutes and makes use of the whole beet, root, greens, and all. I loathe wastefulness in the kitchen and make an attempt to find a use for every little bit of every plant and animal that finds its way to my chopping block. I gently braise the sweet beet roots in butter and chicken broth before stirring in the tender greens with a bit of chopped mint and a splash of apple cider vinegar, which helps to cut the beets' pronounced earthiness. Take care to use young, small beets because their greens are much more tender and softer in flavor than those of larger beets. Beets go well with roast pork, whose natural sweetness complements the earthiness of beets. From time to time, I also pair beets with red meats like lamb. SERVES 4 TO 6

2 pounds baby beets with their greens

3 tablespoons clarified butter (page 59)

2 cups Chicken bone Broth (page 120)

2 tablespoons chopped fresh mint

2 tablespoons apple cider vinegar

Remove the greens from the beets, trim off any tough stems or wilted bits, and finely chop the greens. Set the greens in a bowl. Peel the beets and trim away their root tips and any remaining bits of stem. If the beets are small, leave them whole. If they're large, chop them into 1-inch pieces.

Melt the butter in a large skillet over medium heat. Toss in the beets and baste them with the hot butter for 3 to 4 minutes. Pour in the chicken broth, cover, and simmer until the roots yield easily when pierced by a fork, about 10 minutes. Uncover the skillet, toss in the greens and mint, and continue cooking over medium heat for 3 to 4 minutes, until the greens wilt. Sprinkle with the vinegar and serve.

creamed collard greens

There's an old-fashioned charm to the sturdy collard green, whose tough stems and broad leathery leaves spring from garden beds throughout the year. Despite near year-round availability, collards are at their best in the cold months after the first frost, which sweetens the otherwise notoriously bitter green. Here, heavy cream and caramelized onions add luxurious sweetness to counterbalance the collards' briny undertones. SERVES 4 TO 6

2 tablespoons unsalted butter

1 large yellow onion, thinly sliced

2 bunches collard greens, about 24 ounces, stems removed and leaves coarsely chopped

1 cup heavy cream

1/2 teaspoon freshly grated nutmeg

Melt the butter in a cast-iron skillet over medium-high heat. When it froths, decrease the heat to medium, stir in the onion, and fry until fragrant and a bit caramelized at the edges, 6 to 8 minutes.

Toss the chopped collards into the skillet and cook, stirring until slightly wilted, about 2 minutes. Decrease the heat to medium-low, stir in the heavy cream, and simmer for 5 to 6 minutes, until the cream is reduced by half and thickened. Sprinkle with the nutmeg and serve.

cider-braised kale *with* apples *and* sweet cherries ❧

Each year, at the autumn equinox, I serve this dish at our community's annual harvest festival. It's a magical time when throngs of masked mummers line the streets, reveling in song and drink before congregating at the town's center and lighting a bonfire that reaches so wildly high its embers cannot be distinguished from the stars.

The dish itself is a celebration of the equinox, a time when the long days of summer wane into the growing darkness of autumn. It combines a remnant of summer—dried sweet cherries—with the bounty of autumn's apples, greens, and onions. If you don't have any hard cider, substitute sweet cider. SERVES 4 TO 6

2 tablespoons bacon fat

1 small red onion, thinly sliced

1 apple, peeled, cored, and thinly sliced

2 bunches Lacinato kale, stems removed and leaves coarsely chopped

1 cup dried sweet cherries

¼ cup hard cider

1 teaspoon apple cider vinegar

Melt the bacon fat in a cast-iron skillet over medium heat. Toss the red onion into the hot fat and fry until fragrant and softened, about 3 minutes. Stir in the apple and fry until tender enough to pierce with a fork, about 4 minutes. Toss in the kale and cook until barely wilted. It should take only a minute.

Stir the cherries and hard cider into the wilted kale and apple and simmer until the liquid is mostly evaporated, about 5 minutes. Stir in the apple cider vinegar and serve.

pan-fried savoy cabbage *with* bacon

Pale green and crinkly-leafed, Savoy cabbages tend toward a mildness not typically found in their sturdier cousins. That mildness benefits from the pronounced saltiness of bacon and the bittersweet flavor of caramelized shallots, which lift the natural flavor of Savoy cabbage without hiding it. While Savoys will last a month or two in the cold storage of a refrigerator or a root cellar, they do not keep as long as green and red cabbages, which can last 5 months or longer when carefully stored. SERVES 4 TO 6

1 head Savoy cabbage

1 teaspoon unsalted butter

4 ounces bacon, chopped

2 medium shallots, sliced into paper-thin rings

Quarter the cabbage and remove its core with a sharp paring knife. Slice the cabbage crosswise into thin strips no thicker than ¼ inch.

Melt the butter in a large skillet over medium-high heat. When it froths, stir in the bacon and fry until crispy, about 6 minutes. Remove the bacon from the pan with a slotted spoon and set it aside in a bowl.

Toss the shallots into the fat and fry over medium-high heat, stirring frequently, until brown and crispy, 4 to 6 minutes. Using a slotted spoon, transfer the shallots from the pan to the bowl with the bacon.

Put the cabbage into the skillet and fry over medium-high heat, stirring frequently, until wilted and no longer crisp, about 8 minutes. Stir in the reserved bacon and shallots. Serve warm.

maple-glazed root vegetables
with orange *and* thyme

Sweet on their own, parsnips and carrots adopt a deeper complexity when paired with maple and orange, while thyme perfumes the vegetables with its savory aroma. I often serve maple-glazed root vegetables for breakfast with fried eggs and thick slabs of bacon, though it also does well as a side dish with roasted chicken or pork. SERVES ABOUT 4

2 tablespoons clarified butter (page 59)

1 pound carrots, peeled and sliced into matchsticks

1 pound parsnips, peeled and sliced into matchsticks

2 tablespoons maple syrup

1/2 cup orange juice

2 tablespoons chopped fresh thyme

Finely ground unrefined sea salt

Melt the butter in a wide skillet over medium-high heat. Toss the carrots and parsnips into the hot fat, decrease the heat to medium, and fry for 10 to 12 minutes, stirring from time to time, until the edges of the vegetables begin to caramelize.

Stir in the maple syrup and orange juice and continue cooking until the liquid is evaporated, about 2 minutes. Turn off the heat, sprinkle the thyme over the vegetables, and season with salt. Stir once more, then serve.

puree *of* pale roots stewed *in* milk ❦

Stewing roots and potatoes in milk yields a luscious, creamy texture in this puree. Stewing also concentrates the milk, infusing each vegetable with its soft sweetness. Freshly grated nutmeg (always a good match for milk) enlivens that sweetness with its spice. This technique of stewing roots in milk can be easily applied to other root vegetables, such as carrots, for uniquely creamy purees. I typically serve this in place of mashed potatoes alongside roasted chicken or turkey.

This recipe calls for parsley root, a knobby, pale cream-colored vegetable with twisting root tips. You can find it at farmers markets in mid- to late autumn. Its flavor is clean, crisp, and reminiscent of the herb, but richer and sweeter. Parsley root is also lovely when roasted, especially when paired with carrots. SERVES ABOUT 6

1 lemon, halved

1¹/₂ pounds russet potatoes

1¹/₂ pounds celeriac

1 pound parsley root

8 ounces parsnips

4 cups whole milk

1 cup heavy cream

2 bay leaves

1 teaspoon finely ground unrefined sea salt

¹/₂ teaspoon freshly grated nutmeg

Fill a large mixing bowl half-full with cold water and squeeze the juice of the lemon halves into it. Peel and chop the potatoes, celeriac, parsley root, and parsnips into 1-inch cubes, tossing them immediately into the lemon water to prevent them from discoloring.

After you've prepared the vegetables, drain away the lemon water and dump the vegetables into a heavy stockpot. Cover with the milk and cream, and then drop in the bay leaves. Bring to a boil over medium-high heat, then immediately decrease the heat to medium and simmer, covered, for 45 minutes. Remove the cover and continue simmering for another 45 minutes, stirring occasionally, until the vegetables are tender and easily pierced with a fork.

Remove the bay leaves, and then stir in the salt and nutmeg. Puree with an immersion blender until smooth. Serve warm.

roasted pumpkin *with* spiced sorghum syrup ✿

Sorghum is a gluten-free grain that makes a fine syrup with a flavor resembling molasses, with subtle fruity undertones reminiscent of pineapple. I often use it as a replacement for molasses when our jugs run shy. I like the way it pairs with pumpkin and other sweet autumn squash.

I typically use Black Futsu pumpkins, an heirloom winter squash with a deeply ribbed and beautifully bumpy skin. Like most winter squash, its flavor is strikingly sweet, though a subtle and faint nuttiness follows its sweetness. Of course, any winter squash should work well in this recipe, so use what's available to you from local farms or your own garden. SERVES 6

ROASTED PUMPKIN

1 pie pumpkin (about 6 pounds)

1 tablespoon unsalted butter, melted

1 teaspoon coarse unrefined sea salt

SORGHUM SYRUP

2 tablespoons sorghum syrup

1 teaspoon freshly grated nutmeg

1 teaspoon ground allspice

1/2 teaspoon ground cinnamon

1/4 teaspoon finely ground unrefined sea salt

Pinch of cayenne pepper

Preheat the oven to 400°F. Line a baking sheet with parchment paper.

Scrub the pumpkin well to remove any residual dirt clinging to its skin, then split it in half and scrape the seeds from its flesh, composting or otherwise discarding the seeds. Slice the pumpkin into thin crescents about 1/2 inch thick and arrange in a single layer on the baking sheet. Drizzle with the melted butter and sprinkle with the salt. Roast for 30 to 35 minutes, until the flesh softens and the edges of the slices caramelize just a touch.

While the pumpkin roasts in the oven, warm the sorghum in a small saucepan over low heat. Whisk in the nutmeg, allspice, cinnamon, salt and cayenne and continue whisking for about 2 minutes.

Plate the roasted pumpkin and drizzle with the sorghum syrup.

root cellar soup ✣

Every autumn, I buy root vegetables by the case and store them in an exterior closet that keeps an even, but cold, temperature. I leave the dirt on the roots because it helps them to keep for several months, and as I pack the roots into their boxes, I insulate them with old bath towels and newspapers to keep them from freezing during the subzero nights that arrive in January and February. Kept like this, nestled away in their boxes, they'll last all winter long and into the spring, when greens, herbs, peas, and new vegetables begin to appear once more.

I make this soup frequently in the winter, plucking a few onions, celeriacs, beets, and carrots from those boxes, chopping them finely, and letting them simmer in a simple beef broth spiced with allspice, black pepper, and sweet bay. A spoonful of Milk Kefir (page 62) and a sprinkling of fresh dill cut the inherent sweet earthiness of the root vegetables. SERVES 4 TO 6

2 bay leaves

1 tablespoon whole black peppercorns

2 teaspoons allspice berries

2 tablespoons lard or olive oil

1 onion, finely chopped

1 small leek, white and light-green parts only, thinly sliced

1 celeriac, peeled and chopped

2 carrots, peeled and chopped

5 beets, peeled and chopped

2 teaspoons finely ground unrefined sea salt

6 cups Beef Bone Broth (page 117)

1/4 cup chopped fresh dill

Milk Kefir (page 62), to serve

Place the bay leaves, peppercorns, and allspice berries on a 4-inch square piece of muslin or cheesecloth, tie it with a bit of cooking twine, then set the bundle aside.

Melt the lard in a heavy stockpot over medium heat. Stir in the onion and leek and fry them in the hot fat until they release their fragrance and soften, about 3 minutes. Stir in the celeriac, carrots, and beets. Sprinkle them with the salt, then cover the pot and sweat the vegetables for 20 minutes, or until crisp-tender.

Stir in the beef broth, drop in the bundle of bay and spices that you prepared earlier, and simmer the soup for 20 minutes, until the vegetables are tender but not so soft that they fall apart. Pluck out the bundle of spices and stir in the dill. Top each serving with a dollop of kefir.

potato *and* spinach soup *with* jalapeño

This soup came together by accident, a sort of desperate effort to throw lunch together out of a nearly empty pantry and refrigerator. Not wanting to pick up my market basket and walk through the snow to the little health food store a few blocks away, I simply threw a few things together in the pot and hoped for the best. The result was a lovely pale green soup with a kick of jalapeño that softened under the soothing texture of pureed potatoes. SERVES 6

2 teaspoons unsalted butter

4 ounces bacon, finely chopped

1 small red onion, finely chopped

1 jalapeño chile, seeded and minced

2 pounds potatoes, peeled and chopped into 1-inch pieces

8 cups Chicken Bone Broth (page 120)

8 ounces spinach, tough stems removed, leaves coarsely chopped

Finely ground unrefined sea salt

Sour cream, to serve

Melt the butter in a heavy stockpot over medium heat. Toss in the chopped bacon and allow it to render its fat and become crisp, about 6 minutes. Stir in the onion and fry it until it softens and releases its fragrance, about 3 minutes. Stir in the jalapeño and continue frying for 1 to 2 minutes, until the chile is fragrant.

Toss the potatoes into the pot and pour in the broth. Cover the pot and allow the mixture to simmer for 30 minutes, or until the potatoes fall apart when pressed with the tines of a fork. Stir in the spinach, cover the pot once more, and turn off the heat. Let stand until the spinach wilts in the heat of the soup, about 8 minutes.

Puree the soup with an immersion blender until perfectly smooth, with no lumps remaining. Season with salt and serve the soup, topping each bowl with a spoonful of sour cream.

spring vegetable stew ❧

After a long winter of heavy dishes—meats, potatoes, root vegetables, and breads—I look forward to the clean and vibrant abundance of spring. I make this Spring Vegetable Stew with the many firsts that spring brings: the first leeks, beans, peas, and artichokes. They stew together in Chicken Foot Broth, which offers up its delicate but still rich flavor as a companion to the vegetables. At the end, I toss in fresh basil, parsley, and mint, which brighten the stew a bit more with their clean and faintly floral notes. Lemon juice and zest add a punch of sourness that further complements the flavors of the stew.

If you do not have fresh lima beans, peas, and artichoke hearts, you can prepare this soup from frozen vegetables—as I often do in autumn and winter if I've had the forethought to preserve a little of the spring harvest. Keep in mind, however, that if you do make this stew from frozen vegetables, it will not need to cook as long as it does when using fresh ingredients, and can be finished in about 20 minutes start to finish. SERVES 4 TO 6

1 tablespoon lard

1 tablespoon extra-virgin olive oil, plus more to serve

1 large leek, white and light-green parts only, thinly sliced

Finely grated zest and juice of 1 lemon

3 carrots, peeled and diced

4 cups Chicken Foot Broth (page 121)

2 cups lima beans

1 pound English peas, shelled (1 cup)

1 cup baby artichoke hearts, halved

Finely ground unrefined sea salt

¹/₄ cup torn fresh basil

¹/₄ cup torn fresh mint

¹/₄ cup chopped fresh flat-leaf parsley

Warm the lard and olive oil in a heavy stockpot over medium heat. When the lard melts, stir in the leek and lemon zest and fry until they release their perfume and the leek softens, about 4 minutes. Stir in the carrots and fry, stirring from time to time, until crisp-tender, 5 to 7 minutes.

Stir in the broth, lima beans, peas, and artichoke hearts. Cover and simmer until the vegetables become tender, about 30 minutes. Season to your liking with salt, stir in the herbs and lemon juice, and serve.

chapter two

from the pasture

THE PASTURES IN OUR ALPINE VALLEY ERUPT in green every May. The native grasses grow rapidly in the gradually warming weather, nourished by the mineral-rich soil and fed by the runoff from the winter's receding snow. The earth smells of mud, green things, and the first budding wildflowers that will, in their turn, overtake the hills with their blossoms. The white flowers arrive first, then the yellow mule's ears, followed by huge sprays of pink, purple, and brilliant red. Enclosed in the gray and white recesses of winter for six months or longer, the valley finally bursts open in color.

Those of us left in the valley slough off the driving bleakness of winter and the ensuing mud season when everything seems wet, cold, and brown. Wildlife returns to the valley, too, now that it can support life once more. Ranchers, who sent their herds of cattle and sheep farther south to winter in warmer temperatures, bring them back again to graze on the newly verdant pasture, for they know that spring grass provides profound nourishment after a winter of dry hay.

For a long time I didn't understand the natural and seasonal nature of milk and eggs, as they sat in gleaming cases in the dairy aisle of the local supermarket, perpetually available. Yet, as I spent time connecting with local growers, I learned that not only do vegetables and fruits enjoy their given seasons, waxing to a peak before waning again; rather, all foods have their seasons, moving within the rhythm of spring, summer, autumn, and winter. Just as late summer seems to produce the ripest and most robust tomatoes, so too does spring bring the best cream, eggs, and milk that the animals on pasture can provide. Spring brings the richest cream, and autumn the most flavorful milk.

Milk and Cream

In spring, calving begins at the local raw dairy. Having returned from their winter pastures ninety miles away where the altitude is lower and the cold temperatures milder, the cows give birth one by one, leading to many a late night of work for the tireless managers of the dairy where we, and other community members, hold shares. The calves arrive in spring, when the mild weather and rapidly growing green grass can best support their growth. It's this time, too, that the dairy reopens for its shareholders after five months of rest.

The milk and cream arrive in abundance in those first few months, before waning in supply around November, when the cows dry off for the duration of their pregnancy and leave the valley until the grass is green once more. The cream in the chilled 2-quart jars rises to the top of the milk, forming a cream line that can be 5 inches thick at times. Sometimes the cream is so thick it won't pour; rather, you must scoop it out with a spoon. Later, as the calves grow and spring turns to summer, the milk changes ever so slightly—the thick and viscous cream line in those cold jugs of milk shrinks a little week by week. By mid-autumn, pints of thick cream become scarce, and then the milk disappears altogether as winter approaches and the cows rest. We miss the milk, to be sure, but less than you might think. If I've been conscientious, I've made enough butter and cheese to last us until the cows return to pasture with their new calves come springtime.

My husband and I often pack our little boy into the car and drive a few miles down to the dairy to see the doe-eyed Guernseys and Jerseys grazing happily with their calves on green grass beneath the brilliant blue alpine sky. Our little boy knows the cows by name, even as they come and go from the herd. There's Nettle, Sweet Clover, and Buttercup—beautiful animals with deep brown eyes fringed in black. Their soft muzzles push into your hand when you offer them a bit of grass just plucked from the field.

Traditional and seasonal dairying ensures the health of the cows. The milk and cream a cow produces reflects her health, and the quality of nutrients she consumes. Cows are ruminants, grazing animals, and grass represents their natural diet. Rich in vitamins, minerals, and antioxidants, the varied grasses and wild herbs found on a healthy and biodiverse pasture support a cow's optimal health and influence the nutrient quality of her milk and cream. The milk of cows grazing on grass contains more nutrients than the milk of her grain-fed, industrially raised counterparts; grass-fed milk is rich in vitamins A and K2, as well as healthy fatty acids such as conjugated linoleic acid (CLA) and trans-palmitoleic acid.

Raw Milk

Every Wednesday for the last six years, my husband and I have picked up our weekly supply of milk. We'd meet our dairy farmer surreptitiously at first, on street corners. She'd open the hatch of her hatchback and pass us icy cold glass jugs of fresh, frothy milk. It seemed like a subterfuge, as though we were purchasing something on the black market—skirting the law—and oddly incongruent for something as simple and wholesome as milk. When we began picking up our milk, the law in Colorado had only recently changed to allow consumers like us to purchase part of a dairy herd, and in turn acquire raw milk. With the newness of the change, and having felt accustomed to purchasing milk from the store for years, it felt strange to meet on a street corner to pay our dues and pick up the milk.

My family consumes raw milk, butter, cream, and yogurt. There's a richness to raw milk that pasteurized whole milk and cream lack. Raw milk tastes sweeter, with more complex notes than can be found in industrially or even organically produced pasteurized milk. The flavor of raw milk evolves with the seasons, depending on the grasses in the pasture where the cows graze. Just as the grasses change with the seasons, so, too, does the flavor of the milk. Spring brings a subtle but distinct grassiness to the milk, while the milk of autumn tastes sharper and less sweet. I favor autumn's milk for cheese making, while I prefer springtime cream for butter making.

Raw milk hovers in a gray area of legality; most states disallow the sale of raw milk outright, others restrict it to on-farm purchase only, and some allow it to be sold for pets. A handful of states allow retail sales of raw milk. Others, like Colorado, protect access to raw milk through a shareholder program;

that is, the consumer purchases a part of a herd and pays the dairy to manage the herd and milk the cows. Since the consumer owns a part of the herd, he or she is entitled to drink the milk the herd produces. While I favor the legalization of raw milk for retail sale, I also cherish the herd share system because not only does it help consumers to better know their farmers and where their food comes from, it also helps to ensure community support for local farms.

Once widely available and, indeed, the only kind of milk available, raw milk has become increasingly difficult to access since the early part of the twentieth century due to government regulations. A resurgence of interest in local, traditional, and real food is beginning to be met with increased supply from young farmers and dairymen. The primary objection to raw milk rests on a concern for public health and safety; like all foods, raw milk can potentially harbor harmful bacteria. Most bacteria with which we come into contact either in our food or in our environment are beneficial or, at the very least, benign; however, those few pathogenic bacteria can create disease. Healthy, grass-fed cows raised by farmers who honor nature produce healthy milk. Industrially raised cows, fed an unnatural grain-based diet, not only produce fewer nutrients in their milk but are also more likely to produce milk contaminated by potentially harmful microorganisms. Further, many farmers who sell raw milk or who operate herd share programs often test their milk for the presence of harmful microorganisms and also practice optimal techniques to care for their cows. A sick cow is removed from the herd in the rare event she becomes ill, which the farmer does not only to comply with any relevant state laws, but also to ensure that the food they produce meets the quality expected by their customers.

In addition to its rich flavor and mouthfeel, raw milk also offers an assortment of other benefits. Raw milk produced from grass-fed cows contains a plethora of naturally occurring vitamins, antioxidants, food enzymes, and beneficial bacteria that are often destroyed during the pasteurization process. While milk's fat-soluble vitamins help to nourish our bodies, and its beneficial bacteria help to support the immune system, its food enzymes help in our digestion of it, which is why some people who otherwise feel intolerant of pasteurized milk tolerate raw milk more easily.

Store raw milk in the refrigerator for up to 10 days, and use it within about 1 week of opening the jar. Raw milk will begin to sour on its own, due to the presence of naturally occurring beneficial bacteria. Sour milk should smell pleasantly tart like yogurt or buttermilk, and you can use it in place of buttermilk.

Pasteurized and Homogenized Milk

Pasteurization, invented in the 1860s by French chemist and microbiologist Louis Pasteur, applies enough heat to milk that it destroys any microorganisms present.

This process kills existing beneficial bacteria as well as any potentially harmful bacteria; it also destroys heat-sensitive vitamins and food enzymes in the process. When handling large volumes of milk from multiple sources, pasteurization can help to rid the milk of any disease-causing bacteria it may potentially contain; however, small-scale milk production coupled with scrupulous practices both with regard to herd health and the cleanliness of the milking parlor can help to ensure that raw milk is safe.

While pasteurization kills off microorganisms, both beneficial and potentially harmful, naturally existing in the milk, it also provides an avenue for contamination by foreign microorganisms later. As a result of post-pasteurization contamination, pasteurized milk can become a source of food-borne illness.

The times and temperatures at which dairy processors pasteurize milk varies from 145°F for 30 minutes to 280°F for 2 seconds, in a process known as ultrahigh temperature (UHT) pasteurization. Processing milk at the temperatures required for ultrahigh temperature pasteurization can change the nature of the proteins existing within milk, and it also extends the shelf life of milk—making it shelf-stable at room temperature for a year or longer, provided it's kept in a hermetically sealed carton. The heat-sensitive vitamins that were destroyed are then replaced through fortification. Pasteurization also changes the flavor and mouthfeel of raw milk. Raw milk drinkers often complain that pasteurized milk lacks flavor, feels thin, or tastes "cooked."

Cream, being lighter than milk, separates and rises to the top of a bottle of milk, developing the characteristic cream line found in raw milk or pasteurized, but not homogenized, milk. Homogenization is a mechanical process that changes the structure of the fat in milk, making the fat cells smaller so that the milk fat remains suspended within the milk, rather than rising to the top.

In my kitchen, I prefer to use raw milk and raw cream. If the expense or scarcity prevents you from using raw dairy in cooking, consider substituting vat-pasteurized, non-homogenized milk from grass-fed cows. Due to increased interest among consumers, retailers and health food stores are increasingly making this type of milk more available. I avoid UHT milk and do not recommend its use in my recipes.

Cultured and Fermented Dairy Foods

Dairying people across the world recognized the temporary, seasonal nature of milk and, with classic human ingenuity, developed a natural way to preserve milk for winter months when cows went dry. They produced cultured butter and buttermilk, clabbered milk, cheese, kefir, and a wide variety of yogurts that nourished their families when dairy and other fresh foods grew scarce.

Just as beneficial bacteria consume naturally present sugars in vegetables and fruit, producing lactic acid, which acts as a preservative, so, too, can beneficial bacteria transform milk into a long-lasting yogurt or cheese. As the beneficial bacteria do their work, eating milk's natural sugars, they increase the vitamins in the milk, particularly B vitamins like folate, a nutrient critical to women of reproductive age and for their babies, too. After fermentation, dairy foods typically have increased vitamin content coupled with lower levels of carbohydrates.

Some bacteria thrive at room temperature, while other bacteria thrive at slightly elevated temperatures. For this reason, some cultured dairy foods, like sour cream and buttermilk, are produced with mesophilic cultures at room temperature. Others, like classic Bulgarian yogurt, are made with thermophilic or heat-loving starter cultures at a more constant, elevated temperature between 108°F and 112°F.

When you first purchase starter cultures for homemade yogurt, they'll arrive in little packets as a fine, milky powder. Once you add the starter culture to the milk or cream of your choosing and prepare your first batch of yogurt, reserve 1/4 cup of the yogurt to use as a starter culture for future batches. In this way, your starter cultures can be reused indefinitely.

Room-Temperature Yogurts from Northern Europe

Northern Europe is home to a wide variety of different yogurts, each with their own unique characteristics, from runny to thick, sweet to cheese-like. These yogurts are made at room temperature and do not require milk to be heated or kept at a warm temperature for an extended period of time in order to culture properly. With its thin texture and cheese-like flavor, *piima* pairs well with vegetables, while *viili*'s soft sweetness and gelatinous texture make it a lovely match for desserts and honey-sweetened fruit. Exploring these lesser-known varieties of yogurt allows you to experiment with their unique flavors and textures, giving you the opportunity to find a new style you might prefer over those you are used to. You can find starters online though a variety of shops specializing in fermentation.

VIILI
Popular in Finland, *viili* tastes mildly sweet by comparison with other, stronger yogurts, and its viscous, jelly-like consistency appeals to small children.

FIL MJOLK
Fil mjolk tastes mildly of cheese and is less sour than other yogurts. Its thickness makes it particularly well suited to straining for making Yogurt Cheese (page 57), and it pairs well with common herbs like chives, dill, and flat-leaf parsley.

PIIMA
Piima lacks *viili*'s and *fil mjolk*'s thickness. When cultured, it remains thin and takes on a mild cheese-like flavor. It serves as an excellent substitute for buttermilk because they share similar flavors and consistencies.

Preparing Raw Milk Yogurt

Both Scandanavian-Style Room-Temperature Yogurt (opposite) and Slow-Cultured Yogurt (page 56) can be prepared from raw milk, without first scalding the milk, for those who wish to keep the heat-sensitive components of raw milk live and active. To prepare truly raw milk yogurt, simply whisk the starter culture of your choice into your raw milk, or use a pure seed starter described below, and culture it for the length of time required in the recipe.

Due to the protein structure of raw milk and its food enzyme content, raw milk yogurts tend toward runniness, and they rarely develop the thickness associated with yogurts made from heated or scalded milk. Scalding the milk denatures the milk proteins to some extent, and culturing the milk allows those proteins to coagulate more easily, producing a thick yogurt unlike the thin and liquid yogurts produced from unheated raw milk.

PURE SEED STARTER FOR RAW MILK YOGURTS

If you wish to prepare yogurt from raw milk, consider maintaining a pure seed starter that will ensure the integrity of your yogurt's texture and flavor over time. Many consumers seek out raw milk in effort to support small, local farms and for its high-quality nutrition. The use of raw milk, which is extraordinarily rich in beneficial bacteria, can actually change the results of your yogurt after successive reculturing. Those beneficial bacteria may overtake, outnumber, and outcompete with the bacteria in the starter culture you use. As a result, by using raw milk over an extended period of time, you may lose the unique characteristics of the yogurt you intend to culture—such as texture or flavor—and instead produce clabbered milk.

If you wish to maintain the texture and flavor of the yogurt you make but also want to use raw milk, you need to maintain a pure seed starter. By scalding milk, thus killing off any naturally occurring bacteria, you can prepare a pure starter culture to inoculate your raw milk yogurts without compromising the texture or flavor of your yogurt over time.

MAKES ABOUT ½ CUP

½ cup raw milk

1 tablespoon yogurt

Pour the milk into a small saucepan and bring it to a boil over medium-high heat. Immediately turn off the heat and let the milk cool to the temperature required for your starter culture (110°F for thermophilic yogurts like Bulgarian yogurt, and room temperature for Scandinavian-style yogurts like *viili*, *piima*, and *fil mjolk*). Stir in the yogurt and culture it for 8 to 24 hours for thermophilic yogurts or 24 to 48 hours for room-temperature yogurts.

Reserve 1 tablespoon of the pure seed starter in a small container with a tight-fitting lid in your refrigerator and use it to prepare another batch of pure seed starter within 2 weeks; use the remaining ½ cup to culture your raw milk yogurt.

To prepare yogurts from raw milk, follow the instructions for Scandanavian-Style Room-Temperature Yogurt (opposite) or Slow-Cultured Yogurt (page 56), using the pure seed starter to culture the milk, and omitting directions to boil the milk.

scandinavian-style
room-temperature yogurt

The flavor and consistency of the yogurt you make depends on the characteristics of the starter you use. Whether you choose *villi*, *piima*, or *fil mjolk* (see page 53 for more information about these types of yogurt), the instructions remain the same: mix your starter into the milk and then let it sit on your counter, undisturbed, for 24 to 48 hours, or until the yogurt thickens enough to separate cleanly from the walls of the jar when you tilt it. If you make your yogurt using raw milk as a base, refer to Preparing Raw Milk Yogurt, opposite. MAKES ABOUT 1 QUART

4 cups whole milk

¼ cup *viili, piima, fil mjolk,* or mesophilic yogurt starter

Pour the milk into a saucepan and bring it to a boil over medium heat. When bubbles first appear, immediately turn off the heat and allow the milk to cool to room temperature.

Thoroughly whisk the starter into the milk, taking care not to leave any clumpy bits of yogurt lingering in the milk. Pour the milk and starter culture into a quart-size jar, cover it loosely with a lid, and transfer it to a warm spot in your kitchen.

Allow the milk to culture at room temperature for 24 to 48 hours, or until the milk becomes semisolid and pulls away from the sides of the jar when you tilt it (the exception is a *piima*-cultured yogurt, which thickens only slightly and remains liquid after successful culturing).

Cover and refrigerate the yogurt and use it within a month. Remember to reserve ¼ cup of the yogurt to start future batches; store it in a small jar in the refrigerator for up to 2 weeks.

slow-cultured yogurt

Yogurt teems with life. Beneficial bacteria thrive in milk, eating away milk's natural sugars. That beautiful and ancient microbial process produces yogurt's distinct tartness. Most thermophilic yogurts culture for only 8 to 12 hours, but the longer you allow the bacteria to do their work, the more sour and complexly flavored your yogurt will become.

I prefer a strongly sour yogurt and favor culturing milk over a longer period of time—a full day. Over those 24 hours, milk transforms from liquid and sweet to thick and creamy with a striking lemony sourness. If you find that my process produces too strong a yogurt for your liking, consider culturing your yogurt for a shorter period of time. MAKES ABOUT 1 QUART

4 cups milk

¼ cup yogurt from a previous batch or store-bought yogurt with live active cultures

Pour the milk into a saucepan and bring it to a boil over medium heat. When bubbles first appear, immediately turn off the heat and allow the milk to cool to 108°F to 112°F.

Thoroughly whisk the yogurt into the milk so that any clumps dissolve. Pour the milk into a quart-sized jar, cover it loosely, and place it somewhere in your kitchen that maintains a constant temperature of 108°F to 112°F. You might choose a yogurt maker, a food dehydrator, a well-insulated cooler filled with warm water, or even a gas oven with a pilot light. Any method will do, as long as the temperature is steady and hovers between 108°F and 112°F.

Allow the milk to culture undisturbed for at least 8 and up to 24 hours while the beneficial bacteria do their work. After 8 hours the yogurt will taste slightly sour, and after 24, the yogurt will taste strikingly sour and lemony. The milk will have coagulated and will pull away from the walls of the jar in a solid mass when you tip the jar gently.

Cover and refrigerate the yogurt and use it within a month or so; remember to spoon about ¼ cup of the yogurt into a small jar to reserve for future batches.

yogurt cheese

Straining yogurt removes the thin whey, or liquid portion of the milk, from the milk solids that have thickened and coagulated during fermentation. Straining thickens the yogurt further, resulting in an extraordinary luscious consistency. The longer you allow the yogurt to strain, the thicker it will become—ranging from a soft consistency similar to Greek-style yogurt to a firmer texture, similar to cream cheese.

You can use the reserved whey in place of water as a nutrient-dense additive for breads and baked goods, as an addition to your morning smoothie, or as a replacement for vinegar in salad dressings. MAKES ABOUT 2 CUPS

4 cups Scandinavian-Style Room-Temperature Yogurt (page 55), Slow-Cultured Yogurt (opposite), or store-bought plain yogurt

Line a large fine-mesh sieve with a double layer of cheesecloth or a single layer of butter muslin and set it over a large mixing bowl. Pour the yogurt into the sieve, cover it loosely with the overhanging cheesecloth, and let it sit for 8 to 24 hours or until thickened to your liking. Don't worry about leaving your yogurt on the counter overnight at room temperature; the beneficial bacteria and the acidic nature of yogurt will prevent it from going bad during straining. However, if you prefer, you can move the bowl, yogurt, and strainer to the refrigerator.

Spoon the strained yogurt cheese into a jar, cover, and put it in the fridge where it should keep for up to a month or so.

Pour the whey into a separate jar and store it in the back of the refrigerator for up to 6 months, where the colder temperature helps to preserve the bacteria and it remains out of the way.

herb-and-oil-marinated yogurt cheese

After preparing yogurt cheese, I often marinate it with herbs and spices in olive oil, which not only preserves the yogurt, increasing its shelf life, but also infuses it with the distinct flavors of rosemary, black pepper, and lemon. If rosemary and black pepper don't appeal to you, consider substituting other herbs, like garlic chives or thyme; whole dried red chiles or red pepper flakes work well, too.

I favor olive oil made from Mission olives for this dish. Mission olive oil has a mild flavor and is low-wax, so it won't coagulate in the refrigerator like high-wax olive oils. Before you serve the marinated cheese, pull it from the refrigerator and let it stand at room temperature for about 20 minutes. Then spoon out a ball and a bit of oil and spread it on a piece of toasted bread.

MAKES ABOUT 1 QUART

2 cups Yogurt Cheese (page 57)

1 teaspoon finely ground unrefined sea salt

1 lemon

2 teaspoons whole black peppercorns

2 sprigs rosemary

Olive oil, to cover the cheese

Spoon the yogurt cheese into a mixing bowl and beat in the salt. Take 2 tablespoons of the cheese and roll it between the palms of your hands to make a round ball. Drop it into a jar. Continue until all the yogurt cheese is formed into balls.

Finely grate the zest of the lemon and place it in a small bowl. Cut the lemon in half crosswise and squeeze its juice into the bowl containing the lemon zest. Pour the lemon juice and finely grated zest over the cheese. Drop in the whole peppercorns, arrange the rosemary in the jar, and cover with olive oil. Refrigerate for at least 1 day and use within 2 months.

clarified butter

Clarifying butter deepens its flavor and color and concentrates its butterfat by removing its milk solids. The process also helps to extend its shelf life. Store clarified butter at room temperature out of direct light, just as you would store olive oil, coconut oil, or any other concentrated fat. Once you've removed the milk solids from the butterfat, there's little risk of spoilage.

You can apply high heat to clarified butter in ways that would cause regular butter to scorch. MAKES ABOUT 12 OUNCES

1 pound unsalted butter, cut into 1-inch pieces

Place the butter in a wide sauté pan set over low heat. Allow the butter to melt slowly. As it heats, froth and foam will gather on top of the liquid butter. Skim this off and discard it. Continue heating the butter until it becomes perfectly clear, about 10 minutes.

Set a fine-mesh sieve over a bowl and line it with a double layer of cheesecloth or a single layer of butter muslin. Pour the melted butter through the cloth and into the bowl. Discard the milk solids in the cloth, then pour the clarified butter into three 4-ounce jars or one 12-ounce jar and cover tightly. Stored in a cool, dark space, the clarified butter will keep for up to 1 year.

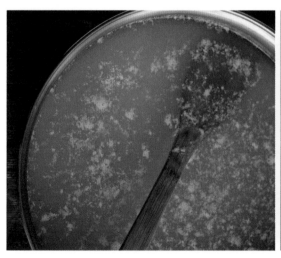

sweet cultured butter *and* true buttermilk

Cows seem to produce the best cream in springtime—thick enough to stand up on a spoon, pale yellow, and blessedly abundant. While the shares of cream I pick up from our local raw dairy will continue to arrive until mid-autumn, the cream in later months lacks the thick viscosity of early spring cream. When the cows graze on fresh, rapidly growing green grass, their cream turns a beautiful pale yellow color. When cultured and churned, springtime cream produces butter of vibrant gold.

I keep freshly churned butter in a little butter bell on my countertop, where it will keep for several weeks provided I exchange the water in the container daily. I freeze the butter, too, in balls weighing about a half pound each that I tuck away until winter, when the dairy in which my family holds a share ceases production. I also make ghee—or clarified butter (page 59)—storing it in 2-quart mason jars in my cupboard and dip into it as I need it.

MAKES ABOUT 1 CUP BUTTER AND 2 CUPS BUTTERMILK

---

4 cups heavy cream

¼ cup buttermilk (store-bought or from a previous batch of butter)

Stir the cream and buttermilk together in a large bowl. Cover the bowl loosely with a kitchen towel and tuck it away in a warm spot on your countertop. Let it stand, undisturbed, at room temperature for 18 to 24 hours, or until it tastes pleasantly sour.

Transfer the bowl to the refrigerator and let the cream chill for about 2 hours.

Whip the cream vigorously for 8 to 10 minutes in a stand mixer using the paddle attachment, until it moves past soft and firm peaks to its breaking point, when bits of coagulated butter separate from the thin, watery buttermilk. Continue beating until those bits of butter form larger clumps, another 3 to 6 minutes.

Line a fine-mesh sieve with a double layer of cheesecloth or a single layer of butter muslin and place it over a bowl. Pour the clumpy bits of butter and the cloudy buttermilk into the sieve to strain it. Pour the buttermilk into a jar, cover, and refrigerate. It should keep for about a month.

Remove the butter from the sieve and put it into the bowl that previously held the buttermilk. Add 2 cups cold water, transfer to the refrigerator, and let the butter harden for 5 to 10 minutes.

Remove the butter from the fridge and drain off the water. Working the butter with the back of a wooden spoon or with a butter paddle, knead the butter repeatedly to remove any residual water or buttermilk. When the butter becomes smooth and waxy and yields no more water when pressed, wrap it tightly in parchment paper and then in foil to seal it and prevent oxidation. Place the butter in the refrigerator. It should keep for up to 2 months, or if frozen, for up to a year.

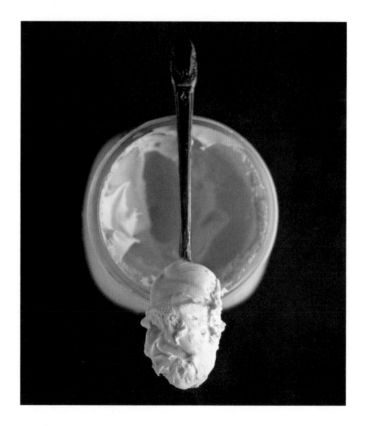

milk kefir

Similar to yogurt in flavor, though stronger, kefir is a traditional cultured dairy product from the Caucasus, a mountainous region at the southwestern gateway where the European continent meets Asia. For generations, the people of the Caucasus have cherished the sour and faintly bitter drink as an elixir of long life. Milk kefir, like all fermented foods, is extraordinarily rich in B vitamins, beneficial bacteria, food enzymes, and antioxidants. It also contains kefiran, a component unique to milk kefir that is responsible not only for the smooth mouthfeel of kefir, but also for many of its medicinal qualities.

Unlike other cultured dairy foods such as yogurt or cheese, kefir requires a symbiotic colony of bacteria and yeasts (SCOBY), also referred to as kefir grains, to culture properly. Despite their name, kefir grains are not grains at all, but rather a collection of beneficial bacteria and yeasts held together in a matrix of proteins, carbohydrates, and fats. Gelatinous in texture, they look like rumpled, overly large curds of cottage cheese. If you culture kefir regularly, your grains will proliferate and reproduce. Always keep the ratio of kefir grains to milk the same and give any excess grains away to a friend in need. Liquid and viscous, kefir is excellent on its own as a beverage, or it can be added to smoothies in place of yogurt. I often use it in place of buttermilk when cooking. A bit of honey tempers its acidity. MAKES ABOUT 1 QUART

1 heaping tablespoon milk kefir grains

4 cups milk

Put the kefir grains into a quart-size jar. Pour in the milk and cover tightly with a lid. Allow the milk to culture at room temperature for 24 to 48 hours, shaking or agitating the jar once or twice a day. The longer the milk ferments, the thicker and more sour it will become.

After the kefir sours enough for your liking, strain it through a fine-mesh sieve and pour it into bottles or jars. Cover and place the kefir in the refrigerator, where it should keep for the better part of a month.

Give the kefir grains in the sieve a quick rinse under running water, place them in a small glass container, cover them with water, and store them in the refrigerator. Milk kefir grains grow and proliferate when cultured regularly. Making milk kefir at least once a week will keep your grains vibrant and healthy.

sour cream ❧

I use sour cream with a heavy hand in my cooking, often spooning a dollop into soups or dressing vegetables and fruit with it. Its billowy softness reminds me of whipped cream, and its velvety tartness balances the fiery heat of chiles while also enlivening the earthy flavor of beans and lentils.

Like most cultured dairy foods, sour cream is easy to make—you simply whisk a starter into fresh cream and let the beneficial bacteria do their work, turning the fresh sweet cream into something thick and sour. I typically use buttermilk to culture my sour cream, but you can substitute any yogurt you might have on hand if no buttermilk lurks in your refrigerator.

MAKES ABOUT 2 CUPS

---

2 cups heavy cream

2 tablespoons buttermilk

Pour the cream into a bowl and whisk in the buttermilk until the buttermilk fully dissolves. Pour the inoculated cream into a pint-sized jar and cover with a lid. Let the cream culture at room temperature for 18 to 24 hours, until thickened and soured to your liking.

Transfer the sour cream to the refrigerator and use it up within about 6 weeks.

bonny clabber ✸

The tradition of preparing bonny clabber—a wild-fermented dairy product eaten like yogurt—was nearly lost in the last century although it was once enormously popular in the hills of Appalachia and in Scotland. As the pasteurization of milk took hold and lawmakers limited the sale of raw milk, bonny clabber fell from favor.

Bonny clabber can only be made from raw milk. Just as yogurt relies on the beneficial bacteria of its starter to culture milk, bonny clabber relies on the beneficial bacteria naturally occurring in raw milk for its transformation from liquid milk to curds and whey. After pasteurization, milk no longer contains its natural complement of beneficial bacteria; it is sterile and will not clabber.

Traditionally served for breakfast, bonny clabber is often sweetened with unrefined cane sugar or molasses and seasoned with nutmeg.

MAKES ABOUT 2 CUPS

4 cups raw milk

Unrefined cane sugar or blackstrap molasses, to serve

Freshly grated nutmeg, to serve

Pour the milk into a quart-sized jar and set it in a warm spot in your kitchen. Cover loosely with the lid. Allow the milk to rest, undisturbed, for 3 to 5 days, or until the curds separate from the whey. At this point, the creamy milk solids will rest at the bottom of the jar and the thin, blue-green liquid whey will float at the top.

Line a fine-mesh sieve with cheesecloth or butter muslin and place it over a large mixing bowl. Pour the curds and whey into the lined sieve and allow to drain for about 8 hours, or until the curds are thick and smooth, resembling Greek yogurt in texture.

Spoon the curds into a serving bowl, sweeten them with unrefined cane sugar or molasses, and sprinkle with freshly grated nutmeg as it suits you. Or spoon the curds into a container, cover tightly, and refrigerate for up to 1 week.

Pour the whey into a glass bottle and refrigerate it for up to 6 months. One way to use the whey is in the brine for Pickled Tongue with Mustard Sauce (page 110).

skyr

Though you might think of skyr as yogurt, it is more accurately described as a soft cheese because it is made with rennet, a complex of enzymes that coagulates liquid milk and causes it to separate into curds and whey. Skyr is traditionally made from skimmed milk, milk from which the cream has been separated for butter making. But don't confuse traditional skimmed milk for the pallid blue skim milk sold in stores; the store-bought version contains a wide variety of additives and synthetic vitamins.

Skyr is pleasantly sour and remarkably thick. I often mix it with honey and fresh fruit for breakfast or a light dessert. MAKES ABOUT 2 CUPS

8 cups milk (not ultrapasteurized)

1/4 cup skyr

2 tablespoons water

3 drops liquid rennet

Warm the milk in a heavy stockpot over medium-low heat until it reaches 110°F. Whisk in the skyr until it fully dissolves into the warm milk.

Pour the water into a little bowl, stir in the liquid rennet, then stir the mixture into the milk with deliberate up and down strokes. Cover the pot and let it sit in a warm place, such as a sink filled with warm water (about 104°F), for 12 hours or until the milk solids coagulate, separating from the yellowish whey. As the water in the sink cools, drain it and replace it with warm water to maintain a consistent temperature.

With a long-bladed knife, cut the curds by making firm slices the length of the pot, about 1 inch apart, then turn the pot 90 degrees and make similar slices across the curds to achieve a cross-hatched effect.

Line a fine-mesh sieve with a double layer of cheesecloth and set it over a large bowl. Spoon the curds into the sieve, cover with a bit of cheesecloth, and allow the curds to drain at room temperature for 6 to 8 hours, until they thicken to the consistency of Greek-style yogurt.

Transfer the curds to a bowl and beat them by hand with a wooden spoon until smooth. Spoon the skyr into a jar, cover, and transfer to the refrigerator, where it will keep for 6 to 8 weeks.

slip

Slip is a sweet clabbered milk made with rennet; however, it lacks the complex acidity of cheeses and other clabbered milks because it requires no bacterial starter culture that would otherwise eliminate its natural sweetness through fermentation. Popular in the nineteenth century, slip was traditionally served in the summer and spring months, when dairy cows produce abundant milk. Slip pairs well with other foods of spring and summer, particularly fresh berries, sweetened, if you like, with a drizzle of honey. Or serve it with honey, unrefined sugar, nutmeg, cinnamon, or cream. MAKES ABOUT 2 CUPS

2 tablespoons water

3 drops liquid rennet

4 cups whole milk (not ultrapasteurized)

Pour the water into a little bowl, stir in the liquid rennet, and set it aside.

Pour the milk into a saucepan and warm it over very low heat until it reaches blood temperature, 98° to 100°F. The milk should be neither hot nor cold to the touch.

Stir the rennet mixture into the warm milk, cover with a lid, and allow it to sit at room temperature for about 6 hours, or until the thin and watery whey separates from the curds.

Place a fine-mesh sieve over a bowl and line it with a double layer of cheesecloth or a single layer of butter muslin. Pour the curds and whey into the cheesecloth-lined sieve and allow the curds to drain for about 6 hours, until they have thickened.

Transfer the curds to a large mixing bowl and whip by hand with a whisk for 1 or 2 minutes, until smooth. Serve the slip at room temperature or slightly chilled. Or cover and store the slip in the refrigerator, but use it up within a day or so; after that, its texture becomes rubbery.

simple herb cheese

This simple fresh cheese requires no starter culture or rennet and instead relies on the acidic nature of white vinegar to cause the milk solids to separate from the whey. Its taste is sweet, milky, and mild, so I like to add fresh herbs to the cheese, though you can skip them if you prefer a plain cheese. I serve the cheese cubed, for a light appetizer or a small snack, though it also melts very well and can substitute for any similar mild-tasting cheese.

MAKES ABOUT 4 (2-OUNCE) SERVINGS

8 cups whole milk
(not ultrapasteurized)

3 tablespoons white vinegar

1 tablespoon snipped chives

1 tablespoon chopped fresh curly parsley

1 teaspoon finely ground unrefined sea salt

1/4 teaspoon freshly ground black pepper

Line a fine-mesh sieve with a double layer of cheesecloth and set it over a large bowl to catch the dripping whey.

Bring the milk to a boil over medium heat, stirring it frequently to prevent scorching. Decrease the heat to low and stir in the vinegar. The milk solids should separate from the whey almost immediately, but continue stirring until the solids separate completely from the greenish-colored whey. Turn off the heat and let the curds and whey rest for about 5 minutes. Pour the curds and whey into the cheesecloth-lined sieve, then stir the herbs, salt, and pepper into the curds.

Twist the cloth together over the curds and knot it tightly so that the curds form a thick, round ball. Give the cheesecloth a good squeeze to wring out more whey. Hang the cloth on a hook or knot it around a spoon handle and suspend the ball above a bowl. Or, hang the cloth on the faucet of your kitchen sink. Allow the remaining whey to drip out of the bundle for 4 hours.

Give the bundle one last squeeze, then unwrap the cheese, place it in an airtight container, and store in the fridge for about a week.

Eggs

Just as cows produce milk within a seasonal cycle, so do hens lay eggs. A hen's natural cycle of egg production waxes and wanes with the movement of the sun. In spring and summer, when days grow long, her egg production increases. In her prime, she will typically lay one egg a day; however, as the days grow dark again in autumn and winter, she lays eggs infrequently until her production halts altogether, and she molts. Slowly, over a period of two months or so, she loses her feathers—around the head at first, then along her neck, breast, thighs, wings, back, and tail. Molting birds are homely birds—scraggly-looking things who eat but do not lay.

The hens in our valley completely cease production of eggs around the time of the winter solstice, during the third week of December. Once they've molted and refreshed themselves in new feathers, their egg production steadily increases until spring, when the eggs arrive in magnificent abundance. Not only do we receive our eggs through our local farm, but every backyard chicken wrangler seems to give my family an extra half dozen here or there until a basket of six or seven dozen sits on my counter, and I think to myself now's the time to make custard.

Consumers don't typically witness this cycle of scarcity followed by plenty. Free-range and organic eggs line the dairy case of every grocery store, giving the false impression that eggs are and should be available year-round. Yet year-round abundance of eggs in grocery stores belies a deception of modern egg production; that is, hens are kept inside, where a cycle of indoor lighting unrelated to waxing and waning of daylight throughout the seasons tricks their bodies into producing eggs whether or not it is seasonally appropriate. Of course, in order to maintain the level of industrial production, the hens do not receive access to the outdoors or to their natural diet of bugs and grubs, and the quality of their eggs—both in flavor and in nutrition—suffers.

I favor pasture-raised eggs for my family, and we pick them up directly from the farm when we can. Whereas industrially raised hens eat a diet of grain, corn, and soybeans, pasture-raised hens enjoy their natural diet of sprouts, grubs, and insects with some supplementation by kitchen scraps or a small amount of chicken feed.

A thing of beauty, the yolk of a pasture-raised egg tastes extraordinary. It stands firm and high in the viscous, clear egg white, and its color positively gleams a vivid and rich orange like that of a marigold.

The Myth of the Vegetarian-Fed Hen

Although the label "vegetarian-fed" stamped across cardboard cartons of eggs at your local health food stores might lead you to believe that chickens are natural herbivores, that label is deceptive. Quite simply, hens, like many other birds, are not natural vegetarians; a well-rounded omnivorous diet for hens supports both their health and the quality of their eggs. The term "vegetarian-fed" gained popularity in the last few decades because consumers realized that unscrupulous industrial egg producers fed animal waste to their laying hens as a way to cut corners, producing the most eggs they could for the cheapest price they could. Feeding industrial animal waste to the hens, understandably, resulted in sick—but expendable—birds. As public uproar against the practice increased, many egg producers opted to feed their hens a vegetarian diet comprised almost entirely of grain and soy. While vegetarian-fed hens do not consume industrial animal waste, they also do not consume their natural diet. And caged or housed in huge indoor facilities, they are denied a natural life under the sun and in the grass.

In her natural state, a hen is an astute forager. She lives outside with her flock. She pecks and scratches her way across the pasture, where she eats insects, worms, and grubs in addition to sprouts, clover, and other forage. Rich in omega-3 fatty acids, antioxidants, and vitamins, her natural foods support her health and the nutrient quality as well as the flavor of her eggs in ways that exclusive grain feeding cannot. A pasture-raised egg contains two-thirds more vitamin A, three times more vitamin E, seven times more beta carotene, and twice the omega-3 fatty acids compared to the egg of a conventionally raised hen.

Storing Eggs

I prefer to pick up our eggs from the farm and store them on the countertop in an egg basket where they'll stay fresh for up to 6 weeks, depending on the ambient temperature of our home. A thin cuticle or bloom covers the exterior of an egg, protecting it from contamination by external sources of bacteria. Light rinsing will not damage this cuticle, and as long as it remains intact, the egg will stay fresh for a period of weeks—even at room temperature. Make sure the egg shell remains intact before you use it; small cracks and breaks can compromise the egg, leaving it open to contamination. Eggs in the United States are typically sold refrigerated after having been dipped in a solution that removes their protective cuticle, leaving them open to microbial contamination unless stored below 40°F. If you purchase refrigerated eggs, keep them in the refrigerator. If you are ever uncertain as to whether your eggs are fresh, fill a bowl of water: a fresh egg will sink, while a rotten egg will float in the water.

shirred eggs *with* gravlax *and* asparagus ❧

On weekends when family arrives to our little mountain town, I often prepare shirred eggs to greet them in the morning as they tumble into the kitchen hungry for breakfast. I butter individual ramekins and drop in a bit of whatever's in season: chopped tomato and basil in summer, mushrooms in autumn, or a bit of bacon or cured meat in winter. I crack open an egg into each of the ramekins, pour a spoonful of cream over the top, and set them in the oven to bake. While my ingredients may change from season to season, my favorite combination includes gravlax and asparagus. SERVES 6

6 ounces chopped Gravlax with Maple, Dill, and Juniper (page 135), or store-bought gravlax

6 asparagus spears, trimmed of woody ends and chopped

6 eggs

1 shallot, finely grated

6 tablespoons heavy cream

1¹/₂ teaspoons freshly ground black pepper

Preheat the oven to 425°F. Butter six 6-ounce ramekins and set them on a baking sheet.

Evenly distribute the gravlax and asparagus among the ramekins. Crack open the eggs one at a time and drop one into each ramekin. Sprinkle a bit of the grated shallot over each egg, pour over 1 tablespoon of cream, and sprinkle with ¹/₄ teaspoon of black pepper.

Carefully transfer the baking sheet holding the ramekins to the oven and bake for 8 to 12 minutes, until the yolks are done to your liking. Baking the eggs for 8 minutes yields runny yolks, while baking for 12 minutes yields firm yolks. Serve immediately.

fresh herb frittata ❦

In spring, when the farmers' fields offer very little, I find both eggs and fresh herbs in abundance at our farmers market. Although a frittata makes a lovely breakfast, I prefer to serve it as a light lunch alongside a salad of crisp just-picked lettuce and young radishes.

I make this frittata with chives, parsley, dill, and chervil—four herbs that I grow year-round, outside in warm weather and inside next to a window in cold weather. If you haven't these same herbs, use what you do have on hand. Basil is lovely, as are marjoram, fennel, and even mint. SERVES ABOUT 6

---

9 eggs

2 tablespoons heavy cream

2 tablespoons chopped fresh flat-leaf parsley

1 tablespoon snipped fresh chives

1 teaspoon chopped fresh dill

1 teaspoon chopped fresh chervil

2 tablespoons unsalted butter

Preheat the oven to 425°F.

Break open the eggs into a large mixing bowl, pour in the cream, and beat them together until loosely combined. Whisk in the herbs.

Melt the butter in a 10-inch ovenproof skillet over medium-low heat; when it froths, pour in the eggs. Let the eggs cook, undisturbed, for 5 minutes, or until the bottom is cooked through but the top is still liquid.

Transfer the skillet to the oven and bake for 5 minutes, until the eggs have set. Invert the frittata onto a plate or leave it in the pan, cut it into wedges, and serve.

yogurt *and* cheddar cheese soufflé *with* chives ✦

This soufflé has a gentle sharpness owing to the combination of yogurt and sharp cheddar cheese. I like the way these two flavors combine with the soft onion-like flavor of fresh chives. Use the sharpest cheddar you can find.

SERVES 4 TO 6

2 cups plus 2 tablespoons finely shredded sharp cheddar cheese

4 eggs, separated

1 cup yogurt

3 tablespoons high-extraction wheat or einkorn flour (see page 157) or unbleached all-purpose flour

1/2 teaspoon finely ground unrefined sea salt

1/2 teaspoon finely ground white pepper

2 heaping tablespoons finely snipped chives

Preheat the oven to 400°F. Butter a 1 1/2-quart soufflé dish and dust it with the 2 tablespoons of shredded cheddar cheese, taking care to coat the bottom and sides of the dish evenly.

In a large bowl, beat the egg yolks with the yogurt, flour, salt, pepper, and chives.

In a separate bowl, whip the egg whites by hand until they form stiff peaks. Fold one-third of the egg whites into the egg yolk and yogurt mixture to lighten the mixture. Fold in the remaining 2 cups of cheddar cheese, followed by the remaining egg whites. Gently pour the soufflé mixture into the prepared dish.

Place the soufflé in the oven and immediately decrease the temperature to 375°F. Bake the soufflé undisturbed for 25 minutes, or until puffed and golden brown on top but slightly wobbly at its center. Serve immediately lest the soufflé fall while you wait to get it to the table.

scrambled eggs *with* salmon roe

Eggs and roe make a natural pairing. Salmon roe brings the essence of the sea, and the chicken eggs temper that direct briny and faintly oily flavor to create something softer and delightfully creamy. Both pair nicely with dill and with sour cream.

Salmon roe is extraordinarily rich in vitamins A and K, the former contributing to reproductive health and the latter to bone and heart health. Like the salmon itself, the roe is rich in omega-3 fatty acids, which help to support heart health and overall systemic wellness. SERVES 4

8 eggs

2 tablespoons sour cream, plus more to serve

2 tablespoons unsalted butter

1/4 cup Smoked Salmon Roe (page 141) or ikura

1 tablespoon chopped fresh dill

1/4 teaspoon finely ground white pepper

Crack the eggs open into a large mixing bowl and whisk them lightly to break up the yolks. Whisk in the sour cream until barely combined.

Melt the butter in a skillet over medium-low heat. When it froths, pour in the eggs. Let them sit, undisturbed, for about 30 seconds. Using a spatula, stir the eggs until they begin to curdle, then fold in the roe, dill, and pepper. Cook a minute or two longer, until the eggs are cooked through but not rubbery, then spoon them onto individual dishes and serve with extra sour cream.

eggs poached *in* fiery tomato sauce ✢

The soft, buttery orange yolk of the egg melts into the fresh tomato sauce, which offers just a little bit of a kick thanks to the inclusion of crushed red pepper flakes. I prepare this dish often in the summertime, especially for lunch; I pair it with a simple green salad spiked with basil and drizzled with olive oil and balsamic vinegar. SERVES 6

TOMATO SAUCE

2 tablespoons extra-virgin olive oil

1 shallot, thinly sliced

2 cloves garlic, thinly sliced

1/2 teaspoon finely ground unrefined sea salt

1/2 teaspoon crushed red pepper flakes

2 ribs celery, finely chopped

1 carrot, peeled and finely chopped

1 tablespoon fresh thyme leaves

1 cup Chicken Bone Broth (page 120)

3 pounds tomatoes, peeled, seeded, and chopped

1 tablespoon balsamic vinegar

EGGS

6 eggs

6 slices toasted sourdough bread

1/4 cup chopped fresh basil

Warm the olive oil in a wide, nonreactive saucepan over medium heat. Toss in the shallot, garlic, salt, and crushed red pepper flakes and sauté until softened and fragrant, about 4 minutes. Stir in the celery, carrot, and thyme and continue sautéing until the celery and carrot have softened, about 8 minutes. Pour in the chicken broth and use a spatula to scrape any bits adhering to the bottom of the pan. Stir in the tomatoes and balsamic vinegar, lower the heat to medium-low, and simmer for 35 to 40 minutes, until the sauce becomes fragrant and the tomatoes soften and lose their form.

Crack the eggs, one at a time, into a small bowl and slip them very gently into the sauce, taking care not to break the yolks. Cover the pan and poach the eggs in the tomato sauce for 3 to 5 minutes, until the whites become firm. Poaching for 3 minutes will yield runny yolks, and 5 will deliver firm yolks.

Place a piece of toasted bread into each of six bowls. Ever so gently, transfer one egg at a time from the sauce to the bowls using a slotted spoon. Evenly distribute the sauce among the bowls, top with basil, and serve.

potherb *and* goat cheese pie *with a* potato crust

I like to serve egg-rich vegetable pies for lunch or for a light dinner. I place heaping wedges onto plates with a scoop of one fermented vegetable or another, depending on what sits in our refrigerator. From time to time I substitute thinly sliced potatoes for a floury crust. It makes for a charming, rustic appearance, and the potatoes grow tender and soft as the pie bakes. My favorite of these pies includes greens and herbs—particularly chard, kale, parsley, and thyme—though mustard greens make a nice substitute for either chard or kale. SERVES 6

1 bunch Swiss chard (about 12 ounces)

1 small bunch curly kale (about 8 ounces)

1/4 cup chopped fresh flat-leaf parsley

1 teaspoon fresh thyme leaves

4 Yukon Gold potatoes

2 tablespoons clarified butter (page 59)

8 eggs

1/4 cup heavy cream

1/2 teaspoon finely ground unrefined sea salt

4 ounces chèvre

Preheat the oven to 375°F.

Trim the Swiss chard of any tough stems or veins, then stack the leaves on top of one another, roll them into a cigar, and slice them crosswise into strips about 1/4 inch wide. Tear the kale leaves away from the tough stems and into small pieces no bigger than 1/2 inch; discard the stems. Put the torn kale in a bowl with the Swiss chard, parsley, and thyme.

Keeping the skins on, slice the potatoes crosswise into 1/8-inch-thick rounds.

Melt the butter in a 10-inch ovenproof skillet over medium-low heat. Swirl the skillet so that the butter lightly coats the bottom and sides. Turn off the heat and carefully arrange the potato slices along the bottom and sides of the pan to form a crust. Tightly pack the greens and herbs into the potato-lined skillet.

Crack the eggs into a mixing bowl and add the cream and salt. Beat them together until uniform in color. Pour the egg mixture over the vegetables, filling the skillet to within 1/2 inch of its rim; you may not need to use all the eggs. Drop the chèvre a teaspoon at a time into the eggs and vegetables.

Transfer the skillet to the oven and bake for 40 to 45 minutes, until the center of the pie no longer wobbles when you gently shake the pan. Allow the pie to rest for 5 minutes before slicing into wedges and serving.

olive oil mayonnaise ❦

I make mayonnaise weekly, using the freshest eggs, a bit of salt, vinegar, and olive oil. You can whisk it together by hand, slowly dripping in the olive oil, or use a food processor to simplify the process. For a few years I struggled with making mayonnaise—the sauce came out too thin or it broke and curdled—that is, until I learned that adding a tablespoon of water helps to emulsify the mayonnaise, producing a remarkably clean, lofty, and light consistency. MAKES ABOUT 2 CUPS

3 egg yolks

¼ teaspoon finely ground unrefined sea salt

1 tablespoon apple cider vinegar

1 tablespoon water

1½ cups extra-virgin olive oil

To Make Mayonnaise by Hand

Drop the egg yolks into a bowl, sprinkle them with the salt, then pour in the vinegar. Whisk together until barely combined, then whisk in the water.

Pour the oil into a small salad dressing cruet or pitcher. With a whisk in one hand and the oil in the other, carefully add the oil to the bowl one drop at a time as you whisk the ingredients. Resist the temptation to pour the oil more quickly. After a minute or two, the egg yolks will begin to thicken and increase in volume. Now you can drizzle the oil into the eggs in a very fine stream as you continue to whisk, but take care not to add the oil too quickly or your mayonnaise will break. Continue whisking until you've incorporated all the oil into the yolks.

Spoon the mayonnaise into a jar, cover tightly, and store it in the refrigerator, where it will keep for about 5 days.

To Make Mayonnaise in a Food Processor

Put the egg yolks in a food processor with the salt, vinegar, and water; pulse once or twice to combine. Continue processing the egg yolks while slowly adding the olive oil drop by drop until well emulsified.

Spoon the mayonnaise into a jar, cover tightly, and store it in the refrigerator, where it will keep for about 5 days.

puffed pancake *with* honey *and* lemon ✤

A puffed pancake is my simple solution to breakfast and brunches. Unlike cooking pancakes on a griddle or in a pan, preparing a puffed pancake requires no painstaking attentiveness, a virtue I lack early in the morning. I simply whip the ingredients together, pour them in a hot pan, and let the oven finish my work. This pancake puffs to 6 inches or higher in a hot oven, like a giant golden crown, but it deflates rapidly once you remove it from the oven, so don't linger in the kitchen too much. SERVES 6 TO 8

2 tablespoons unsalted butter

6 eggs

³/₄ cup whole milk

¹/₄ cup honey

¹/₂ cup high-extraction wheat or einkorn flour (see page 157) or unbleached all-purpose flour

¹/₄ teaspoon finely ground unrefined sea salt

1 teaspoon finely grated lemon zest

1 lemon, cut into 6 or 8 wedges, to serve

Preheat the oven to 425°F.

Melt the butter in a cast-iron skillet over medium heat. When the butter froths, turn off the heat and let it be.

In a large mixing bowl, beat together the eggs, milk, and honey until uniformly combined. Beat in the flour, salt, and lemon zest. Pour the batter into the buttered skillet. Transfer the skillet to the oven and bake for about 25 minutes, until the pancake rises and puffs. Remove the skillet from the oven, let your guests admire the pancake, then cut it into wedges and serve with lemon wedges for squeezing.

chapter three

from the range

I LIVE IN A TINY TOWN WHERE NO STOPLIGHTS EXIST, where you can stand in the center of any intersection and still see where the roads end in all four directions. Crested Butte sits isolated at the end of the road in the womb-like folds of the Rocky Mountains. In this old mining town, I can walk with my husband and son a block or two down the street to where the town proper gives way to expansive alpine pasture between the rising peaks that surround us in three directions.

Many cattle begin their lives nourished on the mountain grasses and clear streams that weave their way through our valley. Later, when the cattle have grown fat on the rapidly growing grass fed by snow runoff, ranchers herd them together, funnel them onto eighteen wheelers, and send them out of the valley of their birth to some of the world's largest feedlots. For a long time I dutifully avoided meats and animal foods; the atrocity of industrialized production and its effects on animals, people, and the environment troubled me very deeply. I wished to remove my participation in such a system. There seemed to be no alternative to an industrialized meat supply other than resolute avoidance of meat. Later, after the birth of my son, I learned of another way— one that respects and honors the natural balance among animals that feed people, the grass that feeds the animals, and how, with the great mindfulness of those who care for them, the animals nourish the grasslands themselves.

As I began to learn, I realized that an agricultural system that removes the animals from the land or ignores their role is fundamentally imbalanced. Plants need the animals as much as the animals need the plants, and, that with a mindful approach, they feed one another, and they all flourish. Even more, I realized that when we approach the raising of animals for food with mindful intent and in good conscious respect for the natural cycles of both the animals and their environment, people prosper, too.

With a mindful approach termed "holistic management," ranchers move their animals from pasture to pasture in a way that mimics the natural movements of herd animals. Holistic management allows animals to consume fresh grass, fertilize the field, and move on. Pastures rest, allowing the sequestering of carbon that in its turn builds the soil. Healthy soil then allows a greater variety of native grasses and flowers to take root, which attracts more fauna, and the cycle that industrial agriculture once uprooted can be restored. Holistic management respects the intricate balance between both animals and plants, building soil, renewing the world's grasslands, and reversing desertification.

Pasture-Raised Chicken and Poultry

The varied diet of pasture-raised poultry, which typically includes forage of sprouts, grasses, grubs, worms, and insects coupled with supplementary chicken feed, enriches the flavor of the birds' meat. While the flavor of conventionally raised chicken or turkey seems mild, the flavor of pasture-raised birds tastes concentrated—as though you taste a bit more chicken in each bite.

Raising poultry on pasture allows the birds to lead a natural life, one in which they can live as nature intended: stretching their legs, pecking at worms, bathing their plumes in soft piles of dirt. Each chicken enjoys expansive space by comparison to conventionally raised birds. That space coupled with clean air, clean water, a natural diet, and access to sunshine means that as a result the birds typically enjoy better overall health.

Leaner than most grocery store chickens, pasture-raised chickens benefit from long, low, and slow cooking, which allows their full flavor to develop while also yielding a luscious, succulent texture to meat that might otherwise be tough. I typically braise, stew, or slow-roast chicken and other birds.

stewed hen *with* leeks *and* prunes ❦

If you ever see a stewing hen for sale at your local farmers market, pick it up in a hurry because the flavor is incomparable. But, like most pasture-raised birds, they require extra care in cooking. After a few years on the pasture, a laying hen will slowly decline in her egg production. Farmers harvest these spent hens and sell them as stewing hens to differentiate them from traditional meat birds. Unlike meat birds, stewing hens have been bred over generations for maximum egg production. Meat birds, by contrast, have been bred for packing muscle meat onto their frames quickly. Typically leaner, lighter, and less dense than meat birds, stewing hens benefit from very long, slow cooking for soups, stews, casseroles, or broth making.

This stew of chicken, leeks, cream, and prunes tastes mild and gentle, perfect for rainy evenings when one craves comfort food. The stronger flavor of a stewing hen works well in this recipe; however, if you cannot find a stewing hen, simply substitute a whole chicken. SERVES 6 GENEROUSLY

---

1 whole chicken, preferably a stewing hen (about 3½ pounds)

Water

2 bay leaves

1 tablespoon whole black peppercorns

6 leeks

3 tablespoons unsalted butter

3 ribs celery, finely diced

½ cup heavy cream

½ cup pitted prunes, very thinly sliced

Finely ground unrefined sea salt

Rinse the chicken under cold water inside and out until the water runs clear. Place the chicken in a heavy stockpot and cover it with cold water. Drop in the bay leaves and peppercorns. Trim the root tips and the dark green leaves from the leeks and add the trimmings to the pot. Slice the white and light green section of the leeks paper thin and set them in a bowl while you prepare the chicken.

Bring the pot with the chicken to a rolling boil over medium-high heat, then cover the pot and lower the heat to medium. Simmer the chicken for 1½ hours, or until the meat loosens from the bone.

Turn off the heat, remove the chicken from the pot, and place it on a platter to cool until you can comfortably handle it. Strain the broth through a colander into a large bowl or pitcher. Wipe the pot clean with a kitchen towel to remove any stray peppercorns or leeks.

Once the chicken is cool enough to handle, remove its skin and pick the meat off the bones. Shred the meat with a fork and set it in a bowl until you need it.

Melt the butter in the stockpot over medium heat. When it begins to froth, stir in the white and light green part of the leeks. Sauté until they soften, about 6 minutes, but do not let them brown. Stir in the celery and continue cooking for 3 to 5 minutes longer, until the celery releases its fragrance. Add the shredded chicken to the pot, then pour in the reserved chicken broth. Simmer, uncovered, for 20 minutes. Stir in the cream and prunes. Cover the pot, turn off the heat, and allow the prunes to soften in the residual heat of the stew. Season with salt, ladle into bowls, and serve.

cider-brined slow-roasted chicken ✿

Slow roasting is my favorite way to prepare poultry. It allows the flavors to develop fully and produces a wildly succulent bird with meat that falls off the bone. Officially, poultry is cooked when it reaches an internal temperature of 165°F; however, when slow-roasting a bird, do not rely on temperature so much as on time. A slow-roasted bird will reach a safe temperature far before roasting is complete, but continue to roast it, basting it occasionally, until the cooking time is finished and the meat develops its characteristic succulence.

Brining also helps to develop moisture and flavor in a roasted chicken, and I favor a brine of apple cider and sage. The brine, coupled with sage butter, helps to gives this slow-roasted chicken a distinct but subtle infusion of flavor. SERVES 4 TO 6

BRINE

3 cups apple cider

3 tablespoons finely ground unrefined sea salt

1 tablespoon whole black peppercorns

2 heaping tablespoons chopped fresh sage

2 bay leaves

1 whole chicken (3 to 5 pounds)

Water

ROAST

2 tablespoons unsalted butter, at room temperature

2 tablespoons chopped fresh sage

1 apple, quartered

1 onion, quartered

1 tablespoon finely ground unrefined sea salt

¹/₄ cup apple cider

To make the brine, heat the cider in a 6-quart stockpot over medium heat until warm to the touch. Whisk in the salt until it dissolves. Stir in the peppercorns, sage, and bay leaves. Cool the cider to room temperature, then drop in the chicken and add water to completely submerge it. Cover the pot, transfer it to the refrigerator, and brine the chicken for at least 8 and up to 12 hours.

Preheat the oven to 250°F.

Remove the chicken from the pot and discard the brine. Brush off any bits of seasoning adhering to its skin. Gently insert a butter knife between the skin and flesh of the bird's breast to loosen it. Tuck the wing tips behind the bird and tie the legs together with 100 percent cotton cooking twine.

Whip the butter with the sage and gently spread the mixture between the skin and flesh of the bird's breast, in the pocket you just loosened with a butter knife. Stuff the bird's cavity with the apple and onion, then sprinkle its skin generously with the salt. Place the prepared bird in a baking dish or roasting pan, add the apple cider to the pan, and roast for 3 hours.

Increase the oven temperature to 375°F and continue roasting the chicken for another 30 to 45 minutes, until its skin crisps and browns. Remove the chicken from the oven, tent it with parchment paper or foil, and allow it to rest for 5 to 10 minutes before carving.

chicken *in* riesling *with* peas ✤

I make this dish in the springtime, when I can pair the last of my overwintered celeriac with the new foods of the season—young carrots, young leeks, peas, and fresh herbs. Deeper in flavor than the breast, the flesh on a chicken thigh also has more fat, which in turn produces moister and more succulent meat. I leave the meat on the bone for this stew, for bones offer up a lot of their richness when cooked in liquid over time. SERVES 6

2¹/₂ pounds bone-in, skinless chicken thighs

¹/₂ teaspoon finely ground unrefined sea salt

¹/₄ cup unsalted butter

1 large leek, white and light green parts only, sliced paper thin

4 carrots, peeled and sliced into matchsticks

2 celeriac, peeled and sliced into matchsticks

2 cups Riesling wine

1 cup Chicken Foot Broth (page 121)

1 pound English peas, shelled (1 cup)

2 tablespoons chopped fresh flat-leaf parsley

2 tablespoons snipped fresh chives

1 teaspoon chopped fresh dill

¹/₄ cup sour cream

Sprinkle the chicken thighs with the salt.

Melt the butter in a large Dutch oven over medium heat. When it froths, add the chicken and cook it for 2 minutes on each side. Remove the chicken from the pan and stir in the leek. Lower the heat to medium-low and sauté the leek for 6 to 8 minutes, until translucent. Add the carrots and celeriac and cook until they soften and become crisp-tender, about 6 minutes. Return the chicken thighs to the pot and pour in the wine and chicken broth.

Cover the pot and simmer the chicken and vegetables for 25 minutes. Remove the cover, stir in the peas, and continue simmering for another 25 to 30 minutes, until the chicken falls apart when pierced with a fork. Stir in the herbs and sour cream and serve warm.

Grass-Fed Meats

Pot roast, stew, and pan-fried steak conjure images of comfort for me, of deep nourishment and of satisfaction. I love to pour a smooth brown gravy over a pile of beef and vegetable hash, or to rub a tenderloin with salt and spice, then set it in the oven to roast until suppertime. I serve beef and lamb once or twice a week at home, depending on the availability of meats from our local ranchers. I pick up meat from them monthly, and it varies depending on the seasons and the schedule for processing the animals. Sometimes ground beef dominates, other times other cuts, and, if we're lucky, pasture-raised veal might make an appearance from time to time.

I like to buy directly from local ranchers who practice holistic management. The manner in which an animal is raised has a distinct effect on the flavor of the meat, the health of the environment, and the nourishment your body receives. What an animal eats influences both the flavor and the quality of its meat, and I prefer the nuanced flavor of grass-fed beef. In a holistically managed system, cattle self-regulate their consumption of their natural diet, and, under the eye of the rancher, they move among pastures so their diet evolves while they continually enjoy access to fresh grass and herbs in new pasture. As the cattle consume a natural nutrient-dense diet of carotene-rich grasses and also enjoy the liberty to travel and exercise along the range, the meat they produce is consequently leaner than the meat of grain-fed beef. It is also richer in critical nutrients such as omega-3 fatty acids, fat-soluble vitamins, conjugated linoleic acid (CLA), and even antioxidants such as beta carotene, which we typically associate only with plant foods.

Cooking Grass-Fed Meats

Grass-fed beef and lamb, like pasture-raised chicken, tend toward toughness. As is the case with many traditional foods, grass-fed meats require a special touch in cooking before they will release their tenderness and exquisite flavor. Adding fat during the cooking process helps to overcome grass-fed meat's natural leanness. I favor lard, tallow, or clarified butter when cooking beef, lamb, and game. These traditional cooking fats remain stable even when cooking requires high or prolonged heat. Braising grass-fed meat by first searing it in a bit of good-quality cooking fat then adding a bit of liquid also introduces a resounding succulence to a traditionally lean meat. In the case of steaks, a split-second sear helps to create a beautiful flavor while leaving the meat itself rare and still moist.

braised short ribs *with* sun-dried tomatoes *and* herbs

Short ribs, my favorite cut of beef, benefit from very long, very slow cooking. A cross-section of beef ribs, the short rib is lined with sinew and fat. This folly of anatomy can make short ribs impossibly tough if cooked improperly, or resolutely tender and rich if prepared well. Cooking meat on the bone, especially over a long period of time, infuses it with flavor, and here that flavor is further enhanced with slow braising in wine and sun-dried tomatoes.

SERVES 4

8 bone-in beef short ribs (about 7¹/₂ pounds)

¹/₂ teaspoon finely ground unrefined sea salt

¹/₂ teaspoon freshly ground black pepper

1 tablespoon unsalted butter or lard, plus more if needed

4 ounces bacon, finely chopped

4 carrots, peeled and diced

6 ribs celery, diced

1 yellow onion, diced

2 cloves garlic, minced

¹/₄ cup sun-dried tomatoes packed in oil

1 tablespoon chopped fresh rosemary needles

1 tablespoon fresh thyme leaves

2 cups dry red wine, plus more if needed

2 cups Beef Bone Broth (page 117), plus more if needed

2 bay leaves

Preheat the oven to 250°F.

Trim the ribs of any sinew or silver skin with a sharp knife, then rinse them and pat them dry. Sprinkle the ribs with the salt and pepper and set them on a plate.

Melt the butter in a Dutch oven over medium heat. When it froths, stir in the bacon and fry it until it releases its fat and turns brown and crispy, about 6 minutes. Remove the bacon with a slotted spoon and set aside in a bowl.

Increase the heat to high and, working in batches to avoid crowding, place the short ribs in the pot. Brown them for 1 minute on each side, then return them to the plate. When all the ribs have been browned, decrease the heat to medium and add the carrots, celery, onion, and garlic to the pot. Fry the vegetables, adding more butter if necessary, until softened and fragrant, about 5 minutes.

While the vegetables cook, combine the sun-dried tomatoes, rosemary, and thyme in a mortar and pound them with a pestle until they form a uniform paste. Alternatively, process the tomatoes and herbs in a food processor until they form a paste.

Stir the tomato and herb paste into the Dutch oven, then return the short ribs and bacon to the pan. Stir in the wine and broth. Drop in the bay leaves, then cover the pot and transfer it to the oven. Leave the pot in the oven for 6 hours, until the meat falls off the bone under the firm pressure of a fork. Check on the contents from time to time and add more wine or broth as necessary to keep the ribs covered. Remove the bay leaves and serve.

roasted lamb *with* leeks *and* potatoes

We buy a whole lamb once a year, in the autumn after the animals have enjoyed an entire summer fattening themselves on green grass. I tuck the bones into the freezer for soup and Scotch broth, but my family enjoys lamb roasts most of all. I often roast lamb with olives and preserved lemon, but my favorite way to prepare it is by pairing it with new potatoes and leeks. I drizzle a simple herb sauce of flat-leaf parsley, mint, and marjoram over the lamb, taking the relatively mild and gentle flavors of lamb, potato, and leek to a new level. If the potatoes you find at the market are small—a little bigger than a marble—consider keeping them whole because it makes such a beautiful and rustic presentation. SERVES 4 TO 6

LAMB

2 medium leeks, white and light green parts only, thinly sliced

1 pound new potatoes, halved

1 boneless leg of lamb (about 3 pounds)

3 cloves garlic, thinly sliced

2 tablespoons extra-virgin olive oil

2 teaspoons finely ground unrefined sea salt

2 teaspoons coarsely ground black pepper

1/2 cup dry white wine

HERB SAUCE

1/2 cup chopped fresh flat-leaf parsley

1/4 cup chopped fresh mint

2 tablespoons chopped fresh marjoram

1 small shallot, finely minced

1/2 cup extra-virgin olive oil

2 tablespoons white wine vinegar

1 teaspoon finely ground unrefined sea salt

Preheat the oven to 400°F.

Line the bottom of a roasting pan with the leeks and potatoes.

Trim the lamb of any excess fat. Using a sharp paring knife, make small 1/2-inch incisions in the meat about 2 to 3 inches apart. Insert a slice of garlic into each slit. Rub the lamb with the olive oil, salt, and pepper. Then truss the lamb tightly with 100 percent cotton cooking twine and place it in the roasting pan on the vegetables. Pour the wine into the pan. Tent the lamb first with parchment paper, then layer aluminum foil over the parchment.

Roast for 30 minutes. Decrease the oven temperature to 350°F, uncover the lamb, and roast for about an hour longer for medium-rare, basting about every 15 minutes with the pan juices. Pull the pan from the oven and allow the lamb to rest for 10 minutes while you prepare the herb sauce.

Stir the parsley, mint, marjoram, and shallot together in a small bowl. Whisk in the olive oil, vinegar, and salt. Carve the lamb and serve it with the leeks and potatoes and the herb sauce.

pan-fried veal *with* shallots

When a farm raises cows for milk and cream, it also produces calves. In holistically and ethically managed small dairies, those calves remain with their mothers, drinking milk and eating grass, for 5 to 6 months; then they are harvested for veal. As there is support for raw, grass-fed, and ethically managed dairy farms, there likewise exists a call to support small-scale, humanely raised veal, for one cannot exist without the other.

Pasture-raised veal is not pale and lackluster like its industrially raised counterpart; rather, it is pink and rosy. It tastes mild and sweet, with a texture that is much more tender than that of beef. Here its mild qualities find balance with the stronger and more assertive flavors of rosemary and crispy shallots. SERVES 4

½ cup high-extraction wheat flour (see page 157), rice flour, or unbleached all-purpose flour

1½ teaspoons finely ground unrefined sea salt

½ teaspoon freshly ground black pepper

4 veal cutlets (4 to 6 ounces each)

2 tablespoons bacon fat

2 sprigs rosemary

3 shallots, sliced paper thin

Whisk the flour, salt, and pepper together in a mixing bowl. Dredge the veal in the seasoned flour until very well coated and set it aside until you need it.

Melt the bacon fat in a cast-iron skillet over medium heat. Drop in the sprigs of rosemary and fry them in the hot fat for about 2 minutes, until they release their fragrance and the needles become crisp. Pluck out the rosemary and discard. Stir in the shallots and fry them, stirring from time to time, until they brown and begin to crisp a bit, 6 to 8 minutes. Remove them from the pan.

Add the veal to the pan and fry the cutlets for 2 to 3 minutes on each side until browned and cooked through but still moist. Plate the veal and top with the crispy shallots.

pot roast *with* apples, sweet potatoes, *and* prunes

Apples, sweet potatoes, and prunes complement grass-fed beef's natural, if subtle, sweetness in this simple pot roast. My family relies on pot roasts frequently, particularly in the fall and winter, when one roast might feed us for several meals.

Nowadays, spices like allspice and cloves seem relegated to baked goods and desserts, though they have traditionally been used to season meats in addition to sweets. I like the way their sweet spiciness forms a bridge of flavors between the beef, apples, sweet potatoes, and prunes in this dish. If you can't find hard cider for this pot roast, substitute sweet apple cider. SERVES 6 TO 8

2 teaspoons finely ground unrefined sea salt

1 teaspoon freshly ground black pepper

$^1/_2$ teaspoon ground allspice

$^1/_2$ teaspoon ground coriander

$^1/_4$ teaspoon ground cloves

1 rump roast (about 4 pounds)

3 tablespoons lard or tallow

1 yellow onion, quartered

3 apples, peeled, cored, and quartered

3 large sweet potatoes, peeled and chopped into 1-inch pieces

2 cups pitted prunes

4 cups Beef Bone Broth (page 117)

2 cups hard apple cider

Preheat the oven to 275°F.

Measure the salt, pepper, allspice, coriander, and cloves into a small bowl, then whisk them together to form a spice rub. Rinse the meat and pat it dry. Rub the spices into all sides of the meat.

Melt the fat in a large Dutch oven over medium-high heat, then place the seasoned meat in the hot fat, searing it for about 3 minutes on each side. Arrange the onion, apples, sweet potatoes, and prunes around the meat, then pour in the broth and hard cider. Turn off the heat, cover the pot, and transfer it to the oven. Leave the pot in the oven for 4 hours, or until the meat becomes tender and the vegetables soften.

Spoon the vegetables into bowls, slice the meat, and layer it over the vegetables. Ladle on a bit of sauce over the roast and serve.

Pasture-Raised Pork

I buy locally raised pastured pork whenever availability allows. It goes quickly at our farmers market, and if you've missed the window on ordering your whole or half pig, you're out of luck until the next year. I buy bacon, hams, sausages, tenderloins, and chops when I can and take the little white paper packages home, where I slice them open with kitchen shears to reveal the rosy meat.

Not only does pasture-raised pork look beautiful, with its pink meat marbled by white fat, but pasture-raised pork tastes remarkable, too—rich, sweet, and buttery with a concentrated pork flavor. While I love to serve pan-fried pork chops or braised pork tenderloin to my family, what I really enjoy is the pork fat. In response to the prominent fear of fat (particularly animal fat) so common in the last few decades, farmers have bred leaner hogs for commercial use. It's a shame, really, because fat provides flavor and succulence to meat so that a smaller amount of meat satisfies more readily. With fat bred out of commercial pork breeds, flavor has been bred out, too.

Fortunately, an interest in pasture-based farming and local food production in recent years has spawned a resurgence of interest in old-world heritage breeds of hogs. At small ranches and farmsteads, you find a revival in heritage breeds like the Gloucester Old Spot, a beautiful pink pig with black spots that was for a long time considered endangered because so few people took the time to breed them. Many small-scale farmers also enjoy the liberty of raising pigs for attributes that may not hold merit in large-scale production—like their ability to weather a cold winter, or for lard production rather than for meat production.

Beyond the revival of heritage breeds, many small farmers also adhere to a system of holistic management that slowly nurtures the health of the pasture's soil and grasses. These pigs, heritage breed or not, live a life on pasture that allows them to exercise in the sunshine, wallow in mud, and root around just as their nature commands them to do. This time spent eating natural grasses, roots, and other forage—often coupled with supplementary feed or kitchen scraps—reinforces both the flavor and nutrient quality of their meat. Further, pigs, like humans, synthesize vitamin D in their skin and fat when they live a life exposed to sunshine. As a result, pasture-raised pork is extraordinarily rich in vitamin D, a nutrient that supports bone health, immunity, and overall wellness.

milk-braised pork tenderloin ⋈

Unless you've purchased heritage-breed pork bred for lard production, pasture-raised pork tends toward leanness because the animals enjoy free and unfettered access to the outdoors, where they can stretch their legs, run, root around, and exercise. Slowly braising pork in milk helps to reintroduce moisture into the meat while further complementing the pork's inherent sweetness. I like the balance that black pepper and sweet bay bring to that sweetness. SERVES 6

1 pork tenderloin (about 2 pounds), trimmed of silver skin or sinew

2 teaspoons finely ground unrefined sea salt

1 teaspoon freshly ground black pepper

2 tablespoons lard

2 cups whole milk

2 bay leaves

Sprinkle the tenderloin with the salt and pepper. Melt the lard over medium-high heat in a heavy pot just wide enough to hold the tenderloin. Place the tenderloin in the hot fat and sear it for 4 to 5 minutes on each side. Decrease the temperature to medium-low, pour in the milk, and drop in the bay leaves. Cover the pot and simmer the tenderloin for 1 1/2 to 2 hours, or until fork tender. Turn the tenderloin occasionally to ensure it cooks evenly and remains uniformly moist.

Transfer the tenderloin to a cutting board and tent it with parchment paper or foil to keep it warm. Increase the heat under the pot to high and reduce the milk by half, until it forms a thick, creamy sauce. Remove the bay leaves. Slice the pork no thicker than 1/4 inch thick and serve it topped with sauce.

home-cured bacon *with* fenugreek, mustard seed, *and* maple sugar ❧

Like the most ardent of do-it-yourselfers, I enjoy curing my own bacon. WhileI enjoy experimenting with flavors and combinations of sweeteners and spices, my favorite will always be maple sugar, fenugreek, and mustard seed—a mix with a sweetness and faint heat that pairs nicely with pork. Fenugreek on its own tastes faintly of maple, so it complements and enhances the maple sugar.

I avoid the use of saltpeter and other curing salts traditionally used to keep cured meat pink and to stave off contamination by botulism. Straight salt works just fine for small-batch home curing provided you will consume the meat within a few weeks or freeze it to use within a few months. If you wish to preserve the meat longer, the use of pink curing salt (not to be confused with Himalayan pink salt, an unrefined sea salt) can ensure that you keep botulism away. Although there are concerns that pink curing salt, which typically contains a combination of sodium nitrate, sodium nitrite, and table salt, might contribute to cancer, this remains a subject of debate.

MAKES ABOUT 2 POUNDS

2 tablespoons coarse unrefined sea salt

¹/₄ cup maple sugar

3 tablespoons mustard seed

3 tablespoons fenugreek

1 slab pork belly (about 2 pounds)

Stir the salt, sugar, and spices together in a small bowl, then rub the mixture onto the pork belly, taking care to thoroughly cover each side.

Tightly wrap the seasoned pork belly in 100 percent cotton cheesecloth and place it in a resealable plastic bag on a plate in your refrigerator. Allow the bacon to cure for 5 days, flipping the bag twice each day.

After 5 days, unwrap the bacon and brush off any excess salt mixture.

If you're fortunate enough to have access to a smoker, smoke the bacon at 200°F for 2 hours, or until it reaches an internal temperature of 150°F. If not, place the bacon on a baking sheet lined with parchment paper and bake it for 2 hours in an oven preheated to 200°F, or until it reaches an internal temperature of 150°F.

Remove the bacon from the smoker or the oven and allow it to cool completely. The bacon will keep in the refrigerator for about 2 weeks or in the freezer for up to 6 months.

To serve, slice the bacon about ¹/₈ inch thick and fry it in a cast-iron skillet until crisp, turning once.

Liver, Kidney, Fat, and Other Odd Bits

Livers, hearts, kidneys, tongues, and other odd bits of animal can leave home cooks feeling squeamish. It's understandable; after all, with the greater reliance on and availability of mild-tasting muscle meats, the more distinctly flavored organ meats are too often forgotten, shuttled away, or discarded. But, not too long ago, every bit of every animal slaughtered found use in the kitchen. Home cooks simply couldn't afford the waste.

Fortunately, interest in nose-to-tail eating has surged as adventuresome eaters begin to find, and source, locally raised meats. To avoid offal is to deprive your tongue of a variety of deeply flavorsome meats. Liver, kidney, heart, and other odd bits are extraordinarily rich in nutrition,

particularly B vitamins, minerals, and, in the case of liver, true vitamin A. Indeed, liver and offal featured prominently and even held near sacred status in the traditional cookery of Europe, the Americas, and Asia.

Liver, kidney, heart, and other organ meats have a strong flavor, with a distinct mineral-like taste that some people find unappealing. Marinating these meats in salt water, lemon juice, or milk helps to clear them of excess blood and softens their distinct flavors without entirely subduing them. In preparing offal in my home, I find that soaking organs like liver and kidney in milk overnight significantly improves their flavor, while heart and tongue, which are properly classified as muscle meats though they're more practically considered among organs, benefit from a simple saltwater brine.

sherried chicken liver pâté
with apples *and* sage ✤

I prepare pâté every few weeks, cap it with clarified butter so that it will keep, and dip into it from time to time when I need a quick lunch or a light snack. I make this version in the fall, when apples from the market tumble through my kitchen door by the bushel, and before all the sage in my garden withers away for winter. The key to a light, perfectly smooth pâté is to puree it until thoroughly smooth, then press it through a fine-mesh sieve or a chinois to remove any grit or remaining sinew. I struggled for years with thick and pasty pâté before learning this technique. SERVES 4 TO 6

1 pound chicken livers, trimmed of any sinew

Milk, to marinate the chicken livers

1 cup plus 2 tablespoons clarified butter (page 59)

1 shallot, finely minced

1 medium apple, cored, peeled, and chopped

2 tablespoons chopped fresh sage

¹/₂ cup dry sherry

Put the chicken livers in a large mixing bowl, cover them with milk, and let them marinate in the refrigerator for at least 4 and up to 12 hours. Drain the livers, discarding the milk, and pat them dry with a kitchen towel.

Melt the 2 tablespoons of clarified butter in a wide skillet over medium heat. Stir in the shallot and fry until translucent, soft, and fragrant, about 4 minutes. Stir in the apple and sage and cook until the apple is tender, about 8 minutes. Add the livers to the pan and cook until browned on the outside but still slightly pink in the center, about 8 minutes. Stir in the sherry and simmer for another 3 to 5 minutes, until most of the liquid evaporates. Turn off the heat and allow the mixture to cool for about 5 minutes.

Transfer the liver mixture to a food processor. Pulse 2 or 3 times, then process continuously, adding the remaining 1 cup of clarified butter about 1 tablespoon at a time through the feed tube.

Transfer the pâté to a fine-mesh sieve or a chinois set over a bowl. Press it through the screen to remove any tough bits. Spoon the pâté into ramekins, cover well, and transfer to the refrigerator for at least 4 hours and up to 5 days. Remove the pâté from the refrigerator 20 to 30 minutes before serving so it can come to room temperature and soften slightly.

goose liver mousse *with* mission figs

In the autumn, migratory birds like the goose gorge themselves in preparation for the long flight south. With this instinctive practice, geese stuff themselves with forage, fattening their livers. After discovering the fattened livers of the autumn goose, farmers began to force-feed geese to produce the delectable treat foie gras. While the ethics behind the production of foie gras will always remain a source of contention, the magnificent, buttery flavor of fattened goose liver is incomparable.

When I can, I buy liver fattened by the goose's instinctual seasonal gorging. Farmers keeping geese sell these livers, which taste a good deal like foie gras but are not as large nor as tender, in the autumn. They disappear from markets quickly, so you must be ever vigilant should you want to pick up a few pounds and tuck them away in your freezer for a special occasion. This mousse is excellent spread thickly on slices of sourdough bread with toasted almonds or home-cured olives offered alongside. MAKES ABOUT 2 CUPS

8 ounces fatty goose livers

Milk, for soaking the livers

$1/2$ cup plus 2 tablespoons unsalted butter

1 shallot, very finely minced

$1/4$ cup chopped dried Mission figs

$1/4$ cup brandy

$1/2$ teaspoon ground coriander

$1/4$ teaspoon ground allspice

$1/4$ teaspoon ground white pepper

$1/2$ cup heavy cream, preferably raw

Trim the livers of any membrane or sinew, slice them into thin strips about $1/4$ inch thick, then toss them in a bowl and cover with milk. Transfer to the refrigerator and let the livers soak for 8 to 12 hours. Drain away the milk and pat the livers dry.

Melt the 2 tablespoons of butter in a skillet over medium heat. When it froths, stir in the shallot and sauté for about 4 minutes, until it softens and releases its fragrance. Decrease the heat to medium-low, toss in the livers, and cook until they brown on the outside and stiffen slightly but remain ever so slightly pink on the inside, 4 to 6 minutes. Stir in the figs and brandy and simmer over medium-low heat until the liquid has mostly evaporated, about 8 minutes.

Let the liver mixture cool for about 5 minutes, then transfer to a food processor and add the coriander, allspice, and pepper. Pulse once or twice to combine, then process continuously, dropping the remaining $1/2$ cup of butter about 1 tablespoon at a time through the feed tube. Then, in a thin stream, dribble in the cream.

Spoon the mousse into a fine-mesh sieve or a chinois set over a large bowl. Press the mousse through the sieve to remove any bits of grit or remaining sinew. Spoon the mousse into individual ramekins or into a serving dish, cover tightly, and refrigerate. It should keep for about 2 weeks. Remember to pull the mousse out of the fridge about 30 minutes before you serve it to give it time to soften.

broiled lamb's kidneys *with* mustard

Kidneys taste strong and mineral-like, which is why they pair nicely with mustard. Like other organ meats, kidneys benefit from a long soaking in milk, which clears them of blood and softens their mineral intensity. These broiled lamb's kidneys are delicious served on buttered toast with an extra dollop of mustard. SERVES 4 TO 6

12 lamb's kidneys

Milk, for soaking the kidneys

1 teaspoon finely ground unrefined sea salt

1 teaspoon powdered mustard

1/4 teaspoon cayenne pepper

Toast points, to serve

Unsalted butter, to serve

English mustard, to serve

Trim away the skin and membrane that surrounds each kidney and cut off any fat that might adhere to them. Split them in half lengthwise and remove the tubes and central fat. Place the trimmed kidneys in a bowl, cover with milk, and transfer to the refrigerator to marinate for 8 to 12 hours, until the milk clears them of blood.

Preheat the broiler.

Drain away the milk, pat the kidneys dry, and sprinkle them with the salt, powdered mustard, and cayenne pepper. Distribute the kidneys in a single layer on a rimmed baking sheet and broil for about 10 minutes, turning once, until both sides are browned. Serve warm with toast points, butter, and mustard on the side.

old-fashioned meat loaf *with* gravy ✢

I often combine liver and other organ meats with ground beef or pork when making meat loaf or meatballs. The rich flavor of liver complements the other meats without overwhelming them, broadening their flavors and elevating them to a robust heartiness. A bit of coriander and allspice help to round out the flavors in this classic meat loaf, while the sweet saltiness of bacon brings it all together. I often serve this with mashed potatoes or root vegetables and a simple brown gravy. SERVES 6

MEAT LOAF

8 ounces beef liver

Milk, for soaking the liver

1¹/₂ pounds ground beef

1¹/₂ pounds ground pork

1 small yellow onion, finely minced

1¹/₂ teaspoons finely ground unrefined sea salt

1 teaspoon ground coriander

¹/₂ teaspoon ground allspice

2 tablespoons chopped fresh curly parsley

2 teaspoons fresh thyme leaves

2 eggs, beaten

¹/₂ cup sourdough bread crumbs

8 ounces bacon (about 8 slices)

GRAVY

3 carrots

2 yellow onions

5 ribs celery

2 sprigs thyme

1 bay leaf

3 cups Beef Bone Broth (page 117)

2 tablespoons unsalted butter

Finely ground unrefined sea salt and freshly ground black pepper

To make the meat loaf, trim the liver of any sinew and drop it into a small mixing bowl. Cover it with milk and let it marinate in the refrigerator for 8 to 12 hours. Drain away the milk and pat the liver dry. Transfer it to a food processor and process it until coarsely ground.

Preheat the oven to 450°F.

Transfer the liver to a large mixing bowl and add the ground meats, minced onion, salt, coriander, allspice, parsley, thyme, eggs, and bread crumbs. Knead the ingredients by hand until well combined. Form the mixture into a loaf and weave or layer the bacon on top. Place the meat loaf bacon side up in a 9 by 4-inch loaf pan and bake for 15 minutes. Decrease the oven temperature to 350°F and continue baking for another 1¹/₂ hours, until the loaf is well browned on top and no longer pink in the middle.

While the meat loaf bakes, prepare the gravy. First peel and chop the carrots and onions into 1-inch pieces, then chop the celery into 1-inch pieces. Place the vegetables in a large saucepan and drop in the thyme and bay leaf. Pour in the broth, bring to a boil over medium-high heat, then decrease the heat to medium-low and simmer, covered, for 30 minutes, or until the vegetables soften enough to fall apart when pressed with the tines of a fork.

Pluck out the sprigs of thyme and bay leaf, then puree the vegetables into the broth with an immersion blender. Season with salt and pepper and strain into a gravy boat. Slice the meat loaf and serve with the gravy.

pan-fried calf's liver *with* caramelized shallots *and* port

I love how the rich and faintly smoky flavor of caramelized shallots pairs with liver, while tawny port adds a touch of sweetness. Calf's liver is milder than beef liver, and marinating it overnight in milk softens its flavor even more. SERVES 4

- 1 1/2 pounds calf's liver
- Milk, for soaking the liver
- 1/4 cup high-extraction wheat flour (see page 157), rice flour, or unbleached all-purpose flour
- 1/2 teaspoon finely ground unrefined sea salt
- 1/2 teaspoon finely ground white pepper
- 3 tablespoons bacon fat or lard
- 6 shallots, thinly sliced
- 1/4 cup tawny port

Trim the liver of any membrane or sinew and slice it into strips about 1/4 inch thick. Place the liver in a large mixing bowl, cover with milk, and allow it to soak in the refrigerator for at least 8 and up to 12 hours. Drain the liver and rinse it well. Discard the milk and pat the liver dry with a kitchen towel.

Whisk together the flour, salt, and pepper in a shallow bowl. Dredge the liver in the seasoned flour and set it on a plate until you are ready to fry.

Melt the bacon fat or lard in a skillet over medium-high heat. Toss the shallots into the hot fat and fry, stirring frequently, until fragrant and caramelized, about 8 minutes. Transfer the shallots to a bowl with a slotted spoon and set them aside.

Add the liver to the skillet and fry until golden brown, about 2 minutes on each side. Return the shallots to the skillet and pour in the port. Decrease the heat to medium-low and continue cooking until the liquid is reduced by half, 3 to 5 minutes. Serve immediately.

pan-fried calf's liver *with* bacon *and* onions

Bacon and onions help to round out the assertive flavor of liver in this classic combination, while parsley provides a much-needed punch of brightness at the very end. The trick to making liver palatable is not to overcook it; liver can become leathery and tough in an instant, but a mindful eye toward temperature and time will give you tender results. SERVES 4

1¹/₂ pounds calf's liver

Milk, for soaking the liver

1 teaspoon finely ground unrefined sea salt

1 teaspoon freshly ground black pepper

2 tablespoons unsalted butter

4 ounces bacon, chopped

3 yellow onions, sliced into rings no thicker than ¹/₄ inch

2 tablespoons chopped fresh flat-leaf parsley

Trim the liver of any membrane or sinew and slice it into strips about ¹/₄ inch thick, then toss it in a bowl and cover it with milk. Transfer the bowl to the refrigerator and soak for at least 8 and up to 12 hours. Drain away the milk and pat the liver dry. Sprinkle it with salt and pepper, then set aside while you prepare the other ingredients.

Melt the butter in a skillet over medium heat, toss in the bacon, and cook until crispy, about 6 minutes. Transfer the bacon to a bowl with a slotted spoon. Toss the onions into the hot fat and fry them until they turn a deep golden brown, about 15 minutes. Stir them frequently to prevent them from scorching. Using a slotted spoon, transfer the onions to the bowl with the bacon and cover it with a kitchen towel to keep them warm.

Add the liver to the skillet and fry for 2 to 3 minutes on each side until cooked through but not overdone. Return the bacon and onions to the skillet and stir to warm them through. Sprinkle with the parsley and serve warm.

pickled tongue *with* mustard sauce

Pickling tongue in brine infuses the meat with the flavors of spices like black pepper, sweet bay, coriander, allspice, and clove. Much like corned beef brisket, pickled tongue benefits from a long, slow simmer—a process that renders an otherwise gnarly and tough piece of meat tender. Traditionally, pickled tongue is served cold, but I prefer it stewed with vegetables and served warm with a creamy mustard sauce.

While pickling tongue and other meats is not a particularly complex process, it does take time. Remember to begin at least 5 days before you plan to serve the dish. SERVES 4 TO 6

PICKLED TONGUE

1 calf's tongue (about 2 pounds) or 2 pounds beef tongue

2 cups whey from Yogurt Cheese (page 57) or Bonny Clabber (page 65)

1/2 cup finely ground unrefined sea salt

1/2 cup unrefined cane sugar

Water

1 tablespoon whole black peppercorns

1/4 cup Sweet Pickling Spice (page 277)

2 bay leaves

Begin preparing your tongue at least 5 days and up to a week before you plan to serve it. First, place the tongue in a large mixing bowl or crock.

Whisk the whey, salt, and sugar together in a pitcher large enough to comfortably hold 2 quarts of liquid. Stir in 6 cups of water and drop in the peppercorns, pickling spice, and bay leaves. Pour the brine over the tongue and cover the bowl securely with a lid or with plastic wrap. Place it in your fridge and allow it to rest for 5 to 7 days.

When you're ready to prepare the meal, lift the tongue from the brine and brush off any spices that might adhere to it. Discard the brine and place the tongue in a heavy stockpot. Pour in enough water to cover the tongue by 3 inches. Cover the pot and bring the liquid to a boil over medium-high heat. Decrease the heat to medium and simmer for 1 1/2 hours, or until the tongue can be easily pierced with a knife.

Remove the tongue from the pot and place it in a large bowl of very cold water until it's cool enough to handle. Do not disgard the cooking liquid. Trim away any gristle on the tongue and peel away the skin with a sharp paring knife.

VEGETABLES

1 celeriac, peeled and chopped into $1/2$-inch pieces

4 carrots, peeled and chopped into $1/2$-inch rounds

1 yellow onion, sliced into $1/4$-inch rounds

2 large waxy potatoes, chopped into $1/2$-inch pieces

1 small green cabbage, cored and quartered

MUSTARD SAUCE

2 tablespoons unsalted butter

1 shallot, minced

$1/2$ cup white wine

1 cup heavy cream

2 tablespoons Dijon-style mustard

2 tablespoons chopped fresh flat-leaf parsley

Return the tongue to the pot and arrange the celeriac, carrots, onion, potatoes, and celery over the tongue. Cover, bring to a simmer over medium heat, and cook for 30 to 45 minutes, until the vegetables are tender.

While the vegetables simmer, prepare the mustard sauce. Melt the butter in a small saucepan over medium heat until it foams. Stir in the shallot, and fry until fragrant and translucent, 2 to 3 minutes. Pour in the wine and simmer until reduced by half, about 5 minutes. Stir in the cream and simmer for 6 to 8 minutes, until the mixture thickens enough to coat a spoon. Whisk in the mustard and parsley.

Cut the tongue into slices no thicker than $1/4$ inch and serve over the vegetables, drizzled with mustard sauce.

stewed beef heart *with* root vegetables *and* porcini mushrooms ⚭

Like most offal, beef heart has a mineral flavor that's easily tempered by soaking in milk or salt water. Sometimes tough, heart benefits from long, slow cooking. I like to serve it braised with root vegetables and mushrooms in red wine and beef bone broth. I tend to favor porcini mushrooms, which my son and I gather in late summer along forest paths, though any mushroom will do, including cremini, button, and even shiitakes. SERVES 6

2 tablespoons coarsely ground unrefined sea salt

4 cups water

1 beef heart, trimmed of any fat or sinew and cut into $\frac{1}{2}$-inch cubes

2 tablespoons lard or bacon fat

1 sprig rosemary

3 sprigs thyme

1 yellow onion, finely chopped

2 cloves garlic, finely chopped

1 celeriac, peeled and finely chopped

2 carrots, peeled and finely chopped

1 cup sliced fresh porcini mushrooms

1 cup Beef Bone Broth (page 117)

1 cup dry red wine

$1\frac{1}{2}$ cups peeled and chopped tomatoes

2 bay leaves

$\frac{1}{4}$ cup chopped fresh flat-leaf parsley

In a large bowl, whisk the salt into the water. Place the trimmed heart in the salt water and put the bowl in the refrigerator for at least 4 hours and up to 1 day to allow the blood to clear. Drain the salt water, then give the heart a good rinse and pat the cubes dry.

Melt the fat in a wide skillet over medium heat and drop in the rosemary and thyme. Let the herbs sizzle in the hot fat for 3 minutes or so, then discard them. Stir the onion into the fat and fry until fragrant and translucent, about 6 minutes, and then stir in the garlic and fry for another 2 minutes.

Add the heart and cook, stirring occasionally, until browned on all sides, about 3 minutes. Transfer to a bowl, then add the celeriac, carrots, and mushrooms to the pan. Sauté until the vegetables are crisp-tender, about 5 minutes. Return the heart to the pan and pour in the beef bone broth, red wine, and tomatoes. Drop in the bay leaves. Bring to a simmer, cover, and turn down the heat to medium-low. Cook for 30 minutes, then remove the bay leaves, sprinkle with the fresh parsley, and serve.

In Defense of Lard

Of all the animal fats, lard is without a doubt the most maligned, the most hated, and the most feared. Butter gets a pass, but lard still remains nearly universally despised. I will share something with you: I cook with lard, I eat lard, and I revel in lard. Toward autumn, ranchers in our valley send their pigs, which have grown fat on forage and kitchen scraps, to the processor for slaughter. I always ask them to reserve the fat for me. I take it home, mince it very finely, and render it on the stove over low heat for several hours until it produces a perfectly creamy, snowy white fat.

At the beginning of the twentieth century, industrially produced vegetable fats like margarine, vegetable shortening, and soy and corn oils began replacing traditional cooking fats like lard, tallow, and butter, and for several decades these modern fats were championed for their perceived health benefits while the animal fats, which nourished prior generations, remained largely ignored, or, in the case of lard, actively discouraged. While many people squirm at the idea of using lard, it simply doesn't deserve its bad reputation. The primary fat found in lard is monounsaturated fat—the very same fat found in olive oil and avocados and which is thought to support cardiovascular health and optimal cholesterol levels. Further, pigs raised outdoors on pasture with plenty of access to natural sunlight manufacture ample amounts of vitamin D in their skin and fat, making lard from pasture-raised pigs one of the best food sources for vitamin D.

In a culinary sense, lard gives braised meats and vegetables a rich mouthfeel and can be used to make pastry with a flakiness difficult to achieve with other cooking fats. It is luxuriously rich, softly flavored, and an excellent source of both monounsaturated fat and fat-soluble vitamins like vitamin D.

home-rendered lard *or* tallow (*with* cracklings) ❦

Animal fat, despite its bad reputation, nourished the robust health of generation upon generation of families across the globe, until modern vegetable
oils replaced them in the early part of the twentieth century. Like offal and
bones, the fat of a freshly slaughtered hog or steer would never be wasted
or cast off as unwanted.

Consider approaching ranchers early in the season, before the harvest,
if you plan to purchase pork fat for rendering lard or beef suet for rendering
tallow. Due to the innate leanness of pasture-raised pork and grass-fed beef,
ranchers often request that butchers add any extra fat to sausage or ground
meat. By requesting it in advance of the harvest, they may set aside a bit for
your larder. When rendering lard, ask for leaf lard—that is, the fat around the
kidneys of the hog. The soft texture and mild flavor of leaf lard make it ideal
for baking. MAKES ABOUT 1 QUART

Water

3 pounds pork fat or
beef suet

Set a large, deep, heavy pot on the stove. Pour about a cup of
water into the pot.

Mince the fat very finely or shred it using a box grater or the
grater attachment of your food processor. The finer the fat, the
more effectively it will render. Add the fat to the pot and turn
the heat to low. Cover the pot and allow the fat to soften and
liquify.

After about 3 hours, turn off the heat. With a spoon, remove
any large pieces of fat from the pot and set them aside. Very
carefully pour the liquid fat through a fine-mesh sieve into a
glass jar. Cover and store in a cool place in your kitchen. The
lard or tallow will keep for several months.

You can make cracklings by cooking the reserved pieces of fat
in a hot skillet over high heat for about 5 minutes, until brown
and crisp.

Bones

Bones bring both flavor and nourishment to the kitchen table. I cook with bones daily, mostly by preparing simple stocks and long-simmered bone broths. My home smells of broth, and of butter. I serve soups and sauces with most meals, so I often cook with stocks and broths. Rich in minerals and amino acids, bone broths can provide a much-needed source of these nutrients and are rich in gelatin, which helps to support both digestive and skin health, especially when used in combination with natural fats and leafy green vegetables.

Bones are typically very inexpensive and make an excellent source of powerful nutrition for families on a budget for that reason; and the silky richness bone broths bring to the table can greatly enhance many dishes.

beef bone broth

The trick to making a good beef bone broth is to roast the bones before simmering them in a pot of water, herbs, and vegetables. Roasting helps to release a significant amount of fat from the bones, which can otherwise leave a greasy film in the broth or infuse it with an odd, flat, and almost acrid flavor. With much of the fat released and a rounder, more complex flavor developed during roasting, the resulting broth has the flavorful complexity of roast beef.

I find that beef bone broth makes an excellent base for hearty soups, stews, and braised meats. When preparing roasted root vegetable soups, I invariably choose this broth because it, unlike milder chicken broth, has the fortitude to complement assertive flavors.

While you can use any beef bones to produce a delicious broth, choosing a variety of beef bones including neck bones, knuckle bones, and a small number of marrow bones will produce the richest broth. **MAKES ABOUT 4 QUARTS**

5 pounds beef soup bones

2 bay leaves

4 sprigs thyme

3 tablespoons whole black peppercorns

2 large yellow onions, quartered

3 carrots, chopped

2 celeriac, peeled and chopped

4 cloves garlic, smashed

1 cup red wine

2 gallons water, plus more as needed

Preheat the oven to 425°F.

Arrange the bones in a roasting pan in a single layer and roast for 45 minutes. Transfer the bones to a heavy stockpot. Toss in the bay leaves, thyme, peppercorns, onions, carrots, celeriac, and garlic. Pour in the red wine and water.

Bring the liquid to a boil over high heat, then immediately lower the heat to medium-low, cover, and simmer for at least 12 and up to 18 hours, adding water as necessary to keep the bones submerged.

Strain the broth through a fine-mesh sieve, discard the solids, and pour the broth into jars. Cover the jars and place them in the fridge; you can remove the fat that hardens on the surface and use it for cooking. Use up the broth within a week, or freeze it for up to 6 months.

bone marrow custard *with* black pepper *and* parsley ❧

Comprised mostly of fat, bone marrow tastes like browned butter—for this reason, you can often find it used for sweet custards and desserts in old cookbooks. Cream and eggs nicely complement roasted marrow in this simple savory custard, while the fresh flat-leaf parsley adds a clean, bright flavor to balance the richness. I often serve this custard for a late but substantial breakfast with sliced fruit, though it pairs nicely with a crisp green salad at lunchtime.

Long leg bones from beef steers provide delicious, buttery marrow. Purchase them precut, or ask your butcher or rancher to cut them 1 inch to 4 inches thick to make scooping out the marrow a little more manageable. While you can remove the marrow from the center of a raw bone, roasting the bones significantly improves the flavor of marrow and makes it a bit easier to remove, too. SERVES 4 OR 6

---

5 pounds beef marrow bones, cut about 1 inch thick

5 eggs

2 cups heavy cream

1 teaspoon finely ground unrefined sea salt

1 teaspoon finely ground black pepper

1 tablespoon minced fresh flat-leaf parsley

Preheat the oven to 425°F.

Put the bones in a single layer in a roasting pan and roast for 30 minutes. Remove the pan from the oven and let the bones cool until they are comfortable to handle.

Decrease the oven temperature to 325°F and grease six 4-ounce or four 6-ounce ramekins with a bit of butter.

Extract the marrow from the bones with a spoon and drop it into a bowl, discarding the bones. Whisk the eggs and cream into the marrow, then pass the mixture through a fine-mesh sieve set over a bowl to remove any coagulated bits of marrow or lumps of egg. Whisk in the salt, pepper, and parsley.

Pour the mixture into the buttered ramekins and place the ramekins in a large baking dish. Fill the dish with enough hot water to reach halfway up the sides of the ramekins. Bake for 45 minutes, or until the sides of the custards are set but the centers remain a touch wobbly. Serve warm.

chicken bone broth

I slow-roast a chicken every Sunday for my family, and I always reserve the chicken's spent carcass to make a simple savory broth that will nourish us throughout the week. Simmered in water and wine with fragrant herbs, the chicken carcass releases the flavor of its bones and marrow into the pot, and the minerals of its bones dissolve into the smooth yellow liquid. With prolonged cooking, the bones will break away and crumble when pressed between your thumb and forefinger, and then you know the broth is finished, for the bones yielded everything they could.

A good broth will solidify and gel when chilled because the prolonged simmering in water made slightly acidic by wine helps to release amino acids and collagen from cartilage-rich joints. This gelatin-rich broth aids with digestion while also yielding beautiful body to any soups or sauces made from the broth. I often drink broth in the morning with a clove of minced garlic and a bit of parsley and sea salt. MAKES ABOUT 4 QUARTS

Carcass of 1 roasted chicken

2 yellow onions, 1 chopped and 1 quartered

4 ribs celery, chopped

3 carrots, chopped

1 tablespoon whole black peppercorns

3 sprigs thyme

6 to 8 sprigs flat-leaf parsley

2 bay leaves

¼ cup white wine

4 to 6 quarts cold water, plus more as needed

Combine the chicken carcass, onions, celery, carrots, peppercorns, thyme, parsley, and bay leaves in a large, heavy stockpot. Pour in the wine, then cover the chicken and vegetables with the cold water. Bring to a boil over medium-high heat, then immediately decrease the heat to medium-low and simmer, covered, for 12 to 14 hours, adding water as necessary to keep the bones submerged. From time to time, skim away any scum that might rise to the surface. The foamy scum isn't harmful, but it can leave the broth with a very faintly acrid or dirty flavor.

Strain the broth, discarding the solids, then pour it into jars, cover, and store it in the refrigerator for up to 1 week or freeze for up to 6 months. As the broth cools, a bit of fat might float to the surface and then harden with chilling. You can scrape it away and discard it, or use it as you would any other cooking fat.

chicken foot broth

Whenever our local rancher processes chickens, I arrive with bags in hand, not for the whole chickens, but to ask for the feet, lest they feed them to the dogs. Chicken feet have very little marketable value. Gnarly and doubtlessly repulsive with their scaly yellow skin and sharp talons, they nevertheless make the best broth. As with other odd cuts of meat, it's easy to cast off the humble chicken foot, but in allowing squeamishness to get the better of you, you also miss out on the powerful nourishment and deep flavor they lend to broth, soups, and sauces.

Chicken feet are an extraordinary source of amino acids, particularly collagen, which is why chicken foot broth gels so readily. Its flavor is rich and concentrated, but somehow still delicate. MAKES ABOUT 4 QUARTS

---

3 pounds chicken feet, scrubbed very well

1 yellow onion, chopped

1 large leek, root tip removed, white and green parts thinly sliced

4 ribs celery, chopped

3 carrots, chopped

1 tablespoon whole black peppercorns

2 sprigs thyme

6 to 8 sprigs flat-leaf parsley

2 bay leaves

¼ cup white wine

4 to 6 quarts cold water, plus more as needed

If necessary, peel away and discard any yellow membrane that adheres to the chicken feet, then chop off the claws. (The process of defeathering chickens often removes that yellow membrane; however, if it remains, it—and the talons—can create off flavors in the broth.)

Combine the chicken feet, onion, leek, celery, carrots, peppercorns, thyme, parsley, bay leaves, and wine in a large, heavy stockpot. Cover the chicken feet with the water. Bring to a boil over medium-high heat, then immediately decrease the heat to medium-low, cover, and simmer for 8 to 12 hours, adding water as necessary to keep the feet submerged. From time to time, skim away any scum that might rise to the surface.

Strain the broth, discarding the solids, then pour it into jars, cover, and store it in the refrigerator for up to 1 week or freeze it for up to 6 months. With chilling, the broth should gel enough that it must be scooped out of the jar with a spoon. This is normal, and the broth will liquefy once you heat it. A thin layer of yellow fat may harden on the surface of the gelled broth; I recommend discarding this fat, as it doesn't lend itself to cooking.

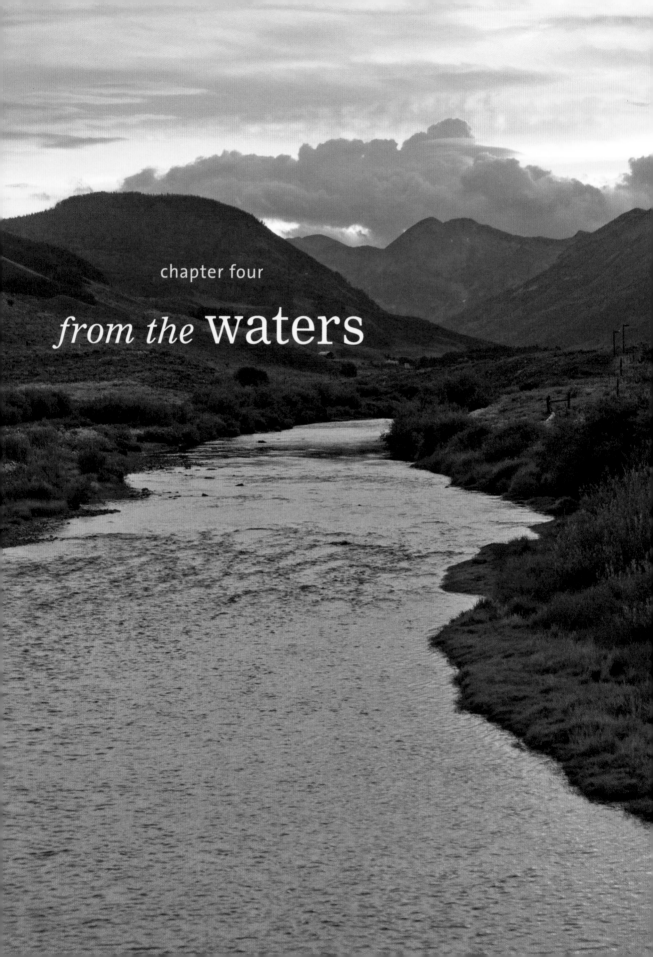

chapter four

from the waters

I SPENT MOST OF MY CHILDHOOD NEAR THE SEA, on a tiny island in the middle of the Pacific Ocean, and I remember very clearly the glistening wet eyes and the gaping mouths of the fish at the local market. My mother would take my sister and me by the hand, and we'd walk down to the Japanese market, where we'd see freshly caught whole fish, fillets, octopus, squid, and occasionally little crabs or other shellfish. Other times, when the season was right, we'd visit the beach and watch local women don their rubber galoshes, hike up their kimonos, and bend over the rocky reef to gather spiny black sea urchins at low tide. They'd pluck the sea urchins from their sandy beds nestled between the coral, crack them open, and scoop out the brilliant bright orange roe that lay at their center. In many ways I miss the beach and a life encircled by the sea.

I live far from the ocean now, away from the waves, the salty sea air, and the fresh fish. Whenever I visit seaside towns, which is not as often as I'd like, I gorge myself on fresh-caught fish and shellfish. While the oceans may be thousands of miles from me in either direction, I set out for the mountain streams and lakes near my home in hopes of catching what I can—trout mostly, though occasionally Kokanee salmon, too, if the season's right.

While I try to buy all our foods locally if possible, I invariably make an exception for fish and shellfish, as well as for California olive oil and citrus fruits. Fish and shellfish provide powerful nourishment—nutrients that can otherwise be challenging to find in high concentration in other foods. Studies of indigenous tribes find that even relatively isolated, landlocked peoples often went to very great lengths to acquire seafood, prizing it for its ability to promote good health, fertility, and robust children. The key behind that traditional wisdom might very well be seafood's high concentration of omega-3 fatty acids, coupled with minerals like iodine and selenium, as well as B vitamins and the fat-soluble vitamin D.

Due to rampant overfishing and pollution of the world's waterways, finding high-quality, uncontaminated, and properly labeled fish can prove distinctly challenging. I typically rely on third-party verification and recommendations, like those of the Monterey Bay Aquarium's Seafood Watch Program or the Marine Stewardship Council, and make my purchases accordingly. Small fish, like sardines or anchovies, often make the best choice because they cost little, do not suffer the contamination with heavy metals that larger and older fish see, and generally come from abundant populations. Shellfish, like oysters and clams, also represent good choices, as do fish farmed in an ecologically sound way.

Finfish

I make a point to serve fish to my family several times a week. Yes, it's wonderfully good for you—rich in vitamins, minerals, and healthy fats. For me, the choice centers less around good health and more around the simple pleasure of good food. I enjoy the distinct marine oiliness of fish, the way the flesh flakes as you press your fork into a well-cooked fillet.

Fish is a tender food and should be cooked carefully. A fillet can go from perfectly cooked to overdone and dry in an instant, so I find quick cooking typically achieves the best results. Also, fish is rich in polyunsaturated fatty acids that, unlike the saturated fats found in beef or the monounsaturated fat in pork, cannot withstand high, prolonged heat without losing many of its benefits. For the most part, finfish, and their fat, call for a delicate approach in cooking. I also favor curing fish in brine, because it develops a wonderful flavor and can help to preserve fish over time. I shave off a bit of gravlax or spoon some cured anchovies over a salad. I often serve small fish—sardines and anchovies—whole and on the bone, but I prefer to serve fillets of larger fish such as salmon, halibut, and arctic char. Very occasionally, I fry fish—whole smelts dressed in bread crumbs or battered hook-and-line-caught Atlantic cod.

grilled sardines *with* preserved lemon gremolata

A fresh sardine bears little resemblance to its oily, overly fishy tinned cousin; rather, it tastes of the sea—briny, but clean. I first tasted a fresh sardine while volunteering in Morocco when I was in my early twenties. Our little camp of idealistic volunteers ate what could be had from local markets— mostly chicken, lamb, potatoes, vegetables, herbs, olive oil, and fresh fish caught just offshore in the Atlantic Ocean. We sliced the sardines open and cleaned them. Then we packed them with garlic and fresh herbs before grilling them over an open flame. Ten years later, I still prefer sardines prepared in this way, as the clean flavor of fresh herbs complements the fish's briny oiliness. I like to serve them with a little chopped preserved lemon, garlic, and parsley. SERVES 4 TO 6

SARDINES

2¹/₂ pounds cleaned sardines, with heads and tails left on

2 teaspoons finely ground unrefined sea salt

1 teaspoon smoked paprika

6 cloves garlic, minced

¹/₄ cup minced fresh flat-leaf parsley

2 tablespoons minced fresh cilantro

1 tablespoon extra-virgin olive oil

GREMOLATA

2 preserved lemons (page 279), seeded and finely chopped

2 tablespoons minced fresh flat-leaf parsley

2 cloves garlic, finely minced

Prepare a hot fire in a charcoal grill or preheat a gas grill to high.

Rinse each sardine, inside and out, and pat it dry.

In a small bowl, stir together the salt, paprika, garlic, parsley, cilantro, and olive oil. Stuff the mixture into the sardines, dividing it evenly, then truss each fish with 100 percent cotton cooking twine.

Oil the grill grate and grill the sardines until the fish is cooked through and the flesh flakes easily when pierced by a fork, about 3 minutes on each side. Transfer the sardines to a serving plate.

To make the gremolata, in a small bowl, stir together the preserved lemons, parsley, and garlic. Serve the gremolata alongside the grilled sardines.

whole mackerel *on* potatoes ✤

An oily fish with firm, white flesh, mackerel speaks of the sea. I like to serve the little fish—each one about 9 inches from head to tail—roasted whole, as in this dish. Mackerel's natural oiliness pairs well with the starchiness of potatoes. SERVES 4

2 pounds fingerling potatoes

6 cloves garlic, coarsely chopped

3 tablespoons extra-virgin olive oil

2 tablespoons coarse unrefined sea salt

4 whole mackerel (about 3¹/₂ pounds) cleaned, with heads and tails left on

1 medium lemon, sliced into rounds no thicker than ¹/₈ inch

4 sprigs rosemary

4 sprigs thyme

Preheat the oven to 425°F.

Cut the potatoes into 1-inch pieces and toss them into a large mixing bowl with the garlic. Add the olive oil and salt and toss gently to coat. Spread the potatoes in a single layer in a 9 by 13-inch baking dish. Roast for 30 minutes, stirring once.

While the potatoes roast, rinse the mackerel well, inside and out, then pat dry with a clean kitchen towel. Stuff each mackerel with a few slices of lemon and one sprig each of rosemary and thyme.

After the potatoes have roasted for 30 minutes, remove the baking dish from the oven and set the herb-and lemon-stuffed fish on the potatoes. Return the dish to the oven and bake for an additional 30 minutes, or until the fish is cooked through and flakes easily when pierced by a fork. Serve immediately.

roasted arctic char *with* sweet orange *and* rosemary sauce ❦

The coldwater fish arctic char tastes like a cross between salmon and trout and is related to both. Like salmon and trout, arctic char has buttery red flesh that lends itself well to smoking, though I often roast the fish on a bed of citrus and herbs and serve it with a simple sweet and tart sauce. Most commercially available arctic char is sustainably farmed in Alaska, Canada, Iceland, or Norway. And like salmon, arctic char offers a favorable ratio of omega-3 to omega-6 fatty acids and is rich in B vitamins. SERVES 4

FISH

8 sprigs rosemary

4 (4- to 6-ounce) arctic char fillets

2 whole oranges with their skin intact, thinly sliced

ORANGE AND ROSEMARY SAUCE

2 tablespoons unsalted butter

1 shallot, minced

Juice of 3 oranges

1 tablespoon honey

1 sprig rosemary

Preheat the oven to 425°F.

To prepare the fish, line a 9 by 13-inch baking dish with the rosemary. Place the arctic char fillets in a single layer on the rosemary and top them with orange slices. Roast for 15 to 20 minutes, or until the fish flakes easily when pierced with a fork.

While the fish roasts, prepare the sauce. Melt the butter in a saucepan over medium-low heat. When it froths, stir in the shallot and sauté until it softens and becomes translucent, about 4 minutes. Stir in the orange juice and honey and drop in the rosemary. Increase the heat to medium-high and simmer, uncovered, until the sauce thickens enough to coat the back of a spoon, about 8 minutes.

Pluck out the rosemary and serve the sauce over the roasted fish.

baked anchovies *with* fennel, tomatoes, *and* basil ❧

Anchovies, like sardines, are underloved by those who've yet to taste them prepared well. The small, silvery fish pair nicely with strong, robustly flavored ingredients like the tomatoes, fennel, and basil in this simple casserole.

I serve these baked anchovies with a loaf of freshly baked Einkorn Wheat and Herb Bread (page 170). Once you've finished with the fillets, tear off a hunk of bread and sop up the remaining juices. SERVES 4 TO 6

¼ cup extra-virgin olive oil

1 yellow onion, finely chopped

2 cloves garlic, thinly sliced

1 fennel bulb, trimmed, cored, and sliced paper thin

8 tomatoes, peeled, seeded, and chopped

½ cup dry white wine

2 bay leaves

2 pounds cleaned anchovies

1 teaspoon finely ground unrefined sea salt

3 tablespoons chopped fresh basil

Preheat the oven to 350°F.

Warm the olive oil in a skillet over medium-low heat. Stir in the onion and garlic and sauté until softened, about 4 minutes. Stir in the fennel and continue sautéing for 1 to 2 minutes, until fragrant. Stir in the tomatoes, wine, and bay leaves. Increase the heat to medium and simmer the sauce for 8 to 10 minutes, until the tomatoes soften slightly. Turn off the heat.

Arrange the anchovies in a shallow 10-inch round casserole dish and sprinkle them with the salt. Pour the sauce over the anchovies and sprinkle with the basil.

Bake the anchovies for 35 to 40 minutes, or until cooked through. Serve warm.

pollock *and* bacon cakes *with* green onion *and* young garlic mayonnaise ❧

In springtime the gardens sprout with green onions, baby leeks, and young garlic. They arrive in heavy bunches, bundled in twine, from our CSA. I use them with unyielding abandon because these younger alliums offer a softer, fresh flavor that I long for after relying on root cellar crops for the colder months. I often grill the green onions, or slice them and serve them fresh as you might do with carrots or ribs of celery, but I also like to whisk them into a simple mayonnaise and serve them with fish cakes.

Pollock, with its mild-flavored creamy white flesh, marries well with the sweet smokiness of bacon and the brightness of spring's first alliums and freshest young herbs. If you can't find pollock, substitute cod. SERVES 4 TO 6

MAYONNAISE

1 clove young garlic, minced

3 egg yolks

$^1/_4$ teaspoon finely ground unrefined sea salt

1 tablespoon freshly squeezed lemon juice

1 tablespoon water

1$^1/_2$ cups extra-virgin olive oil

2 green onions, white and green parts, finely chopped

FISH CAKES

1$^1/_2$ pounds pollock fillets

1 teaspoon unsalted butter or lard

8 ounces bacon, finely chopped

4 green onions, white and light green parts only, thinly sliced

1 tablespoon chopped fresh curly parsley

1 egg, beaten

$^1/_2$ teaspoon finely ground unrefined sea salt

$^1/_2$ teaspoon smoked paprika

1$^1/_2$ cups stale sourdough bread crumbs

To make the mayonnaise, drop the garlic and egg yolks into a bowl, sprinkle them with the salt, then pour in the lemon juice. Whisk together until barely combined, then whisk in the water.

Measure the oil into a small salad dressing cruet or pitcher. With a whisk in one hand and the oil in the other, slowly drizzle the oil into the bowl, one drop at a time, as you whisk the ingredients together, taking care not to pour in the oil too quickly. After a minute or two, the egg yolks will thicken and increase in volume. Now you can drizzle the oil in a very fine stream as you continue to whisk. Continue whisking until you've incorporated all the oil into the yolks. Fold the green onions into the mayonnaise, cover, and set aside until you're ready to serve.

To make the fish cakes, preheat the oven to 450°F.

Place the pollock in a single layer in a baking dish and bake for 15 minutes, or until the fish flakes easily when pierced with the tines of a fork. Remove the fish from the oven, cover it loosely with a clean kitchen towel, and allow it to cool to room temperature.

Melt the butter in a wide cast-iron skillet over medium heat, then stir in the bacon. Fry the bacon until it renders its fat and crisps, about 6 minutes. Turn off the heat and, using a slotted spoon, transfer the bacon from the skillet to a waiting bowl or plate, but do not discard the rendered bacon fat.

Chop the fish very coarsely just to break it up and put it into a large mixing bowl. Add the crisped bacon, green onions, parsley, beaten egg, salt, paprika, and $1/2$ cup of the bread crumbs. Mix gently by hand until the ingredients hold together. Form the mixture into twelve equal-size patties, each about 1 inch thick.

Spread the remaining 1 cup of bread crumbs in a shallow dish. Dredge the fish cakes in the crumbs, coating them on both sides. Set the cakes on a large plate.

Line a serving plate with a kitchen towel. Set the skillet with the reserved bacon fat over medium heat. Once the fat is hot, fry the cakes in batches for 2 to 3 minutes on each side, or until deep golden brown. As each cake is done, place it on the towel-lined serving plate to drain, covering the plate loosely with a bit of parchment paper or foil to keep the cakes warm.

Serve the fish cakes with the mayonnaise alongside.

fried smelts *with* aïoli

Very small, pale silvery-gold fish, smelts are excellent when fried and eaten whole—head, tail, and all. Their thin bones crisp in the hot fat, then break with a crunch as they melt away in one bite. Smelts are underappreciated but make for a truly sustainable seafood choice.

Dredging the smelts very lightly in bread crumbs seasoned with paprika, salt, and lemon and then frying them in hot lard crisps the fish, without hiding their flavor with a thick egg-rich batter. I like to serve them dipped in a simple aïoli seasoned with a touch of cayenne pepper. SERVES 4 TO 6

AÏOLI
1 egg yolk

2 cloves garlic

1/4 teaspoon finely ground unrefined sea salt

1/4 teaspoon cayenne pepper

1 tablespoon freshly squeezed lemon juice

2 teaspoons water

3/4 cup extra-virgin olive oil

SMELTS
1 1/2 pounds cleaned smelts

2 eggs

1 cup sourdough bread crumbs

1 teaspoon finely ground unrefined sea salt

1 teaspoon smoked paprika

1 teaspoon finely grated lemon zest

Lard, for frying

TO SERVE
2 tablespoons chopped fresh flat-leaf parsley

1 lemon, quartered

To make the aioli, combine the egg yolk with the garlic, salt, cayenne pepper, lemon juice, and water in a food processor; pulse once or twice to combine. Process continuously as you slowly drizzle in the olive oil, drop by drop, until all the oil is added and the aïoli is well emulsified. Spoon the aïoli into a little container, cover, and set it aside until you're ready to serve.

To prepare the smelts, rinse the fish inside and out, then pat them dry with a clean kitchen towel.

Beat the eggs in a bowl and set aside. In a shallow dish, stir together the bread crumbs, salt, smoked paprika, and lemon zest. Add enough lard to a cast-iron frying pan so that it reaches about 3/4 inch up the pan's side when melted. Heat the fat over medium-high heat to about 350°F, or until bubbles appear when you drop in a few bread crumbs.

Working in batches if necessary to avoid crowding the skillet, dip the smelts in the beaten egg, dredge them in the seasoned bread crumbs, then place them in the hot fat. Fry until the fish are golden brown, about 2 minutes on each side. Transfer to the towel-lined plate to allow any excess fat to drain away.

Plate the fried smelts and sprinkle with the parsley. Serve with the quartered lemon for squeezing and the aïoli for dipping.

gravlax *with* maple, dill, *and* juniper

Like corned beef, yogurt, sauerkraut, and other fermented or naturally cured foods, gravlax was born of necessity. Before freezer cases and fish farms, salmon offered only a short season of abundance, forcing the seafaring communities of northern Europe to preserve it for long-term storage by burying it in sand at the high tide line—hence the literal translation of "grave salmon." No longer buried in sand, gravlax is cured with a dry rub of salt and sugar, with spices or herbs added to the rub at the cook's discretion.

The salt and sugar tighten the protein fibers of the fish, leaching out its juice to produce a sweet and salty brine that cures the fish. I prepare gravlax at home, slicing off a bit here or there to serve with breakfast or as a light starter before supper. Any combination of coarse salt and sugar works to preserve the fish, but I love the gentle flavor introduced by maple sugar, dill, and juniper berries. SERVES 4 TO 6 AS AN APPETIZER

½ cup coarse unrefined sea salt

½ cup maple sugar

2 tablespoons chopped fresh dill

2 tablespoons crushed juniper berries

2 (8-ounce) skin-on wild-caught salmon fillets

Stir together the salt, sugar, dill, and juniper berries.

Spread a 14-inch piece of cheesecloth on your countertop, and then lay one salmon fillet flesh side up on the waiting cloth. Pour half the salt mixture over the fish and sandwich the other fillet flesh side down on top of the first.

Season the outside of the salmon fillets with the remaining salt mixture and wrap the sandwiched fillets in the cheesecloth as tightly as you can.

Place the wrapped salmon in a resealable plastic bag and set the bag on a plate. Place a second plate over the first to weight down the fish and refrigerate. Turn the bag once a day for 3 days.

After 3 days, remove the fish from the plastic bag and unwrap the cheesecloth. Brush off the curing mixture from the fish, then pat the fillets dry with a clean kitchen towel. The gravlax will keep in the fridge in an airtight container for about 1 week before its flavor begins to suffer. Slice it very thinly, as needed, just before serving.

pan-seared halibut *with* melted cherry tomatoes *and* tarragon

During the first few weeks of summer, tomatoes trickle slowly into the farmers market, a few baskets at a time. Such a short supply after months of cold-weather crops like roots and greens means those first few tomatoes command hefty prices and seem to disappear the instant the market opens. So I wait to purchase tomatoes until late summer, when their newness wears off and baskets at the market overflow with a seemingly continuous supply of marble-sized cherry tomatoes or even the heftier golden Amana tomatoes that can weigh 2 or 3 pounds each. The price of tomatoes falls as the supply increases, and I buy them by the case. I call on close friends and we preserve as much as we can, but I also serve them with nearly every meal—a few dropped into an omelet, roasted with fennel for soup, tossed with greens for salad, and, frequently, as a simple sauce for fish or meat.

While creamy white-fleshed fish like halibut pair beautifully with mild flavors, buttery sauces, and a very light introduction of lemon or fresh herbs, they also marry well with more robust and assertive flavors like tomato. I reserve this dish for late in the summer, when bright, ripe cherry tomatoes are both inexpensive and abundant. Once they hit the hot pan, they nearly melt and their flavorful juices concentrate in the heat, becoming syrupy and thick. I like to throw in a handful of tarragon at the very end, though both basil and flat-leaf parsley also work well. SERVES 4

FISH

4 (4- to 6-ounce) halibut fillets

1/2 teaspoon finely ground unrefined sea salt

1/2 teaspoon freshly ground black pepper

1 teaspoon chopped fresh thyme leaves

1 tablespoon clarified butter (page 59)

Sprinkle the halibut with the salt, pepper, and thyme. Set the fillets on a plate and let them rest a bit while you prepare to cook the fish.

Melt the butter in a wide skillet over medium-high heat. Once the butter melts, arrange the halibut skin side down in the hot fat and sear for 4 or 5 minutes, until the skin crisps and browns. Flip the fish and continue cooking for another 2 to 3 minutes, until it flakes easily when pierced by a fork. Transfer the halibut to a serving plate and tent it with parchment paper or foil to keep it warm.

TOMATOES

2 tablespoons extra-virgin olive oil

1 shallot, minced

2 cloves garlic, minced

1 pound cherry tomatoes, halved

$1/4$ cup coarsely chopped fresh tarragon

To prepare the tomatoes, set the skillet you used to cook the fish over medium heat and pour in the olive oil. Toss in the shallot and garlic and cook, stirring frequently, until fragrant and translucent, about 6 minutes. Toss in the tomatoes and sauté them with the shallot and garlic until they soften and release their juice, about 2 minutes. Add the tarragon and continue cooking, stirring frequently, for 1 minute.

Uncover the waiting halibut. Spoon the melted cherry tomato mixture over the fish and serve immediately.

salmon baked *in* cream *with* sweet bay, thyme, *and* dill

A rich and buttery fish, salmon pairs beautifully with cream. While heavy cream may threaten to overpower the delicate nature of most fish, salmon's distinct flavor shines, and the cream melts into a simple sauce as it bakes. A sprinkling of parsley and dill infuse the rich sauce with a sparkle of brightness. SERVES 4

4 (6-ounce) wild-caught salmon fillets

4 bay leaves

1 cup heavy cream

2 tablespoons chopped fresh thyme leaves

2 tablespoons chopped fresh dill

Preheat the oven to 400°F.

Place the salmon fillets in a single layer in a small baking dish or gratin dish. Top each fillet with a bay leaf. Pour the heavy cream over the salmon and sprinkle with the thyme and dill. Bake until the fish flakes easily when pierced with a fork and the cream thickens, about 15 minutes.

Discard the bay leaves and serve, spooning warm cream and herbs over the fish.

potted salmon mousse *with* roe

A touch of homemade sour cream lightens the rich, smoky flavor of the salmon in this potted salmon mousse. A little cayenne pepper and a heaping spoonful of salmon roe round out the flavor. Serve the mousse with Yogurt and Dill Crackers (page 183). **MAKES ABOUT 2 CUPS**

3 tablespoons cold water

1 teaspoon plain gelatin

6 ounces smoked salmon

1¼ cups sour cream

1 teaspoon freshly squeezed lemon juice

½ teaspoon finely ground unrefined sea salt

¼ teaspoon cayenne pepper

2 tablespoons (about 1 ounce) Smoked Salmon Roe (opposite) or ikura

1 tablespoon chopped fresh dill

Pour the water into a small dish and sprinkle the gelatin over it. Let the gelatin soften for about 5 minutes, then transfer the mixture to a small saucepan. Warm the gelatin and water over medium heat, whisking continuously until the gelatin has fully dissolved, then set it aside.

Combine the salmon, sour cream, lemon juice, salt, and cayenne pepper in a food processor and blend until smooth. As the food processor continues to run, slowly drizzle in the gelatin. Turn off the food processor and spoon the salmon mixture into a large mixing bowl. Fold in the roe and chopped dill, then spoon the mousse into four 4-ounce ramekins or a pint-size bowl. Cover and refrigerate for at least 4 hours or up to 3 days before serving.

smoked salmon roe ❧

At once luxurious and humble, smoked salmon roe tastes of the sea, of campfires, and of smoldering wood. A simple rub of salt and sugar enhances the roe's flavor by reducing its bitterness while also helping to tighten and strengthen the thin exterior membrane that surrounds each tiny egg. I like to smoke salmon and its roe over alder, though applewood also infuses the roe with a pleasant flavor and aroma.

Salt, sugar, and smoke help to preserve the roe, and it will store in the refrigerator for about 3 weeks before its flavor begins to suffer. I like to serve it spooned over fried or scrambled eggs, or on crackers with a spoonful of Yogurt Cheese (page 57) and a sprinkling of chopped dill or chives. MAKES ABOUT 2 CUPS

2 tablespoons unrefined cane sugar

2 tablespoons coarse unrefined sea salt

3 pounds wild-caught fresh salmon roe in their skeins

In a shallow dish, stir together the sugar and salt.

Rinse the skeins of roe in a gentle stream of filtered water or spring water (tap water treated with chlorine, fluoride, or other chemicals may adversely affect the flavor of the delicate roe). Pat the skeins dry and dredge them lightly in the sugar-salt mixture. Set them in a dish to cure for 20 to 30 minutes. Meanwhile, preheat your smoker to 180°F.

Drain off any liquid from the skeins of roe and brush off any excess salt and sugar. Transfer the skeins to the smoker and smoke for 30 minutes. Remove from the smoker and refrigerate the skeins for 10 minutes. Slit open each skein and gently scrape the thin membrane with a spoon to remove the roe. Spoon the roe into a jar, cover, and store it in the refrigerator for up to 3 weeks.

fried roe *with* homemade tartar sauce

Roe is typically sold cured, as caviar, but if you're lucky enough to befriend a fisherman or to fish yourself, you'll be able to enjoy the unrivaled lusciousness of fresh roe in its skein. A skein of roe holds within its thin, slippery membrane thousands of tiny translucent spheres, little eggs bursting with the concentrated flavor of fish.

I typically use salmon roe for this dish, though the roe of any fish will work well as long as it remains in its skein. Shad roe also does nicely.

SERVES 4 TO 6

BRINE

1½ pounds fish roe in its skeins

2 heaping tablespoons coarse unrefined sea salt

2 cups water

TARTAR SAUCE

1 cup Olive Oil Mayonnaise (page 80)

2 tablespoons finely minced pickles, such as Spiced Sour Pickles with Garlic and Dill (page 265)

1 tablespoon chopped fresh dill

TO FRY THE ROE

1 cup high-extraction wheat flour (see page 157), rice flour, or unbleached all-purpose flour

2 teaspoons finely ground unrefined sea salt

2 teaspoons smoked paprika

2 teaspoons finely grated lemon zest

¼ cup chopped fresh flat-leaf parsley

2 cups clarified butter (page 59) or lard

1 lemon, quartered

To brine the roe, place the skeins of roe in a mixing bowl. In a separate bowl, whisk the salt with the water and pour the brine over the roe to sweeten them and remove any residual bitterness. Put the bowl in the refrigerator and allow the roe to soak in the brine for at least 4 and up to 12 hours. Drain off the brine and gently pat the roe dry.

To prepare the tartar sauce, in a small bowl, stir together the mayonnaise, pickles, and dill. Cover and set in the refrigerator until you're ready to serve.

To fry the roe, in a shallow dish, whisk the flour with the salt, paprika, and lemon zest. Dredge the skeins of roe in the seasoned flour until well coated. Heat the fat in a 10-inch cast-iron skillet over medium-high heat to 375°F. Gently place the roe in the pan, taking care to avoid fat splatters. Fry the roe for about 3 minutes per side until crisp and brown, then drain on a kitchen towel. Sprinkle with the parsley and serve with lemon wedges and the tartar sauce.

Shellfish

I've always loved shellfish—cracking open a bright red-orange crab claw to reveal its sweet, stringy flesh, slurping a fresh oyster with mignonette, or peeling whole shrimp and eating them with a squeeze of lemon juice. In addition to their strong mineral-like marine flavor and their mild sweetness, which lends itself well to so many dishes, shellfish invariably rank among some of the most nutrient-dense foods available to us. Oysters are extraordinarily rich in zinc, while clams are rich in iron and shrimp in iodine.

Spectacularly rich in vitamins, minerals, and good fats and relatively easy to gather and cultivate, shellfish have been considered a sacred food by many traditional peoples, particularly for pregnant and breastfeeding women and small children.

oyster *and* potato stew ⚓

On cold days in winter, I ladle soups and stews into my family's empty bowls to help combat the bone-chilling cold. We favor simple broths, vegetable soups, and heartier meat stews, but, when I can, I make this stew. Once a month I order five dozen oysters, which we eat raw on the half shell or lightly broiled, but we also enjoy them served simply in an old-fashioned oyster and potato stew. Milk and cream complement the oysters' natural sweetness, while potatoes add body to an otherwise humble broth.

Oysters do not benefit from long cooking, which is why they're often preferred in their raw and unadulterated form, so take care not to leave them simmering in the milky broth for too long. Turn off the heat and ladle the soup into bowls just as the edges of each oyster begin to ruffle. SERVES 4 TO 6

1 tablespoon unsalted butter

1 leek, white and light green parts only, thinly sliced

1 large russet potato, peeled and chopped into 1/2-inch cubes

2 cups shucked oysters with their liquor

2 cups whole milk

1 bay leaf

1/4 teaspoon cayenne pepper

1 cup heavy cream

Finely ground unrefined sea salt

Melt the butter in a heavy stockpot over medium heat. When it foams, stir in the leek and fry until softened, about 3 minutes. Stir in the potato, oyster liquor, milk, and bay leaf. Bring to a simmer, cover, and cook for about 30 minutes, or until the potatoes are tender.

Stir in the oysters and cayenne pepper. Simmer them until the edges of the oysters begin to curl and ruffle, only a minute or two. Stir in the heavy cream, season with salt, ladle into soup bowls, and serve.

broiled oysters *with* bacon, mushrooms, *and* spinach ❧

Marrying oysters with mushrooms allows the flavors of the sea and the soil to come together in an extraordinary way. One complements the other, and in a single bite you taste the richness of both the ocean and the earth. While I generally eat oysters raw, I love the richness they develop when broiled, too. While I find that the fruity sweetness of the Kumamoto oyster balances nicely with the salty flavor of bacon, any oyster variety will do. Take care not to overcook them, lest their plump bodies become rubbery in the heat of the oven. I generally choose the thick-stemmed trumpet mushroom to bake with oysters, but any mushroom you come across will work nicely. Serve this dish with slices of crusty bread. SERVES 4 TO 6 AS AN APPETIZER

2 dozen oysters

2 tablespoons unsalted butter

4 ounces bacon, chopped

2 cloves garlic, thinly sliced

2 cups chopped mushrooms

2 cups chopped spinach

2 tablespoons chopped fresh flat-leaf parsley

1 teaspoon fresh thyme leaves

1/2 cup sourdough bread crumbs

Preheat the broiler.

Shuck the oysters, leaving them on the half shell and reserving their liquid. Lay the oysters in a single layer in the bottom of a gratin dish.

Melt the butter in a wide skillet over medium heat. When it froths, toss in the bacon and cook until browned and crisp, about 6 minutes. Remove the bacon from the pan with a slotted spoon and layer it over the oysters. Stir the garlic and mushrooms into the skillet and fry them over medium heat until softened, about 3 minutes. Toss in the spinach, then pour in the reserved oyster liquor. Simmer until the liquid is reduced by half, about 6 minutes. Using a slotted spoon, remove the spinach and mushrooms from the skillet and spread them evenly over the oysters. Sprinkle with the parsley, thyme, and bread crumbs. Broil for 2 to 3 minutes until lightly browned, then serve.

mussels *with* apples *and* cream

In my home, mussels make an almost instant meal. Little sweet-fleshed mussels open up in the heat of simmering hard apple cider in a matter of just a few minutes. Apple, leek, and cream seem like natural accompaniments for mussels, which not only taste of the sea, but, like most shellfish, also taste faintly sweet. SERVES 4 TO 6

4 pounds mussels

1 cup hard apple cider

1 tablespoon unsalted butter

1 small leek, white and light green parts only, minced

1 small apple, cored and chopped

1/2 cup heavy cream

2 teaspoons chopped fresh thyme leaves

Scrub the mussels very well to remove any bits of sand, seaweed, or other remnants from the sea. Remove the mussels' beards and any stringy bits that remain. Discard any mussels that remain open after you handle or tap them, because they are dead. Rinse them well and put them in a large, heavy saucepan. Pour in the hard apple cider. Cover the pan, bring the cider to a simmer over medium heat, and cook until the mussels open, 6 to 8 minutes. Spoon the mussels into a serving dish and cover them to keep them warm, reserving the liquid in the saucepan. Discard any mussels that remain closed after cooking.

Melt the butter in a skillet over medium heat. When the butter turns frothy, stir in the leek and apple. Decrease the heat to medium-low and sauté until softened and fragrant, about 5 minutes. Strain the liquid in the saucepan through a fine-mesh sieve and into the skillet with the leeks and apples. Stir in the heavy cream and thyme. Simmer, stirring frequently, until the liquid thickens and is reduced by half, about 10 minutes. Pour over the mussels and serve.

salt-roasted clams *with* garlic butter ⚜

Roasting clams on a bed of salt and herbs until they open allows them to develop a rich flavor undiluted by steam or liquid. Once the salt cools and can be comfortably handled, you can spoon it into a glass jar to reuse it for salt roasting in the future. A simple garlic butter enriches the notorious leanness of the clams.

Clams number among the best seafood choices for consumers concerned about the environmental impact of their food choices because they're abundant and can generally be farmed without pollution, as well as wild harvested without seriously impacting the oceanic ecosystem. SERVES 4 TO 6

CLAMS

4 pounds littleneck clams

Coarse unrefined sea salt, to line the baking dish

2 sprigs rosemary

2 sprigs thyme

GARLIC BUTTER

2 tablespoons unsalted butter

2 cloves garlic, thinly sliced

$1/4$ teaspoon crushed red pepper flakes

$1/2$ cup white wine

2 tablespoons chopped fresh flat-leaf parsley

1 teaspoon chopped fresh oregano

Preheat the oven to 350°F.

Scrub the clams under cold water to remove any grit or other debris adhering to them. Discard any clams that do not close when you tap on them.

Line a large baking dish with coarse sea salt to a depth of $1/2$ inch. Scatter the rosemary and thyme over the salt and nestle the clams in a single layer into the bed of salt and herbs. Roast for 10 to 15 minutes, until the clams open, discarding any clams that fail to open after 15 minutes.

As the clams bake, make the garlic butter. Melt the butter in a small saucepan over medium heat. When it foams, stir in the garlic and red pepper flakes and fry until the garlic softens, just a few minutes. Pour in the white wine and simmer until it reduces by half, about 6 minutes.

Plate the clams in shallow bowls. Pour the butter sauce over the clams, sprinkle with the parsley and oregano, and serve.

potted shrimp *with* orange *and* spice ❦

Fat, like salt and sugar, helps to preserve foods for the long term. Stored in spiced butter, little shrimp will keep for 2 months or longer. I like to use Oregon pink shrimp for their tiny size; their delicate flavor blossoms when the shrimp are paired with assertive spices such as coriander, cayenne, and smoked paprika. These little shrimp are available cooked, peeled, and frozen. However, if you can't find them, use an equivalent amount of finely chopped cooked shrimp of your choice.

While the season for pink shrimp lasts from midspring to midautumn, you can find the shrimp frozen year-round. Oregon's mindful approach to the commercial fishing of pink shrimp ensures that the catch remains a sustainable choice. Serve the potted shrimp over toasted bread or crackers.

MAKES 2 PINTS

1 cup plus 2 tablespoons clarified butter (page 59)

1 pound cooked, peeled, and frozen Oregon pink shrimp, thawed

2 tablespoons sherry

1 bay leaf

1 shallot, finely minced

2 teaspoons finely grated orange zest

¼ teaspoon cayenne pepper

½ teaspoon ground coriander

¼ teaspoon smoked paprika

½ teaspoon finely ground unrefined sea salt

Melt the 2 tablespoons of clarified butter in a wide skillet over medium-low heat. Stir in the shrimp and sauté until the shrimp curl and release their liquid, about 6 minutes. Stir in the sherry and continue cooking until the liquid in the pan evaporates, 6 to 8 minutes. Spoon the shrimp into two pint-size jars and set the jars on the counter while you prepare the spiced butter that will cap and preserve the shrimp.

Melt the remaining 1 cup of clarified butter in the now-empty skillet over medium-low heat. Stir in the bay leaf, shallot, orange zest, cayenne, coriander, paprika, and salt. Cook the mixture for about 5 minutes, until richly fragrant, then discard the bay leaf. Pour the spiced butter over the shrimp, cap the jars, and store them in the fridge. The shrimp will keep for up to 2 months.

Remove the jars from the refrigerator 60 to 90 minutes before you plan to serve to allow enough time for the butter to soften.

spot prawns *with* almonds *and* garlic

Garlic, parsley, and lemon are natural matches for the sweet flavor of spot prawns, but adding a handful of chopped almonds provides both crunch and a warming, toasted flavor. Large coral-colored spot prawns inhabit the cold waters of the Pacific Ocean. Caught in traps that minimize impact on both other species and the prawns' habitat, spot prawns remain one of many sustainable seafood choices available to consumers. Succulent spot prawns often come with little sticky bits of red-orange roe clinging to their abdomen and legs. As I shell the prawns, I strip the shells of any roe, for its flavor heightens that of the prawns while also supplementing the meal with additional vitamin A and omega-3 fatty acids. SERVES 4 TO 6

1 lemon

1/2 cup coarsely chopped blanched almonds (see page 244)

1/4 cup olive oil

2 cloves garlic, finely chopped

1/4 teaspoon crushed red pepper flakes

2 pounds spot prawns, shelled and deveined

2 tablespoons chopped fresh flat-leaf parsley

Grate the zest of the lemon very finely and place it in a small bowl, then cut the lemon in half crosswise and squeeze its juice into a separate bowl.

Warm a large cast-iron skillet over medium-high heat. Toss in the almonds and toast them, stirring frequently, until they begin to brown just a bit at the edges, about 4 minutes. Stir the olive oil, garlic, red pepper flakes, and lemon zest into the skillet with the almonds. Stir continuously until the garlic softens and becomes fragrant, about 4 minutes. Toss in the spot prawns and sauté until their bodies curl and their flesh becomes opaque, about 3 minutes. Stir in the lemon juice and parsley. Serve warm.

chapter five

from the fields

ALONG THE RURAL COLORADO HIGHWAYS, vast fields of grains grow—first with the greenness of spring, which slowly fades into the amber colors of late summer and autumn. They wave and roll in the winds that sweep through the plains under the cloudless blue sky for which Colorado is known. Grains and beans are beautiful foods: flavorful, inexpensive, and able to keep well in the cupboard and pantry for several months without deteriorating. When the vibrant colors of the kitchen garden begin to fade as cold weather approaches, we lean more heavily on grains and beans, which are naturally satiating. I use beans and grains less frequently in the summer, when an abundance of fruits and vegetables keeps the kitchen table overflowing with fresh things to eat.

I love to use both grains and beans in my cooking: whole grains for their wonderful chewy texture and beans for their pleasant starchiness. They pair well with meats and help extend small amounts of otherwise expensive cuts. While grains and pulses, which include dry beans, dry peas, and lentils, can provide beautiful nourishment and deep, satiating meals, they are not without complications. Grains, beans, and lentils are seeds, ready to sprout into plants given the right condition of moist, faintly acidic soil. The very thing that prevents them from sprouting in suboptimal conditions and also helps preserve them for months in the pantry is what also detracts from the nourishment they can offer to the plate. While grains, beans, and lentils are certainly rich in vitamins and minerals, they also contain antinutrients—naturally occurring components that can inhibit digestion or the absorption of certain minerals. These antinutrients can make grains and pulses difficult to digest and can lock up their minerals, preventing your body from fully absorbing them.

Traditional methods of preparing grains, those handed down by our great-great-grandmothers and described in old and worn cookbooks, emphasize preparing pulses largely through soaking, and fermenting grains by preparing sourdoughs and similar slow-rise breads that derive their unique flavor and texture from natural and wild yeasts and bacteria.

These methods help to deactivate antinutrients, like food phytate, which binds minerals and prevents their absorption, and enzyme inhibitors that can otherwise make grains, beans, and lentils difficult to digest. These methods also enhance both the flavor and texture of grains, beans, and pulses.

High-Extraction Flours and Sifting

The bulk of a grain's antinutrients rest within the bran, or the outer layer of the grain. The bran and germ also contain fatty acids as well as minerals, leaving the fragile polyunsaturated fat found within that layer of bran prone to oxidation once ground and exposed to air. Traditional people in Europe and the high mountains of central Asia often sifted their freshly ground flour to partially remove the bran, which was fed to livestock. This eliminated the bulk of the antinutrients found in the grain, but it removed much of the grain's vitamins and minerals as well.

While grinding flour and sifting it twice through progressively smaller screens approximates this traditional practice, purchasing high-extraction flour (available online and in some well-stocked grocery stores) is an easy alternative. In preparing high-extraction flours, millers sift away most, but not all, of the bran and germ after the flour is ground. The resulting flour is lighter than whole grain flour and, thanks to the absence of the bran and germ, it stores well at room temperature, as all-purpose and bread flours do, without loss in flavor or quality. Whole grain flours, on the other hand, should be stored in the refrigerator or freezer to prolong their shelf life, preserve their flavor, and retain heat-sensitive nutrients.

I use high-extraction flour in balance with freshly milled flours that I grind at home; high-extraction flour lightens otherwise heavy loaves, while freshly milled whole grain flours provide my breads and baked goods with hearty flavor and texture. I also use high-extraction flour in recipes that do not allow the time needed for sour leavening, and it is a good option for dredging meats prior to pan-frying them and for thickening sauces and gravies.

Sourdough

I fell in love with sourdough baking several years ago, and my love of the tart, complexly flavored, chewy bread fueled my persistence despite several failures during those early months. Until the twentieth century, most breads found their flavor and their rise not through commercial bakers' yeast, but with wild yeast. Baking with wild yeast requires patience and care, as the microbial composition of each sourdough starter differs, if only slightly, depending upon the environment in which the yeast was captured. Baking with sourdough requires finesse and skill, as well as a level of patience as you get to know your starter, its rising times, and the flavor it gives your breads and other baked goods.

Once I developed my starter and baked regularly, the ease with which baking came to me multiplied. What once felt daunting now felt relaxed, and tending a sourdough starter—just a little jar of flour and water—seems routine.

For the most part, I rely on crusty old-world, artisan-style loaves of bread, not only for their beautifully rugged appearance, but also because they, surprisingly, require minimal effort. I like the potent sour flavor that accompanies very long, slow rises. I begin most of my breads the night before, pouring flour, water, and sourdough starter into a wide bowl. I swirl it together with my bare hand, because it's easier than washing an extra utensil, and I love the stickiness that develops in the dough as I work the ingredients with my fingertips. I let it rest overnight, punch it down, knead the dough for certain breads, or simply form it, score it with a serrated bread knife, and bake it.

Most sourdough breads benefit from less rather than more; that is, less kneading and less handling overall allow the yeast and bacteria to work their magic on the dough's flour and water. As microbes in your starter eat away at the carbohydrates present in the flour, they release carbon dioxide, which in turn helps the dough to rise. When you knead the bread or overhandle it, the pockets of air produced during its rising time collapse, and the bread can become dense. Occasionally, overhandling the dough and collapsing the air pockets works in your favor—particularly when making sandwich-style loaves that rely on a tight crumb so that they slice more easily.

Working with Sourdough

When I first began baking with sourdough, I found myself producing miserable loaves of overworked dough that baked into dense bricks—at once tough on the outside, desperately heavy, and too moist on the inside. My family indulged me, smiling through loaf after loaf of miserably executed bread. With time and great patience, I picked up a few tricks that helped to produce the kind of bread I wanted—rich in flavor, crisply crusted, and with a light and airy crumb.

KEEP YOUR STARTER REFRIGERATED
For a very long time I kept my sourdough starter on my countertop. I baked frequently, about once a day, and fed the starter each time I baked, so I didn't feel it necessary to refrigerate it. Yet, with time, my loaves of sourdough bread seemed to lack rise and spring. Upon the recommendation of a friend and artisan baker, I began refrigerating my starter to slow down the microbial activity of the yeast and bacteria. Now my starter always remains in the refrigerator unless I will bake with it within 4 hours, and my sourdough buns and loaves of bread have found their spring once more.

KEEP YOUR STARTER'S JAR ONLY HALF FULL

When you feed your sourdough starter, not only do you increase its volume by adding more flour and water to the jar, but you also feed the bacteria and yeasts. As they eat the carbohydrates provided in the new flour, they will produce gas that will cause the starter to double in volume. If your starter fills more than half the jar at the time you feed it, it can expand over the lip of your jar, creating quite a mess.

To prevent your starter from overflowing its jar, feed your starter when you plan to bake, first removing a portion of the starter equivalent to the amount of flour and water you will feed it, then adding more flour and water to the jar. If you don't have time to bake with each feeding, remove some starter as if you were going to bake with it. You can compost or otherwise discard the excess starter, or use it for crumpets (page 177), pancakes (page 175), noodles (page 176), or pie crust (page 178).

BROWN LIQUID OR HOOCH ON YOUR STARTER

If a brown liquid appears floating on top of your sourdough starter, simply pour it off. Sourdough bakers call this liquid "hooch," and it is harmless; however, it often signifies that you've fed your starter too much water in relation to flour or have let your starter sit too long between feedings. A sourdough starter is relatively resilient; it will bounce back quickly once you resume proper care of it.

ALLOW FOR A LONG RISE

In general, allow your breads to rise over a long period of time. This develops flavor; it also improves the nutritional quality of the bread by reducing the glycemic load and increasing the B vitamins. Depending on the ambient temperature of your home, the microbial composition of your starter, and the frequency with which you feed it, your sourdough may require more or less rising time than general recipe guidelines suggest. Few sourdoughs will rise in less than 8 hours, and most require closer to 12.

KEEP YOUR DOUGH MOIST

As the dough rises, if it remains exposed to the air, its surface will dry out, the moisture level within the dough itself will become uneven, and the dough will not rise reliably. Once I set my dough in a bowl for its initial rise, I cover the bowl tightly with plastic wrap so that no moisture escapes. If you live in a humid climate, you may be able to cover it with a kitchen towel; however, keep an eye on the dough and make sure that it doesn't dry out. When I set the dough to rise for a second time, I cover it with a mixing bowl to prevent it from drying out. Moisture is critical to good bread.

RESIST THE URGE TO ADD MORE FLOUR

Artisan-style sourdough breads, like most of the breads included in this book, rely largely on moisture for their characteristic crumb and crust. The light, airy crumb and crinkly crust are produced largely through the high water content of the dough. While your dough may seem sloppy or too wet, resist the urge to add more flour in an effort to help form the dough, because you'll collapse the air bubbles developing within the dough and produce a bread with a thick, tight crumb and a brick-like texture.

Sourdough Starter

Nothing more than flour and water, sourdough starter gives many classic artisan-style breads their classic flavor and their rise. While flour remains shelf-stable on its own, when you introduce it to water, whisking the two into a thick, doughy slurry, they attract wild bacteria and yeast. As the tiny microorganisms eat the sugars in the flour, they transform the flour's natural, if subtle, sweetness into sourness. Similarly, as the yeast eat the flour, they produce gas, which allows the bread to rise, developing an airy crumb and a crisp bubbled crust. As your starter ages, it will develop its own unique flavor and characteristics that depend upon the environment of your home and the frequency with which you feed it. No two starters will give precisely the same results in flavor, rise, or texture.

Once established, your starter will become as forgiving as an old friend—even after several weeks of neglect—and will spring back to its original liveliness with a little care. While a sourdough starter thrives on any kind of flour, I find that most starters do best when fed on high-extraction or all-purpose flour rather than whole grain flour, which can leave the starter with an off-putting flavor.

For newcomers to sourdough baking, pinching a bit of an established starter from a friend or purchasing a starter online can help to ensure that your starter becomes established more quickly and with less room for error. Remember, once established, your starter will rise and fall with every feeding, so make sure that your jar remains no more than half full, lest it expand, lift the lid of your jar, and create a mess.

> High-extraction wheat flour (see page 157), unbleached all-purpose flour, or bread flour
>
> Filtered water
>
> Sourdough starter, purchased or given by a friend (optional)

Begin your sourdough starter by whisking $1/4$ cup flour with 3 tablespoons filtered water in a small bowl. If you happen to have a bit of sourdough starter given to you by a friend, whisk that in, too. Pour the slurry into a 2-quart glass jar with a loose-fitting lid and let it sit for 12 hours. Come back to the jar and whisk in another $1/4$ cup flour and 3 tablespoons water, cover the jar, and let it sit at room temperature for another 12 hours. The next day whisk $1/2$ cup flour and $1/3$ cup water into your starter, and continue whisking $1/2$ cup flour and $1/3$ cup water into your starter twice a day until it begins doubling in volume within 12 hours of each feeding, typically in 3 to 5 days.

Once your starter doubles with each feeding, you can begin preparing sourdough breads and other baked goods. Either bake with it immediately, or transfer it to the refrigerator. Feed the starter 1 cup flour and $2/3$ cup water at least twice a week, or each time you bake in order to keep it lively.

PROOFING YOUR STARTER BEFORE BAKING

Before baking with your starter, you want to ensure that the yeast in the starter is lively and active so that it can help your bread to rise and develop good flavor. To proof your starter, remove it from the refrigerator and feed it with 1 cup water and $2/3$ cup flour. Allow it to rest at room temperature until it doubles in volume, about 12 hours. Then remove the amount of starter called for in the recipe and return the remaining sourdough starter to the refrigerator.

whole wheat *and* spelt sourdough bread

A sturdy, rough-textured whole grain bread, this loaf requires no kneading. Gently handling the dough and leaving it to rise and develop its gluten structure through slow, long fermentation allows the bread to develop a lighter texture than usually found in 100 percent whole grain breads. MAKES 1 LOAF

1 cup proofed and bubbly sourdough starter (opposite)

2 cups whole wheat flour

1 1/2 cups whole spelt flour, plus more for working the dough

2 teaspoons finely ground unrefined sea salt

1 cup warm water

Extra-virgin olive oil, for greasing

Pour the sourdough starter into a large mixing bowl and add the flours and salt with the warm water. Stir it with your hand until it forms a shaggy, loose dough. Cover the bowl tightly with plastic wrap and set it aside in a warm spot in your kitchen until the dough doubles in bulk, usually 8 to 12 hours.

Punch down the dough and form it into a round ball. Then pour a bit of olive oil into another large mixing bowl, place the ball of dough in the oiled bowl, and cover it tightly with plastic wrap. Allow the dough to rise once more for about 3 hours.

Preheat the oven to 425°F.

Flour your work surface, then gently scoop the dough out of the bowl and onto the surface. Working very gently and very swiftly, form the dough into a ball (boule), but take care not to deflate the dough too much by handling it roughly. Place it on a baking sheet and, using a serrated bread knife, score the top of the boule with an X about 1/2 inch deep.

Bake for 45 minutes, until it perfumes your kitchen with its aroma and it turns golden brown on top. Let the bread cool on a wire rack before slicing and serving. Once the bread is cool, store it in a paper bag with the opening folded shut.

sprouted three-grain bread ✂

Sprouted grains lend a nutty and very subtle sweetness to this sandwich
bread. Sprouting releases enzymes that break down the complex starches
found in the grains; as a result, sprouted grain breads are naturally, though
very mildly, sweet without the addition of too much sweetener. MAKES 1 LOAF

1 cup spelt berries

1/2 cup einkorn berries

1/2 cup soft white wheat
berries

2 tablespoons apple cider
vinegar

1/4 cup proofed and bubbly
sourdough starter (page 160)

2 tablespoons honey

2 cups bread flour high
extraction wheat flour
(see page 157), or all-purpose
flour, plus more for working
the dough

1 1/2 teaspoons finely ground
unrefined sea salt

Extra-virgin olive oil,
for greasing

Pour the grains into a mixing bowl that's large enough to
accommodate double their volume, cover them with warm
water by 2 inches, and stir in the vinegar. Move the bowl to
a warm spot in your kitchen and let them soak for at least
12 and up to 24 hours.

Drain the grains using a fine-mesh sieve. Keep them in the
sieve, set the sieve over a bowl, and at least twice a day for
2 to 3 days, spray them with cool water and stir them with your
hand to moisten all the berries. When you see tiny, pale sprouts
appear at the tips of the grains, you can prepare the bread. Take
care not to let the sprouts grow longer than 1/8 inch, or else
they might give the bread a gummy texture.

Place the sprouted grains in a food processor and process until
they form a bulky dough. Plop the grains into a large mixing
bowl and add the sourdough starter, honey, flour, and salt.
Mix well, then turn out onto a floured work surface and knead
for 15 minutes.

Grease the mixing bowl with a bit of olive oil and place the
dough in the bowl. Cover tightly with plastic wrap and let
the dough rise until doubled in bulk, about 12 hours.

Grease a 9 by 5-inch loaf pan with a bit of olive oil. Punch down
the dough and turn it onto a floured work surface. Shape the
dough into a loaf and place it in the loaf pan. Cover the pan with
plastic wrap and allow the dough to rise until the top pushes
up against the plastic and peeks out above the edge of the pan,
about 3 hours.

About 20 minutes before you plan to bake, preheat the oven
to 350°F.

Brush the top of the loaf with a bit of olive oil, then bake for
45 minutes, or until the crust is light golden brown. Let the loaf
cool in the pan for 10 minutes, then turn it out onto a wire rack
to cool completely before slicing.

bohemian rye bread

The most striking notes of a classic rye bread are those not of the rye itself, but of caraway, a fragrant seed with an aroma reminiscent of cumin and anise. This recipe combines wheat flour with rye flour to lighten the loaf, but it remains blessedly dense, with a deep brown crumb and crispy crust speckled with caraway and coarse sea salt. Slice the bread thinly, slather it with mustard, and top it with cheese and salami. MAKES 1 LOAF

BREAD

1 cup whole milk

1 tablespoon lard, plus more for greasing

1 tablespoon blackstrap molasses

2 tablespoons caraway seeds

1$\frac{1}{2}$ teaspoons unrefined sea salt

1 cup proofed and bubbly sourdough starter (page 160)

2 cups rye flour

2 cups bread flour, plus more for working the dough

GLAZE

1 egg

1 tablespoon honey

2 tablespoons water

1$\frac{1}{2}$ teaspoons caraway seeds

1 teaspoon coarse unrefined sea salt

To make the bread, warm the milk in a saucepan over medium-low heat until it reaches a temperature that is neither hot nor cold to the touch, 98° to 100°F. Melt the lard in the milk, then whisk in the molasses, caraway, and salt.

Pour the milk mixture and sourdough starter into a large mixing bowl and stir in the flours, about $\frac{1}{2}$ cup at a time, until the dough becomes too thick to mix with a spoon. Turn it out onto a floured work surface, cover with the bowl, and let the dough rest for 10 minutes.

Uncover the dough, knead in any remaining flour, and continue kneading until the dough is smooth and elastic. Form the dough into a ball. Grease a large mixing bowl with a bit of lard, then drop in the ball of dough. Tightly cover the bowl with plastic wrap, set it in a warm spot in your kitchen, and leave it there, undisturbed, for 8 to 12 hours, until the volume of the dough doubles.

Flour your work surface and gently ease the dough out of the bowl and onto the surface with a spatula. Cover it with the mixing bowl and let it rest for 20 minutes. Flour a baking sheet and transfer the dough to the sheet. Gently shape the dough into a torpedo, cover with a kitchen towel or plastic wrap, and let it rise until doubled in bulk, about 3 hours.

Place a baking stone in the oven and preheat the oven to 425°F.

To glaze the loaf, in a small bowl, whisk the egg with the honey and water. Brush the glaze onto the loaf and sprinkle with the caraway and salt. Transfer the baking sheet to baking stone in the oven and bake for 45 minutes, until the bread is fragrant and brown. Remove the loaf from the oven and allow it to cool on a wire rack before slicing and serving. Store in a paper bag with the opening folded closed.

molasses-glazed black bread

Rich, dark, and dense, black bread combines the hearty earthiness of rye with the sweet mineral-rich notes of molasses. I slice it and serve it with slabs of fresh butter, nearly as thick as the bread itself, alongside bowls of Root Cellar Soup (page 42); the pronounced flavors of beet, allspice, and sweet bay complement this bread's humble charm. Cracked rye berries add texture to the bread, but remember to begin soaking them about a day in advance of baking. Like most traditional breads, this one requires resolute patience for the best results. MAKES 1 LOAF

BREAD

Water

1/2 cup purchased cracked rye berries

1 tablespoon unsalted butter, plus more for greasing

2 tablespoons blackstrap molasses

1 tablespoon caraway seeds

1 tablespoon fennel seeds

1 1/2 teaspoons finely ground unrefined sea salt

2 cups dark rye flour

2 cups unbleached bread flour, plus more for working the dough

1 tablespoon Dutch-process unsweetened cocoa powder

1 cup proofed and bubbly sourdough starter (page 160)

GLAZE

1 egg

1 tablespoon blackstrap molasses

2 tablespoons water

In a small saucepan, bring 2 cups of water to a boil over high heat. Pour the cracked rye berries into a mixing bowl, pour the boiling water over them, and cover the bowl. Let the rye berries soak, well covered, in the hot water at least 12 and up to 18 hours, until plumped. Drain off the water and reserve the berries.

Warm 1 cup of water in a small saucepan over medium-low heat until it reaches a temperature that is neither hot nor cold to the touch, 98° to 100°F. Melt the butter in the water, then whisk in the molasses, caraway, fennel, and salt. In a separate bowl, whisk together the rye flour, bread flour, and cocoa.

Pour the liquid ingredients and sourdough starter into a large mixing bowl and stir in the flour mixture about 1/2 cup at a time until the dough becomes too thick to mix with a spoon. Turn it out onto a floured work surface, cover with the bowl, and let the dough rest for 10 minutes.

Uncover the dough and knead in the cracked rye and any remaining flour. Continue kneading until the dough is smooth and elastic, about 10 minutes. Form it into a ball.

Grease a large mixing bowl with butter, then drop the ball of dough into the bowl. Cover the bowl with plastic wrap to prevent the dough from drying out. Set the bowl in a warm spot in your kitchen and leave it there, undisturbed, for 8 to 12 hours, or until the dough doubles in volume.

Flour your work surface and gently ease the dough out of the bowl and onto the surface with a spatula. Cover it with the mixing bowl or plastic wrap and let it rest for 20 minutes.

Flour a baking sheet and plop the dough on top of the sheet. Gently shape the dough into a ball (boule), cover it with a kitchen towel or plastic wrap, and let it rise until doubled in bulk, about 3 hours.

Preheat the oven to 425°F.

To glaze the loaf, in a small bowl, whisk the egg with the molasses and water. Paint the glaze onto the loaf. Transfer the baking sheet to the oven and bake for about 45 minutes, until the bread is deeply fragrant and dark brown. Remove the loaf from the oven and allow it to cool on a wire rack before slicing and serving.

german-style sunflower bread

In the summer, my husband and I find a small patch of space in our garden and give it to our little boy. Like most parents, we want to instill in him a sense of duty, of responsibility, and of joy, too. Gardening fulfills these purposes, along with so many others. In his patch of dirt he enjoys the freedom to grow what he chooses, selecting varieties, sowing seeds, tending plants. He experiences both success and failure, hardship and reward. Though the plants he chooses vary from season to season, he always adds a sunflower or two to the plot. They sprout, grow tall, and lean against the fence posts, their blooms following the sun across the bright blue Colorado sky. Though our season remains short, we can usually coax a few seeds from those big yellow blossoms before the snows set in.

We roast the seeds, salt them, and eat them out of hand. We also make this German-style bread, kneading the hulled seeds into a rye-based dough sweetened with just a touch of honey. Topped with a sprinkling of sunflower seeds, it's a pretty little loaf. Once you break through that crackled brown crust, you're met with a soft but rustic crumb and the grassy, nut-like flavor of the sunflower seeds scattered throughout. MAKES 1 LOAF

BREAD

1¹/₂ cups water

1 tablespoon unsalted butter

2 tablespoons honey

2 teaspoons finely ground unrefined sea salt

1 cup proofed and bubbly sourdough starter (page 160)

2 cups rye flour

3 cups bread flour, plus more for working the dough

¹/₂ cup sunflower seeds

Extra-virgin olive oil, for greasing

To make the bread, warm the water in a saucepan over medium-low heat until it reaches a temperature that is neither hot nor cold to the touch, 98° to 100°F. Stir in the butter and honey, allowing them to melt and dissolve into the warm water. Whisk in the salt and sourdough starter.

Pour the mixture into a large mixing bowl. Add scoops of the flours, about ¹/₂ cup at a time, stirring well with each scoop, until the dough turns too stiff to mix with a spoon. Sprinkle your work surface with a bit of flour, then turn out the dough onto the floured surface. Cover the dough with the mixing bowl to prevent it from drying out and let it rest for 10 minutes.

Uncover the dough and knead in any remaining flour and the sunflower seeds until the dough becomes smooth and elastic, about 10 minutes. Form the dough into a ball.

GLAZE

1 egg

1 tablespoon honey

2 tablespoons water

2 tablespoons sunflower seeds

Grease a large mixing bowl with just enough olive oil to leave a thin film and place the dough in the bowl. Tighly cover the mixing bowl with plastic wrap and allow the dough to rise at room temperature until doubled in bulk, usually 8 to 12 hours, depending on the liveliness of your sourdough starter.

Flour your work surface and gently ease the dough out of the bowl and onto the surface with a spatula. Cover it with the mixing bowl and let it rest for 20 minutes. Sprinkle a baking sheet with flour. Remove the mixing bowl from the dough and gently shape the dough into a ball (boule). Cover it with a length of plastic wrap or a kitchen towel to prevent it from drying out and allow it to rise until doubled in bulk, about 3 hours.

Place a baking stone into the oven and preheat the oven to 425°F.

To glaze the loaf, in a small bowl, whisk the egg with the honey and water. Brush the glaze onto the loaf and sprinkle the loaf with the sunflower seeds. Using a serrated bread knife, score the loaf with an X about $1/2$ inch deep, then transfer the baking sheet to the baking stone in the oven. Bake for about 45 minutes, until the bread is nicely browned on top. Remove the loaf from the oven and allow it to cool on a wire rack before slicing and serving. Store the bread in a brown paper bag with the opening folded shut.

einkorn wheat *and* herb bread ❧

Einkorn wheat is an ancient grain, among the first cultivated by the first farmers who abandoned a nomadic lifestyle of hunting and gathering to toil in the fields of the Fertile Crescent. Unlike modern varieties of wheat, einkorn remains in its natural, original state, unadulterated by generations of hybridization and selective breeding. Einkorn is typically richer in antioxidants and beta carotene than modern wheat varieties, and some people who are otherwise sensitive to wheat do not exhibit sensitivity to this ancient grain.

I bake with einkorn frequently, and my favorite way to use it is in a classic herb bread. Einkorn tastes more complex and less sweet than wheat flour, and this natural complexity balances nicely with a variety of garden herbs in this simple, no-knead sourdough bread. Due to its high liquid content, no-knead dough tends to spread rather than rise, so don't worry if your dough loses its form as it rests. Simply shape it just prior to baking and you'll have beautiful results. MAKES 1 LOAF

¼ cup proofed and bubbly sourdough starter (page 160)

1½ cups water, at room temperature

3 cups whole einkorn flour

2 cups high-extraction einkorn flour (see page 157) or bread flour, plus more for working the dough

2 teaspoons finely ground unrefined sea salt

2 teaspoons dried parsley

2 teaspoons dried chives

1 teaspoon dried dill

½ teaspoon dried thyme

In a small mixing bowl, whisk together the sourdough starter and water. In a large bowl, stir together the flours, salt, parsley, chives, dill, and thyme until uniformly combined. Make a well in the center of the flour mixture and pour in the liquid ingredients. Mix by hand until you have a loose, shaggy dough. Tightly cover the bowl with plastic wrap and let the dough rest at room temperature for 12 to 18 hours, or until it doubles in volume. The longer you let it rest, the sourer the bread will taste.

Generously flour your work surface and scoop the dough out of the mixing bowl and onto the surface. Cover the dough with the bowl to prevent it from drying out and allow it to rest for 2 to 3 hours.

Preheat the oven to 425°F.

Flour your hands very well, and then flour a baking sheet. Scoop the dough onto the baking sheet and form it into a ball (boule). Generously sprinkle flour over its surface. Using a serrated bread knife, score the dough's surface with a hash mark about ½ inch deep. Bake the bread for 1 hour, or until its crust is light amber in color. Transfer the bread to a wire rack and allow to cool completely before slicing and serving.

sweet spiced buns *with* currants

The aroma and mystery of hot cross buns mesmerized me during childhood, and just once a year I'd dig into my mother's tattered and worn cookbooks, pull out her mixing bowls, and work my way through flour, eggs, and currants until I'd satisfied my want.

Though I only occasionally grace these spiced buns with a cross, I still make them once a year out of habit, toward the spring equinox, when I can use the last of winter's oranges and the first of spring's eggs. These days I spice them with orange, cardamom, cloves, and allspice, adding in a scoop of unrefined sugar to alleviate their sourness. I often serve them with breakfast, or with tea in the late afternoon. MAKES ABOUT 1 DOZEN LARGE BUNS

DOUGH

1¹/₂ cups proofed and bubbly sourdough starter (page 160)

3¹/₂ cups bread flour, high-extraction wheat flour (see page 157), or unbleached all-purpose flour, plus more for working the dough

3³/₄ cups whole grain spelt flour

2 eggs, beaten

1 cup unrefined cane sugar

2 teaspoons finely ground unrefined sea salt

1¹/₂ teaspoons ground allspice

1 teaspoon ground cardamom

¹/₄ teaspoon ground cloves

2 teaspoons finely grated orange zest

1 cup dried currants

Extra-virgin olive oil, for greasing

GLAZE

1 egg

1 tablespoon honey

2 tablespoons water

To make the dough, beat together the sourdough starter and flours in a large mixing bowl, then cover the bowl tightly with plastic wrap and let it sit on your counter for 8 to 12 hours. Punch down the dough and form a well at its center.

In a separate bowl, beat the eggs with the sugar until smooth, light, and uniform in texture. Beat in the salt, allspice, cardamom, cloves, and orange zest. Pour the egg mixture into the well at the center of the sourdough starter and flour mixture. Beat to form a smooth, wet batter. Fold in the currants.

Generously flour your work surface, then turn out the dough onto the surface. Knead the dough well, incorporating enough flour to form a smooth, elastic dough, about 15 minutes. Let it rest, covered, for 10 minutes, and then knead for 5 minutes longer. Form the dough into a large ball.

Rub a large mixing bowl with olive oil, then place the ball of dough in the bowl, cover the bowl with plastic wrap, and let the dough rise until doubled in bulk, about 4 hours.

Dust a baking sheet with flour. Once the dough has doubled in bulk, punch it down and tear off pieces by the handful, forming the dough into about a dozen balls, each 2 to 3 inches in diameter. Place the balls on the baking sheet, spacing them about 2 inches apart. Let the buns rise, covered, for another 45 minutes, until puffed.

About 20 minutes before you plan to bake, preheat the oven to 400°F.

To make the glaze, in a small bowl, beat the egg, then whisk in the honey and water. Paint the buns with the glaze. Bake for 20 minutes, or until the buns are dark brown and deeply fragrant. Transfer them to a wire rack to cool. You can serve the buns barely warm with butter, or allow them to cool to room temperature.

Beyond Bread

As you tend a sourdough starter, it will grow in volume with each feeding and quickly double in volume. If you find you have excess sourdough starter but don't care to bake bread, you can put the starter to other uses where its tart flavor can find a natural complement. Some of my favorite uses for sourdough starter are to make biscuits and muffins, herbed noodles, and blueberry pancakes.

You do not need to proof your sourdough starter when making these recipes because dishes such as pancakes and crumpets achieve their lightness through the reaction that occurs when alkaline baking soda meets the acidic starter.

sourdough blueberry pancakes
with buttered orange syrup ✤

Sourdough starter introduces a pleasant, mild tartness to pancakes,
are an easy way to use extra sourdough starter when you don't feel like
baking bread. I dot these pancakes with fresh blueberries and pair them
with a sweet, warm syrup flavored with butter and orange. SERVES 4 TO 6

SYRUP

4 large oranges

2 tablespoons unsalted butter

¼ cup unrefined cane sugar

PANCAKES

2 cups sourdough starter (page 160)

1 tablespoon honey

½ teaspoon baking soda

¼ teaspoon finely ground unrefined sea salt

Lard or unsalted butter, for frying the pancakes

1 cup blueberries

To make the syrup, finely grate the zest of the oranges. Place the zest in a small bowl, then cut the oranges in half crosswise and squeeze their juice into the same bowl.

Melt the butter in a saucepan over medium heat. When it froths, whisk in the sugar. Allow the sugar to cook in the butter for 1 to 2 minutes, until fragrant and syrupy, and then stir in the orange juice and zest. Simmer the mixture until it reduces by half, about 15 minutes. Cover the pan to keep the syrup warm while you make the pancakes.

Preheat the oven to 200°F.

To make the pancakes, in a bowl, beat the sourdough starter with the honey, then beat in the baking soda and salt. Wait for about a minute until the batter bubbles and increases in volume as the baking soda and sourdough starter react.

Melt about a tablespoon of fat in a skillet over medium-low heat. Pour about ¼ cup of the pancake batter into the hot fat and drop a few blueberries onto the pancake. Let the pancake cook undisturbed until the center of the batter begins to form bubbles, then flip the pancake and continue cooking on the second side for 1 to 2 minutes more, until a toothpick inserted into the center comes out clean. Transfer the pancake to an ovenproof plate, cover with a kitchen towel, and set the plate in the oven to keep warm while using up the remaining batter and blueberries; add more fat to the skillet as needed. Serve the pancakes with the warm orange syrup.

herbed sourdough rye noodles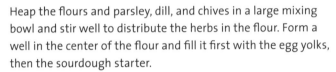

On long winter afternoons, I often undertake larger projects like noodle making. While mixing sourdough starter with flour and herbs requires only a few minutes, rolling out and cutting the dough into ribbon-like strips can be time-intensive, so save this recipe for a slow afternoon. Plunged into boiling water or stock, they'll cook in only a few minutes. SERVES 6 GENEROUSLY

2 cups all-purpose flour
or high-extraction flour
(see page 157), plus more
for working the dough

1 cup rye flour

1 tablespoon dried parsley

1 teaspoon dried dill

1 teaspoon dried chives

4 egg yolks, beaten

1 cup sourdough starter
(page 160)

Unsalted butter or sour
cream, to serve

Heap the flours and parsley, dill, and chives in a large mixing bowl and stir well to distribute the herbs in the flour. Form a well in the center of the flour and fill it first with the egg yolks, then the sourdough starter.

Beat all the ingredients together until they form a smooth dough. Cover the bowl with plastic wrap to prevent the dough from drying out and leave it in a warm spot on your kitchen counter for at least 12 and up to 16 hours.

The next day, generously flour your work surface and plop the dough on the surface. Form the dough into a ball and cover it with the mixing bowl. Allow it to rest for 10 minutes. Uncover and split the dough into four equal portions.

Working one piece at a time, roll out the dough until it's no thicker than 1/8 inch. Pass it through a pasta machine until it is thin enough for you, then cut the pasta sheet into noodles the length and width that you prefer. Gently arrange the noodles on a drying rack and continue rolling and cutting until you've exhausted the dough. The noodles should dry within 8 to 12 hours, depending on their thickness and the ambient humidity of your home. Store the dry noodles in resealable bags at room temperature for 1 week, or transfer to the freezer, where they'll keep for up to 6 months.

When you're ready to serve the noodles, bring a pot of water of broth to a boil and plunge the dry noodles into the water. Let them simmer, covered, for 2 or 3 minutes, or until they rise to the water's surface. Drain and serve the noodles with butter or sour cream.

sourdough crumpets

Surprisingly easy to make, sourdough crumpets come together quickly for a simple breakfast bread. I lean on this recipe on busy mornings because they require only four simple ingredients that I always have on hand: starter, salt, baking soda, and butter.

Crumpets are yeasty little griddle cakes that, when split open, reveal plenty of nooks and crannies in their crumb, perfect for collecting jam and melted butter. The air bubbles that form the crumpet's characteristic texture develop as a result of a simple chemical reaction: the combination of acidic sourdough starter with alkaline baking soda. Because the chemical reaction that gives crumpets their bubbles happens instantly, take care to use the batter quickly after mixing it. To serve the crumpets, split them in half, toast them, and spread them with butter and jam. MAKES ABOUT 8

---

2 cups sourdough starter (page 160)

1 teaspoon finely ground unrefined sea salt

1 teaspoon baking soda

2 tablespoons unsalted butter

Butter two egg rings and set them aside.

Pour the sourdough starter into a mixing bowl and beat in the salt and baking soda. The acidity of your starter will combine with the baking soda and your batter will start to puff and bubble, so don't abandon the batter and work quickly.

Melt the butter in a cast-iron skillet over medium heat. When it froths, set the rings in the pan and pour 2 tablespoons of batter into each mold. Allow the batter to cook until bubbles begin to appear in the center, about 3 minutes. Remove the ring molds, gently pushing out the crumpets, flip over the crumpets, and brown the other sides for about 2 minutes, until puffed and a toothpick inserted into the centers comes out clean. Transfer the crumpets to a plate and continue cooking more until you exhaust the batter.

Store any extra crumpets in the refrigerator in a container with a tight-fitting lid for up to 3 days.

simple sourdough pie crust &

I bake pies—both savory and sweet—frequently in every season, but more often in the cold months, when the warmth of the oven can heat the entirety of our little home. I bake hand pies and turnovers, potpies and fruit pies, and I almost always use this simple recipe for the crust. I like its pleasant tartness, which complements savory pies and balances the sweetness of dessert pies.

When I prepare this crust I typically use high-extraction flour (see page 157). If you don't have high-extraction flour on hand, substitute 2 cups all-purpose flour and 1 cup whole-wheat flour. MAKES 2 DOUGH DISKS, EACH ONE ENOUGH FOR A 9-INCH PIE

3 cups all-purpose flour, high-extraction wheat flour (see page 157), plus more for rolling the dough

1 teaspoon finely ground unrefined sea salt

¼ cup unsalted butter, at room temperature

¼ cup sourdough starter (page 160)

Cold water

Pour the flour into a large mixing bowl and whisk in the salt. Using a pastry blender or a fork, work the butter into the flour until its texture begins to resemble coarse cornmeal. Beat in the sourdough starter, followed by cold water, 1 tablespoon at a time, until the dough is smooth, pliable, and pulls away from the sides of the bowl.

Form the dough into a ball, then divide it in half. Shape each half into a disk, wrap it in plastic wrap, and refrigerate for at least 8 and up to 24 hours.

To Roll Out the Dough

Remove the disk(s) from the refrigerator and let sit at room temperature for 30 minutes, until slightly softened. Cut two large sheets of parchment paper and generously flour one sheet. Place a disk of dough in the center, dust it with flour, and lay the second parchment sheet on top. Roll out the dough to the dimensions specified in the recipe you're following, or to 10 inches in diameter for a 9-inch pie. If rolling out the second disk, do so in the same way, using two new sheets of parchment paper. (The rolled-out dough can be refrigerated, sandwiched between the parchment sheets, for a few hours or wrapped in plastic wrap and frozen for up to 3 months.)

Soaked Flour

I have a love of old-fashioned butter-milk biscuits, soda breads, and other simple baked goods with a tender crumb and lovely flavor. I prepare them in our home in the colder months, when the valley's hens lay eggs less frequently. Soaking flour, like fermenting it through sourdough baking, helps to improve its digestibility and mitigate the effects of antinutrients. Yet, beyond the obvious nutritional benefits of soaked-flour baked goods, there exists another benefit: soaking flour in a slightly acidic medium, like buttermilk or yogurt, produces a remarkably light and tender crumb and a creamy flavor.

brown soda bread *with* whiskey-soaked currants *and* flaked oats 🌾

At its simplest, soda bread needs nothing more than flour, buttermilk, salt, and baking soda. I like to dress up my soda bread, dropping in a spoonful of caraway seeds or a handful of raisins. One of my favorite versions combines flaked oats with whiskey-soaked currants. I like the rustic, chewy texture the oats give to the otherwise uniform crumb of soda bread. MAKES 1 LOAF

4 cups white whole wheat flour, plus more for working the dough

1/2 cup flaked or rolled oats, plus more to top the loaf

1 3/4 cups buttermilk

1 cup dried currants

Whiskey, for soaking the currants

1 teaspoon baking soda

1 teaspoon finely ground unrefined sea salt

Heavy cream, for glazing the loaf

Unsalted butter, to serve

Pour the flour into a large mixing bowl and stir in the flaked oats. Slowly dribble 1 1/2 cups of the buttermilk into the flour and oats, stirring until a soft, shaggy dough forms. Tightly cover the mixing bowl with plastic wrap and let it sit in a warm spot in your kitchen for at least 12 and up to 18 hours.

Preheat the oven to 450°F.

Spoon the currants into a small bowl and cover them with whiskey. Let soak for 15 minutes.

Meanwhile, finish the bread dough. Pour the remaining 1/4 cup buttermilk into the soaked flour, then spoon in the baking soda and salt. Beat until the dough forms a uniform mass. Flour a work surface and turn out the dough onto the surface. Drain the currants, discarding the whiskey, and knead them into the dough. Flour your hands well and form the dough into a ball. Brush the dough with heavy cream and dust the top with flaked oats. With a serrated bread knife, score the dough with an X about 1/2 inch deep.

Line a baking sheet with parchment paper and place the dough on the baking sheet. Bake for 25 minutes, decrease the oven temperature to 400°F, and continue baking for 20 minutes longer, until the bread is browned and fragrant. Remove from the oven and let cool before slicing and serving with plenty of butter.

barley *and* poppy seed kefir bread ✤

When my son was very young, we'd burrow beneath the quilts of his bed and read our favorite poems together. "A poppy's red in its barley bed," we'd repeat from Christina Rossetti's poem "What is Pink?" The image of a poppy, tall, red, and strong against the fields of waving yellow grain, remained with me.

Kefir, like sourdough starter, is a rich source of beneficial bacteria and yeast. While its yeast content varies depending on the individual complement of microbes in each household's kefir grains, the hearty strains of yeast typically offer enough strength to give bread its rise; however, if you're concerned that your kefir is not strong and yeasty enough to make bread rise, add 1/4 to 1/2 teaspoon baker's yeast to the kefir and honey when you stir them into the flour prior to the bread's first rise. MAKES 1 LOAF

3 cups high-extraction wheat flour (see page 157), bread flour, or all-purpose flour, plus more for working the dough

2 cups barley flour

2 teaspoons finely ground unrefined sea salt

2 tablespoons poppy seeds

2 1/2 cups milk kefir (page 62)

1 tablespoon honey

1 tablespoon unsalted butter, melted

Extra-virgin olive oil, for greasing

GLAZE

1 egg

1 tablespoon honey

1 tablespoon water

1 tablespoon poppy seeds

Pour the flours into a large mixing bowl and stir in the salt and poppy seeds. Make a well in the center and pour in the kefir, honey, and melted butter. Stir until the mixture is loosely combined. Flour a work surface and turn out the dough onto the surface. Knead for 5 minutes, incorporating more flour if necessary to maintain the dough's elasticity without reducing its stickiness. Form the dough into a ball.

Grease a large mixing bowl with a bit of olive oil, then place the ball of dough in the bowl. Tightly cover the bowl with plastic wrap and allow it to sit in a warm spot in your kitchen for at least 18 and up to 24 hours.

Grease a 9 by 5-inch loaf pan with a bit of olive oil.

Flour your work surface once more, then turn the dough out onto the surface. Shape the dough into a loaf and place it in the prepared loaf pan. Tightly cover the pan with plastic wrap and allow the dough to rise for 3 to 4 hours, until it increases in volume.

Preheat the oven to 350°F.

To make the glaze, in a small bowl, whisk together the egg, honey, and water. Uncover the dough, brush it lightly with glaze, and sprinkle it with the poppy seeds. Bake for 40 to 50 minutes, until browned. Let the bread cool in the pan on a wire rack, then turn it out of the pan, slice, and serve.

buttermilk spelt drop biscuits ⚘

The aroma of freshly baked biscuits, all sweet and buttery, fills our home from time to time—mostly on lazy weekends, when I plan to wake slowly and make a large, but very late, breakfast. Having completed the bulk of the work the night before, I spoon the dough onto a hot baking stone, close the oven, and wait. In a short time—only long enough to set the table and pour a glass of milk for my son—the biscuits puff in the oven, their tops browning just a little. I pull them from the oven, set them in a little basket lined with an old kitchen towel, and my family sets to work breaking the biscuits in half, smearing them with the freshly made butter that always seems to be on hand in summer, and drizzling them with orchard blossom honey.

MAKES ABOUT 1 DOZEN

---

1 cup high-extraction wheat flour (see page 157) or all-purpose flour, plus more for working the dough

1 cup whole grain spelt flour

8 tablespoons unsalted butter, 6 tablespoons cold and 2 tablespoons melted

1 cup buttermilk

1 teaspoon baking soda

1 teaspoon finely ground unrefined sea salt

Whisk the flours together in a large mixing bowl. With a pastry cutter or fork, work the cold butter into the flour a tablespoon at a time, until the flour resembles cornmeal in texture. Beat in the buttermilk with a wooden spoon until a thick dough forms. Cover the bowl with plastic wrap and allow it to rest at room temperature for at least 8 and up to 12 hours.

Preheat the oven to 450°F.

Dust your work surface with flour and turn out the dough onto the surface. Knead in the baking soda and salt. Knead in enough flour to make the dough workable, but take care not to overwork the dough or your biscuits will be too tough.

Scoop up 2 to 3 tablespoons of dough with a spoon and drop the mound onto a baking sheet. Continue dropping spoonfuls of dough onto the baking sheet, spacing them about 2 inches apart. Brush the mounds with the melted butter and bake for 10 minutes, until the biscuits puff and their tops begin to brown. Serve warm.

yogurt *and* dill crackers

Dill and yogurt make a natural marriage, for the herbaceous and faintly floral notes of dill pair nicely with the tart creaminess of yogurt. Here the two come together in a simple, flaky homemade cracker. Soaking flour in yogurt not only infuses the crackers with the yogurt's tart and cheese-like flavor, but it also tenderizes the crumb. The crackers are not only both flaky and tender, but also redolent with flavor. While we eat them out of hand at home, I also like to float a few in bone broth—chicken, beef, or whatever I happen to have on hand—with a sprinkling of parsley and minced garlic when any member of my family feels under the weather. MAKES ABOUT 5 DOZEN 1¹/₂-INCH CRACKERS

1¹/₂ cups whole wheat pastry flour, plus more for working the dough

¹/₂ teaspoon finely ground unrefined sea salt

1¹/₂ teaspoons dried dill

6 tablespoons unsalted butter, 4 tablespoons at room temperature, 2 tablespoons melted

¹/₂ cup yogurt

Put the flour into a large mixing bowl and whisk in the salt and dill. Beat in the 4 tablespoons of room-temperature butter until the flour resembles cornmeal in texture. Beat in the yogurt until the mixture forms a thick dough. Cover the bowl tightly and allow it to rest in a warm place in your kitchen for at least 8 and up to 12 hours.

Position racks in the upper and lower thirds of the oven and preheat the oven to 450°F. Line two baking sheets with parchment paper.

Divide the dough into four portions. Flour your work surface and roll out each piece of dough to an even ¹/₁₆-inch thickness, then use a pizza cutter or sharp knife to cut the dough into 1¹/₂-inch squares. Place the squares on the prepared baking sheets, spacing them about ¹/₂ inch apart.

Brush the squares with the 2 tablespoons of melted butter and prick them with the tines of a fork to prevent them from puffing as they bake. Bake for 6 to 8 minutes, until the crackers are just tinged with gold around their edges. Pull them from the oven and cool them on a wire rack. Store the crackers in an airtight container for up to 2 weeks.

Porridges and Cooked Whole Grains

Porridges of slowly simmered whole grains provide deep and satisfying breakfasts, while savory pilafs flavored with bone broths, herbs, and vegetables can provide interest to evening meals. I use whole grains readily in my cooking, more so in the cold months than in the warm months. Soaking grains in slightly acidic, or soft, water not only improves the bioavailability of the minerals they contain, but it also softens them a bit, reducing their cooking time and improving their texture and flavor. Remember, soaking requires additional time, so begin the day or evening before you plan to cook them. Despite the additional planning required to accommodate soaking, the process of soaking grains allows a great deal of flexibility to the cook's schedule, as there's no precise point at which your grains are ready; rather, there's a window of optimal soaking periods. Soaking grains also decreases cooking time by about 20 percent.

GRAIN	CONTAINS GLUTEN	FLAVOR	NUTRITION	HOW TO PREPARE IT FOR COOKING AND BAKING
Amaranth*	No	Mild, flavorless	B6, folate, calcium, iron, magnesium, phosphorus, zinc, copper, selenium	Soak 1 cup amaranth with 2 tablespoons vinegar in enough warm water to cover by 2 inches for at least 12 and up to 24 hours.
Barley	Yes	Sweet, nutty	Thiamin, riboflavin, niacin, B6, iron, magnesium, phosphorus, zinc, copper, manganese, selenium	As an additive to sourdough breads and other baked goods. Soak 1 cup hulled barley with 2 tablespoons vinegar in enough water to cover by 2 inches for at least 8 and up to 24 hours.
Buckwheat*	No	Full-flavored, earthy	Niacin, B6, folate, pantothenic acid, copper, manganese, magnesium, iron, phosphorus	Soak 1 cup buckwheat groats with 2 tablespoons vinegar in enough warm water to cover by 2 inches for at least 8 and up to 12 hours.
Einkorn	Yes	Sweet, faint salt and mineral undertones, rich wheat flavor	Thiamin, riboflavin, vitamin B6, iron, phosphorus, beta carotene, magnesium, manganese, zinc, potassium	In sourdough breads and baked goods, soaked flour breads and baked goods. Soak 1 cup einkorn wheat berries with 2 tablespoons vinegar in enough water to cover by 2 inches for at least 8 and up to 24 hours.
Millet	No	Mild, slightly grassy, sweet	Thiamin, niacin, B6, folate	Soak 1 cup millet with 2 tablespoons vinegar in enough warm water to cover by 2 inches for at least 12 and up to 24 hours

GRAIN	CONTAINS GLUTEN	FLAVOR	NUTRITION	HOW TO PREPARE IT FOR COOKING AND BAKING
Oats	Possibly, often due to cross-contamination	Sweet, nutty, faint grass notes	Manganese, phosphorus, iron, zinc, copper, thiamin, niacin, folate, riboflavin	As an additive to sourdough breads and other baked goods. Soak 1 cup hulled, flaked, or steel-cut oats with 2 tablespoons vinegar in enough water to cover by 2 inches for at least 18 and up to 24 hours.
Quinoa*	No	Grassy	Vitamin E, thiamin, niacin, B6, folate, iron, magnesium, phosphorus, zinc, copper, manganese	Soak 1 cup quinoa with 2 tablespoons vinegar in enough warm water to cover by 2 inches for 12 to 24 hours.
Rice	No	Mild and nutty; some varieties offer floral notes	Magnesium, manganese, selenium, phosphorus, niacin, B6	Soak 1 cup brown rice with 2 tablespoon vinegar in enough warm water to cover by 2 inches for at least 8 and up to 24 hours, or sprout.
Rye	Yes	Bold, rich	Niacin, manganese, selenium, iron	In sourdough breads and baked goods, soaked flour breads and baked goods. Soak 1 cup rye berries with 2 tablespoons vinegar in enough water to cover by 2 inches for at least 8 and up to 24 hours.
Spelt	Yes	Wheat-like	Thiamin, niacin, magnesium, manganese, copper, zinc	In sourdough breads and baked goods, soaked flour breads and baked goods. Soak 1 cup spelt berries with 2 tablespoons vinegar in enough water to cover by 2 inches for at least 8 and up to 24 hours.
Teff	No	Rich, chocolaty	Thiamin, niacin, B6, folate	Soak 1 cup teff with 2 tablespoons vinegar and enough water to cover by 2 inches. Soak for at least 12 and up to 24 hours.
Wheat	Yes	Sweet and bread-like	Thiamin, niacin, folate, B6, manganese, selenium, phosphorus, magnesium, iron	In sourdough breads and baked goods, soaked flour breads and baked goods. Soak 1 cup wheat berries with 2 tablespoons vinegar in enough water to cover by 2 inches for at least 8 and up to 24 hours.

* Denotes a pseudocereal rather than a true cereal grain. Pseudocereals are the seeds of broadleaf plants rather than grasses and can be cooked similarly to true cereal grains.

baked oats *with* pistachios, dried figs, *and* honey ❧

Dense, chewy, and cake-like, these oat bars are always a favorite in my home. I reserve them for busy weekends when visiting guests stumble out of their slumber and into the kitchen for breakfast. They cut away a square, then top it with honey or yogurt and more fruit. It's a favorite of my father, and one I always make especially for him when he visits—sometimes substituting walnuts for pistachios, or apricots and raisins for figs. SERVES 6 TO 8

8 cups steel-cut oats

1 cup pistachios

1/4 cup yogurt

1 teaspoon ground cinnamon

1/2 teaspoon finely ground unrefined sea salt

6 eggs, beaten

1 cup milk

1/2 cup honey

1 orange

1 cup chopped dried Mission figs

2 tablespoons unsalted butter, plus more for greasing

Spoon the oats into a large mixing bowl, toss in the pistachios, and cover with warm water by 2 inches. Stir in the yogurt and cover the bowl with a kitchen towel. Set the bowl in a warm spot in your kitchen and allow the oats and pistachios to soak for at least 8 and up to 12 hours.

Drain the oat mixture in a fine-mesh sieve, rinse well, and return it to the mixing bowl.

Preheat the oven to 375°F and grease a 9 by 13-inch baking dish with butter.

Stir the cinnamon, salt, eggs, milk, and honey into the oat mixture until well blended. Finely grate the zest of the orange, placing it in a bowl. Cut the orange in half crosswise and squeeze the juice into the bowl holding the zest. Stir both the orange zest and juice into the oat mixture, then fold in the figs. Spoon the mixture into the prepared baking dish and smooth the top. Cut the butter into small pieces and scatter them over the surface.

Bake for 40 to 45 minutes, until golden brown at the edges and slightly wobbly at the center. Allow to cool for 5 minutes before serving. Baked oats will keep, covered, in the refrigerator for up to 1 week. (To reheat leftovers, cut a square of the baked oats. Drop a tablespoon of butter into a skillet and heat it over medium heat until frothy. Place the oat square in the skillet and cook until warmed through, about 3 minutes.)

barley *in* broth *with* bacon *and* kale

Cooked barley and ribbons of kale swirl together in this thick broth-based soup. Barley brings its earthy flavor and pleasant, chewy texture to a broth punctuated by bacon, carrots, celery, and garlic. SERVES 4 TO 6

1 cup hulled barley

1 tablespoon apple cider vinegar

1 tablespoon extra-virgin olive oil

2 ounces bacon, finely chopped

1 yellow onion, finely chopped

3 carrots, peeled and finely chopped

3 ribs celery, finely chopped

2 cloves garlic, finely chopped

1/2 cup dry white wine

6 cups Chicken Bone Broth (page 120)

1 small bunch Lacinato kale (about 8 ounces)

Finely ground unrefined sea salt and freshly ground black pepper

Toss the barley into a mixing bowl and cover with warm water by 2 inches. Stir in the vinegar, cover the bowl, and allow the grains to soak at room temperature for at least 8 and up to 12 hours.

Drain the barley and rinse it well.

Heat the olive oil in a saucepan over medium heat and toss in the bacon. Allow the bacon to cook until crispy, about 6 minutes. Stir in the onion, carrots, celery, and garlic. Sauté until the vegetables are fragrant and crisp-tender, about 2 minutes. Stir in the soaked barley and the wine and stir continuously until the wine has evaporated, about 8 minutes. Decrease the heat to medium-low, then stir in the chicken broth, cover, and simmer until the barley is cooked through, about 40 minutes.

While the barley cooks, prepare the kale by trimming away any tough stems or veins. Stack the leaves one on top of another and roll them into a cigar. Slice the leaves crosswise into ribbons about 1/8 inch thick.

Once the barley is tender, turn off the heat. Stir in the kale and cover the pot. Allow the kale to wilt in the residual heat of the broth for 3 to 5 minutes. Season with salt and pepper and serve.

wild rice *with* currants *and* toasted walnuts

I love the way the chewy, dark sheath of wild rice opens up to a tender, soft grain when I simmer it in stock or broth. Its flavor, at once nutty and vegetal, marries well with leek and herbs—most notably thyme, whose perfumed green notes elevate and balance the grain's heaviness. Wild rice is rich in protein, B vitamins, and minerals like manganese, magnesium, phosphorus, and zinc. SERVES 4 TO 6

1½ cups wild rice

2 tablespoons apple cider vinegar

½ cup chopped walnuts

1 tablespoon unsalted butter

1 leek, white and light green parts only, thinly sliced

3 ribs celery, diced

2 teaspoons fresh thyme leaves

½ cup dried currants

2 teaspoons finely ground unrefined sea salt

3 cups Chicken Bone Broth (page 120)

Pour the wild rice in a mixing bowl, cover it with warm water by 2 inches, and stir in the vinegar. Cover the bowl with a kitchen towel, set it in a warm spot in your kitchen, and allow the rice to soak for at least 8 and up to 12 hours.

Drain the rice and rinse it well.

Preheat the oven to 375°F and line a baking sheet with parchment paper.

Scatter the walnuts on the baking sheet and toast them in the oven for 10 to 12 minutes, until deeply fragrant, stirring them once or twice to prevent scorching. Remove the nuts from the oven and transfer them to a bowl. Reduce the oven temperature to 350°F.

Melt the butter in an ovenproof saucepan over medium heat. When it froths, stir in the leek, celery, and thyme and fry until the leek softens, about 2 minutes. Stir in the soaked rice and sauté for 1 to 2 minutes, until lightly fragrant. Stir in the walnuts, currants, and salt. Pour in the chicken broth. Cover and bake for 30 to 40 minutes, or until the rice is tender. Serve warm.

Beans and Lentils

I love the sweet, earthy qualities of beans and lentils, the way they plump in cooking, and the near endless heirloom varieties that are available. Blessedly inexpensive, beans and lentils on their own are beautiful foods, but they also make a masterful pairing with small amounts of meat—extending otherwise expensive grass-fed and pasture-raised meats. I often pair beans and lentils with broth, as the mineral-rich saltiness of broth helps to balance the otherwise earthy flavor of legumes and makes the perfect medium with which to cook hard beans into a delicate tenderness.

Like grains, beans and lentils are seeds; that is, they're the start of new plants. Legumes provide rich nutrition comprised of B vitamins and minerals, but also antinutrients that can prevent you from fully absorbing the nutrients they contain. These antinutrients, notably food phytate, exist to prevent the bean or lentil from sprouting prematurely in conditions that do not support the growth of the plant; however, when the environment meets those conditions (notably warmth and moisture), the humble legume that has held strong to its complement of nutrients begins to release enzymes that deactivate those antinutrients and release the nutrients. The key to preparing beans both for optimal nourishment and optimal digestibility rests in very long periods of soaking in frequently changed very warm water coupled with long cooking times that leave beans utterly tender.

With several heirloom varieties of dry beans, dry peas, and lentils available, each with its own unique flavor and texture, pulses can add great variety to the dinner table. Pulses are also typically rich in a variety of minerals, from phosphorus, which supports bone health, to zinc, which supports fertility and immunity. They are also rich in folate, a nutrient critical to women of reproductive age for its role in the prevention of birth defects.

BEAN	FLAVOR	NUTRITION	PREPARATION METHOD
Anasazi beans	Earthy	Vitamin E, thiamin, riboflavin, vitamin B6, folate, iron, magnesium, phosphorus, zinc, copper manganese	Soak 1 cup beans in warm water to cover by 2 inches with a pinch of baking soda for at least 18 and up to 24 hours. Change water every 8 to 12 hours and keep warm.
Black beans	Sweet, earthy	thiamin, folate, iron, magnesium, phosphorus, potassium, copper, manganese	Soak 1 cup beans in warm water to cover by 2 inches for at least 18 and up to 24 hours. Change water every 8 to 12 hours and keep warm.
Cannellini beans	Nutty, mildly earthy	Folate, magnesium, niacin, potassium, riboflavin, thiamin, vitamin B6, zinc	Soak 1 cup beans in warm water to cover by 2 inches with a pinch of baking soda for at least 18 and up to 24 hours. Change water every 8 to 12 hours and keep warm.

BEAN	FLAVOR	NUTRITION	PREPARATION METHOD
Chickpeas	Grassy, earthy	Thiamin, vitamin B6, folate, calcium, iron, magnesium, phosphorus, potassium, zinc, copper, manganese	Soak 1 cup beans in warm water to cover by 2 inches for at least 18 and up to 24 hours. Change water every 8 to 12 hours and keep warm.
Cranberry beans	Nutty, buttery	Thiamin, riboflavin, niacin, folate, iron, magnesium, phosphorus, potassium, zinc, copper, manganese	Soak 1 cup beans in warm water to cover by 2 inches with a pinch of baking soda for at least 18 and up to 24 hours. Change water every 8 to 12 hours and keep warm.
Fava beans (dried)	Faintly bitter, buttery, nutty	Folate, iron, magnesium, phosphorus, copper, manganese	Soak 1 cup beans in warm water to cover by 2 inches for at least 8 to and up to 12 hours. Change water once, after 4 to 6 hours of soaking, and keep warm.
Great Northern beans	Mildly nutty, slightly grainy texture	Thiamin, vitamin B6, folate, calcium, iron, magnesium, phosphorus, potassium, copper, manganese	Soak 1 cup beans in warm water to cover by 2 inches with a pinch of baking soda for at least 18 and up to 24 hours. Change water every 8 to 12 hours and keep warm.
Lentils	Earthy	Thiamin, riboflavin, niacin, vitamin B6, folate, iron, magnesium, phosphorus, potassium, copper, manganese	Soak 1 cup beans in warm water to cover by 2 inches for at least 8 and up to 12 hours. Change water once, after 4 to 6 hours of soaking, and keep warm.
Marrow beans	Sweet, faint bacon-like flavor	Folate, magnesium, niacin, potassium, riboflavin, thiamin, vitamin B6, zinc	Soak 1 cup beans in warm water to cover by 2 inches with a pinch of baking soda for at least 18 and up to 24 hours. Change water every 8 to 12 hours and keep warm.
Navy beans	Soft, sweet, earthy	Thiamin, riboflavin, folate, B, calcium, iron, magnesium, phosphorus, potassium, zinc, copper, manganese	Soak 1 cup beans in warm water to cover by 2 inches with a pinch of baking soda for at least 18 and up to 24 hours. Change water every 8 to 12 hours and keep warm.
Pinto beans	Earthy	Vitamin E, thiamin, riboflavin, vitamin B6, folate, iron, magnesium, phosphorus, zinc, copper manganese	Soak 1 cup beans in warm water to cover by 2 inches with a pinch of baking soda for at least 18 and up to 24 hours. Change water every 8 to 12 hours and keep warm.
Split peas	Earthy, sweet	Thiamin, niacin, folate, iron, magnesium, phosphorus, potassium, zinc, copper, magnanese	Soak 1 cup beans in warm water to cover by 2 inches for at least 8 and up to 12 hours. Change water once, after 4 to 6 hours of soaking, and keep warm.

lentils *with* sausage *and* mustard greens ❧

Lentils go well with pork, and pork goes well with greens. They all come together in this simple one-dish meal that sees the three further complemented by a tablespoon of toasted mustard seeds. Soaking the lentils in advance, which increases mineral availability, requires a little advance planning. SERVES 4 TO 6

1 cup French green lentils, picked over

2 tablespoons mustard seeds

1 tablespoon lard or extra-virgin olive oil

1 onion, thinly sliced

8 ounces fresh Italian-style pork sausages, casings removed

2 bunches mustard greens (about 16 ounces), trimmed and sliced into ribbons about ¼ inch thick

Balsamic vinegar, to serve

Finely ground unrefined sea salt and freshly ground black pepper

Pour the lentils into a mixing bowl. Pour in warm water to cover by 2 inches. Cover the bowl with a kitchen towel, set it in a warm spot on your kitchen counter, and allow the lentils to soak for at least 8 and up to 12 hours.

Drain the lentils and rinse them well. Pour them into a heavy stockpot and pour in enough fresh water to cover them by 2 inches. Bring the water to a boil over medium-high heat, then decrease the heat to low and simmer the lentils, uncovered, for about 45 minutes, or until the lentils soften and become tender. Drain the lentils and set them in a bowl while you prepare the other ingredients.

Heat a very wide skillet over high heat. When it is very hot, toss in the mustard seeds and toast them for about 2 minutes, or until they release their fragrance and begin to brown a bit. Decrease the heat to medium and add the lard to the pan. Once the lard melts, stir in the onion and fry it until it begins to brown a bit at the edges, about 5 minutes. Stir the sausage into the onion and continue stirring until the meat is cooked through and browned, about 8 minutes. Pour the lentils into the skillet and stir them into the sausage and onion until warmed through.

Turn off the heat, stir in the mustard greens, and cover the skillet. Allow the greens to wilt, undisturbed, in the residual heat of the skillet for about 5 minutes. Uncover and stir once again. Serve with a drizzle of balsamic vinegar and a sprinkling of salt and pepper.

spiced lentil soup *with* roasted tomatoes

Fragrant with spice and the robust sweetness of roasted heirloom tomatoes, this lentil soup warms the belly and soothes the soul during the chilly days of early autumn, when the last of the tomatoes and eggplant can still be plucked from the garden's vines. Soaking the lentils first in slightly acidic water quickens cooking time and improves the availability of trace minerals, including iron, zinc, and magnesium. SERVES 6 TO 8

2 cups French green lentils, picked over and rinsed well

3 pounds heirloom tomatoes, halved and seeded

1 pound eggplant, peeled and cubed

2 tablespoons extra-virgin olive oil, plus more to serve

2 tablespoons clarified butter (page 59)

1 yellow onion, thinly sliced

3 ribs celery, thinly sliced

1 teaspoon powdered mustard

$1/2$ teaspoon ground cumin

$1/2$ teaspoon ground coriander

Pinch of ground cloves

2 bay leaves

8 cups Chicken Bone Broth (page 120)

1 small bunch curly kale (about 8 ounces), stems removed, leaves coarsely chopped

Finely ground unrefined sea salt

Pour the lentils into a mixing bowl. Pour in warm water to cover by 2 inches. Cover the bowl with a kitchen towel, set it in a warm spot on your kitchen counter, and allow the lentils to soak for at least 8 and up to 12 hours.

Drain the lentils and rinse them well.

Preheat the oven to 425°F.

Arrange the tomatoes and eggplant on a rimmed baking sheet, drizzle with the olive oil, and roast for about 30 minutes, or until the tomatoes begin to brown a bit at their edges.

Melt the clarified butter in a heavy stockpot over medium heat. Stir in the onion and celery and fry until softened and fragrant, 3 to 4 minutes. Stir in the powdered mustard, cumin, coriander, and cloves and continue frying for 1 to 2 minutes, until deeply fragrant.

Pour in the chicken broth, drop in the bay leaves, and stir in the soaked lentils. Cover and simmer for 20 minutes. Stir in the roasted tomatoes and eggplant and continue simmering, covered, for 20 to 25 minutes, until the lentils soften and become tender.

Turn off the heat, stir in the chopped kale, and cover. Allow the kale to wilt in the residual heat of the soup for 5 minutes. Drizzle olive oil into the soup to suit your taste, season with salt, and serve.

pea *and* ham hock soup *with* browned butter *and* thyme ⁑

Browned butter, with its nutty aroma, complements the down-home flavor of ham hock, reinforcing its smokiness without disguising it. The ham hock comes from the joint where the haunch of the pig meats the foot. It is relatively inexpensive, but, like other cuts of meat on the bone, it releases a succulent flavor that is concentrated by long and slow cooking. Ham hock marries well with pulses and with split peas in particular, whose earthiness provides a subtle flavor in this simple but ultimately satisfying soup. Serve with a dollop of sour cream and a slice of buttered bread. SERVES 6

2 cups split peas, picked over and rinsed well

1/4 teaspoon baking soda

2 tablespoons unsalted butter

1 yellow onion, finely chopped

3 ribs celery, chopped

2 carrots, peeled and chopped

1 tablespoon fresh thyme leaves

1 ham hock (about 1 1/2 pounds)

2 1/2 quarts Chicken Bone Broth (page 120)

Pour the peas into a large mixing bowl, cover them with hot water by 2 inches, then stir in the baking soda. Cover the bowl loosely with a kitchen towel and let the peas soak at room temperature for at least 12 and up to 18 hours, refreshing the peas with hot water once or twice. Drain the peas using a sieve and rinse them well.

Melt the butter in a heavy stockpot over medium heat. Let the butter froth and foam and keep it on the heat until its color transforms from flaxen yellow to a warm, toasty brown and it releases a perfume reminiscent of freshly cracked nuts, about 3 minutes. Watch it closely lest you burn the butter. Reduce the heat to medium-low and stir in the onion, celery, and carrots. Sauté for 3 to 4 minutes, or until the vegetables soften a bit. Stir in the thyme and continue cooking for 1 to 2 minutes more, or until the vegetables take on the perfume of the thyme.

Stir the soaked split peas into the vegetables, add the ham hock to the pot, and pour in the chicken broth. Cover and simmer for 1 1/4 hours, or until the peas fall apart when pressed with a fork. Turn off the heat, remove the ham hock from the pot, and take the meat off the bone with a fork, chopping any large hunks of meat into bite-size pieces. Return the meat to the pot and puree the soup with an immersion blender until perfectly smooth. Serve hot.

cranberry bean *and* einkorn soup *with* basil

The cranberry bean is a small, meaty little bean that plumps into a pleasant roundness once cooked. It makes a natural pairing for einkorn, an ancient variety of wheat that has a complex, nutty flavor. These two heavy and satiating foods find balance with robust tomatoes, vibrant green herbs, and a punch of pancetta's pleasant saltiness in this easy, thick soup. It's perfect for late summer, when herbs and tomatoes are often at their best. I make it in winter, too, when my family longs for both warmth and the brightness of summer foods. In those dark days, I rely on the jars of yellow, orange, and red heirloom tomatoes I had the foresight to put up in the summer. **SERVES 6**

- 1 cup cranberry beans
- 1 cup einkorn wheat berries
- 1 tablespoon extra-virgin olive oil
- 4 ounces pancetta, finely chopped
- 2 sprigs thyme
- 1 sprig rosemary
- 2 cloves garlic, thinly sliced
- 1 small yellow onion, finely chopped
- 2 cups crushed tomatoes
- 6 cups Chicken Bone Broth (page 120) or Chicken Foot Broth (page 121)
- 1/2 cup chopped fresh basil
- 1/2 cup chopped fresh flat-leaf parsley

Toss the cranberry beans and einkorn wheat berries into a mixing bowl and cover with hot water by 2 inches. Cover the bowl and let the beans and grain soak at room temperature for at least 12 and up to 18 hours, draining the water and replenishing it with more hot water at least once.

Drain the mixture and rinse it well.

Warm the olive oil in a heavy stockpot over medium heat. Toss in the pancetta and cook until crisp, about 6 minutes. Stir in the thyme and rosemary and fry them for 1 to 2 minutes, until they release their fragrance and the rosemary needles crisp, then pluck them out with a pair of tongs and discard them. Add the garlic and onion to the pot and cook until softened and deeply fragrant, about 3 minutes.

Add the beans and grain to the pot, then stir in the crushed tomatoes and broth. Decrease the heat to medium-low, cover, and simmer for 1 1/4 to 1 1/2 hours, until the beans are tender.

Remove from the heat, stir in the basil and parsley, and serve.

sweet molasses baked beans *with* bacon *and* toasted mustard seeds

In my version of New England baked beans, I deviate from tradition, favoring tiny, plump marrow beans instead of Great Northern beans or navy beans. I like their buttery, bacon-like flavor, which pairs nicely with mustard and molasses. Long, slow cooking is the key to this dish. Once they're boiled until tender, the beans benefit from baking slowly so that they enjoy several hours to fully absorb the flavors of the mustard, onion, molasses, and tomato. Substantial enough as a main course, these beans can be served with a loaf of bread and some fresh vegetables for a simple dinner. I typically use a classic bean pot, but a covered casserole dish or clay baker should also work well.

SERVES 6

1 pound marrow beans

1/4 teaspoon baking soda

1/4 cup mustard seeds

4 ounces bacon, chopped

1 large yellow onion, finely chopped

2 tablespoons blackstrap molasses

1/2 cup unrefined cane sugar

2 tablespoons tomato paste

2 teaspoons apple cider vinegar

3 cups Chicken Bone Broth (page 120)

Pour the beans into a large mixing bowl, cover with hot water by 2 inches, and stir in the baking soda. Cover the bowl and allow it to sit on the kitchen counter for at least 18 and up to 24 hours, changing the water two to three times.

Drain the beans and rinse them well.

Pour the soaked beans into a large stockpot, cover them with water by 2 inches, cover the pot, and boil over medium-high heat until tender, 1 to 1 1/2 hours. Drain the beans and pour them into a 5-quart Dutch oven or covered casserole dish.

Preheat the oven to 325°F.

Set a large skillet over medium-high heat. When it is hot, add the mustard seeds and toast for 2 to 3 minutes, until they begin to pop, tossing frequently to prevent scorching. Lower the heat to medium, drop the bacon into the pan the bacon, and fry until releases its fat and crisps, about 6 minutes. Transfer the bacon to a plate with a slotted spoon, then add the onion to the pan. Fry the onion in the bacon fat until it softens, about 3 minutes. Turn off the heat and stir in the molasses, sugar, tomato paste, vinegar, and the crisp bacon. Fold this mixture and the chicken broth into the beans, cover, and bake for 6 hours, until the beans are completely tender and the liquid reduces to a sweet syrup.

white bean *and* butternut squash mash *with* garlic *and* sage

Creamy white beans marry nicely with winter squash and garlic, allowing the herbaceous notes of fresh sage to come forth. Starchy and satisfying like any good comfort food, this mash pairs well with roasted poultry and a simple pan sauce or gravy. SERVES 4 TO 6

1 cup navy beans

Pinch of baking soda

1 butternut squash (about 2 pounds)

4 large cloves garlic, in their skins

Extra-virgin olive oil, for brushing

2 tablespoons unsalted butter

2 teaspoons chopped fresh sage

1/2 cup Chicken Bone Broth (page 120)

1/2 cup heavy cream, preferably raw

Put the beans in a mixing bowl and pour in enough hot water to cover them by 2 inches. Stir in the baking soda, cover the bowl, and allow the beans to soak at room temperature for at least 18 and up to 24 hours.

Drain the beans and put them in a large stockpot. Pour in enough water to cover the beans by 2 inches and bring to a boil over medium-high heat. Cover and simmer for about 1 1/2 hours, or until the beans become tender. Drain the beans.

Preheat the oven to 425°F. Line a baking sheet with parchment paper.

Split the squash in half lengthwise and scrape out its seeds. Stuff the cavity of each squash half with 2 cloves of garlic, then carefully invert them onto the baking sheet. Brush a bit of oil over the squash's skin to help loosen the skin from the flesh as the squash roasts. Roast the squash in the oven for 45 minutes, or until the flesh yields easily when pressed with a fork. Remove the squash from the oven and allow it to cool until it becomes comfortable to handle.

Take each clove of garlic from the squash's cavity and press it gently between your thumb and forefinger to remove the garlic from its papery skin. Discard the skin. Add the garlic to a food processor. Scoop the flesh of the squash from the skins and drop it into the food processor.

Melt the butter in a skillet over medium heat, stir in the sage, and sauté for 2 to 3 minutes, until fragrant. Stir in the cooked beans and chicken broth and simmer until the broth reduces by half, 5 to 10 minutes.

Pour the beans and cream into the food processor with the squash and puree until smooth. Serve warm.

slow-baked cannellini beans *with* preserved lemon, rosemary, *and* smoked paprika

I grow rosemary in a little ceramic pot on my deck, and, as the days of summers stretch on into weeks, the rosemary grows with unruly passion before opening up into little blue-purple flowers. As it grows, I use the rosemary generously—tossing it into marinades, sprinkling it over vegetables, or infusing it into oils and vinegars. I like it here most of all, combined with cannellini beans, lemon, and smoked paprika for a deceptively humble dish of baked beans that tastes at once rich and smoky, as well as vibrant and herbaceous. SERVES ABOUT 6

2 cups cannellini beans

1/4 teaspoon baking soda

2 tablespoons extra-virgin olive oil

2 tablespoons lard

1 small yellow onion, sliced into paper-thin rounds

6 cloves garlic, thinly sliced

1 preserved lemon (page 279), seeded and chopped

3 cups Chicken Bone Broth (page 120)

1 teaspoon finely ground unrefined sea salt

1 tablespoon smoked paprika, plus more for sprinkling

2 sprigs rosemary

2 bay leaves

Toss the beans into a large mixing bowl, pour in enough water to cover them by 2 inches, and stir in the baking soda. Cover the bowl with a kitchen towel and let the beans soak at room temperature for at least 18 and up to 24 hours.

Drain the beans and rinse them well.

Put the soaked beans in a large stockpot and pour in enough water to cover the beans by 2 inches. Cover the pot, bring to a boil over medium-high heat, and cook until tender, 1 to 1 1/2 hours. Drain the beans and pour them into a 5-quart Dutch oven or covered casserole dish.

Preheat the oven to 325°F.

Warm the olive oil and lard in a skillet over medium heat. When the lard melts, stir in the onion and garlic and fry for 5 to 6 minutes, until deeply fragrant and beginning to brown. Pour this mixture into the beans, then stir in the chopped preserved lemon. Stir in the broth, salt, and paprika, then tuck the rosemary and bay leaves into the beans. Cover and bake for 6 hours.

Pluck out the rosemary and bay leaves with a fork and serve hot, sprinkled with smoked paprika.

marrow beans *with* swiss chard *and* lemon ❧

I treasure the salty and faintly metallic flavor of Swiss chard, and both the plant's leaves and stems can bring a different flavor and a different texture to cooking. I like to use them separately, sautéing the tough stems in olive oil, as you might do with celery or onion. The stems soften a bit, losing their tough texture. The leaves, by contrast, grow dull with extended cooking, so I prefer to add them at the very end so they wilt in the heat of the warm beans and chicken broth but maintain their bright color. A bit of lemon helps to brighten the otherwise earthy flavors of beans and greens. SERVES 4 TO 6

1 1/2 cups marrow beans

1/4 teaspoon baking soda

1 large bunch Swiss chard (about 12 ounces)

1 tablespoon extra-virgin olive oil

2 cloves garlic, minced

1/4 teaspoon crushed red pepper flakes

Finely grated zest and juice of 1 lemon

1 1/2 cups Chicken Bone Broth (page 120)

Finely ground unrefined s ea salt

Pour the beans into a large mixing bowl, cover with hot water by 2 inches, and stir in the baking soda. Cover the bowl with a kitchen towel and allow it to sit on the kitchen counter for at least 18 and up to 24 hours.

Drain the beans and rinse them well.

Put the soaked beans in a large stockpot and pour in enough water to cover the beans by 2 inches. Bring them to a boil over medium-high heat, cover, and simmer until tender, about 1 1/2 hours. Drain the beans and set aside.

Using a sharp paring knife, separate the chard stems from the greens. Finely chop the stems and set them in a small bowl. Stack the leaves on top of one another, roll them into a cigar, and slice crosswise into strips 1/4 to 1/2 inch wide.

Warm the olive oil in a large skillet over medium heat. Toss in the garlic and chopped chard stems and sauté until the garlic softens and the color of the chard stems turns ever so slightly more vibrant, about 2 minutes. Stir in the red pepper flakes and lemon zest and cook for a minute or two, then add the beans to the skillet. Sauté the beans for 3 to 5 minutes, until they acquire the flavor of the garlic and lemon.

Grab chard leaves by the handful and drop them into the hot pan. Stir once or twice to mix them with the beans, then add the broth. Cover and simmer until the chard leaves wilt, about 3 minutes. Remove from the heat, stir in the lemon juice, and season with salt. Serve hot.

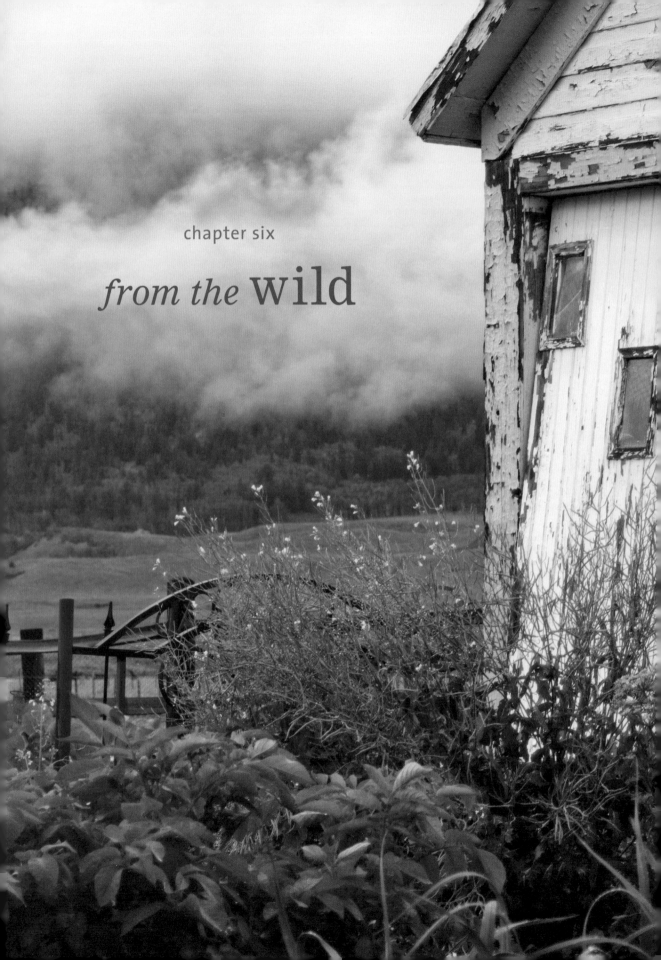

chapter six

from the wild

I ENJOY A LOVE OF WILD FOODS, and when the season beckons, I take my basket into the hills that surround our home, on the hunt for the hidden treasures found in the soft wooded mountainsides and valleys. The foods that the wilderness offers vary. Spring brings nettles. Summer brings tiny wild strawberries that grow on the sun-drenched slopes and red raspberries that hang heavy on their dense canes in good years. Later, as the rains of late summer guide us into autumn, edible mushrooms appear, hidden in the dense underbrush of the forest floor. We find oyster mushrooms, chanterelles, and porcini in our mountains. Or I pick edible weeds in my garden: salty lambs-quarters, lemony purslane, and bitter dandelion greens. All of these enjoy a place at our table, paired with the vegetables from the kitchen garden.

We head to the waters, too, and fish for trout in the mountain streams and lakes. And on good years, friends who hunt share elk, venison, rabbit, or wild goose. We eat together in the waning light of evening—I share my cooking, they share the meat they've hunted, and we fill our bellies with wild things.

dandelion greens salad *with* roasted nectarines *and* warm red onion vinaigrette ❦

Dandelions arrive in my yard during the summer months, a little later than they appear in areas with milder climates. Their fringed yellow heads speak of warmth and sunshine and remind me that soon other wildflowers will appear, and the bees will surely follow. Though dandelions attract pollinators like bees, we dig them up to make more room for native wildflowers. I reserve the tender greens for salads while saving the soft yellow blossoms for sweet fritters.

When foraging for wild dandelion greens, take care to source them from areas you know to be free from pesticides, such as your own yard, and avoid dandelions growing near waterways, in public parks, or near the roadside, as they may contain chemical residue. SERVES 4 TO 6

4 medium nectarines, pitted and quartered

1 teaspoon extra-virgin olive oil

8 ounces bacon, chopped

1 small red onion, minced

1 teaspoon brown mustard seeds

¹/₄ cup red wine vinegar

6 cups loosely packed dandelion greens, rinsed well and trimmed of tough stems

Preheat the oven to 400°F.

Arrange the nectarines in an 8-inch square baking dish and roast them for 15 to 20 minutes, turning once, until they release their juice and begin to caramelize around the edges. Remove them from the oven and let them cool while you prepare the rest of the salad.

Line a plate with a paper towel or clean kitchen towel.

Warm the olive oil in a skillet over medium heat, drop in the bacon, and fry until it crisps and renders its fat, 6 to 8 minutes. Remove the bacon from the pan with a slotted spoon and let it drain on the lined plate.

Stir the onion into the bacon fat and fry it over medium heat for 3 minutes, or until soft and translucent. Stir in the mustard seeds and sauté for 1 minute. Remove the skillet from the heat and whisk in the vinegar to make the vinaigrette.

Arrange the dandelion greens on a serving plate and place the nectarines on top. Top with the crisped bacon and dress with the warm vinaigrette. Serve immediately.

tomato, cucumber, *and* purslane salad

A small creeping plant with oblong waxy leaves, purslane grows unwanted in garden beds, out of cracks in sidewalks, and along gravel paths. While others might discard purslane as a nuisance or as a weed, I cherish it. Our vegetable grower bundles the purslane she collects from her farm into hefty bunches, tying them with twine and setting them into our CSA box in the early summer, though I collect as much as I can on my own.

The last of the purslane finds its way into our box at about the same time as the first tomatoes. Their flavors marry well; the sweet tomatoes benefit from the refreshing, lemony flavor of purslane. SERVES 4

1 1/2 pounds tomatoes, preferably large heirloom tomatoes, such as Zapoteca, Brandywine, or German Zebra

1 large cucumber

1 bunch purslane (about 6 ounces)

1 lemon

2 tablespoons chopped fresh oregano

2 tablespoons extra-virgin olive oil

Finely ground unrefined sea salt

Slice the tomatoes in half crosswise and spoon out and discard their seeds. Chop the tomatoes into 1/2-inch bites and drop them into a large salad bowl. Slice the cucumber in half lengthwise and spoon out and discard its seeds. If the peel of your cucumber tastes particularly bitter, you may want to peel it. Chop the cucumber into 1/2-inch pieces and add it to the salad bowl with the tomatoes.

Rinse the purslane well under running water and pat it dry. Remove any tough bits of stem and chop the purslane coarsely. Add it to the salad bowl. Cut the lemon in half and squeeze its juice through a strainer over the vegetables. Sprinkle the salad with the oregano and olive oil. Toss all the ingredients together gently (lest you bruise the tomatoes), sprinkle with salt, and serve.

stinging nettle soup *with* cream ❧

Nettle is a wild and almost vicious leafy green plant that grows throughout Europe, Asia, North Africa, and North America. Seemingly innocuous, its thin serrated leaves can elicit a powerful reaction on the skin, hence its name. If you make the mistake of touching it with your bare arm or hand, your skin will erupt in tiny red bumps that sting and burn temporarily. Yet if you're mindful and use gloves as you pick the leaves from the stem, you'll save your skin, and you can use the vibrant green leaves in this vividly green soup with a soft spinach flavor. Fortunately, cooking deactivates the reactive compounds in nettle, enabling you to reap their potent array of vitamins and minerals without fear of a sting. SERVES 4 TO 6

2 tablespoons unsalted butter

1 small yellow onion, finely chopped

1 pound russet potatoes, peeled and coarsely chopped

8 cups Chicken Foot Broth (page 120)

1 large bunch (about 8 ounces) stinging nettles

1 cup heavy cream, preferably raw

Finely ground unrefined sea salt

Melt the butter in a heavy stockpot over medium heat. When it froths, stir in the onion and fry it until the onion softens and releases its fragrance, about 4 minutes. Add the potatoes and broth. Cover and simmer until the potatoes soften and fall apart when pierced with a fork, about 30 minutes.

While the potatoes cook in the broth, don a pair of kitchen gloves and pluck the nettle leaves from their stems. Discard the stems and place the leaves in a bowl.

Once the potatoes soften, add the nettle leaves to the pot, cover once more, and cook for 8 to 10 minutes, or until the leaves wilt completely in the heat of the soup and their color darkens. Turn off the heat and puree the soup with an immersion blender until completely smooth and uniform. Stir in the heavy cream and season with salt. Serve hot.

trumpet mushrooms *with* lemon, garlic, *and* thyme ✿

As summer inches its way toward autumn and the weather begins to cool, I pack a picnic lunch for my family and we head into the forests surrounding our little mountain town to forage for mushrooms. After particularly snowy winters or wet summers, wild mushrooms appear in abundance; in dry years, they can be more difficult, though not impossible, to find. It's a fun hunt, foraging in the wilds on foot in hopes of finding a cache that other hunters neglected. I take the mushrooms home and make mushroom stew and mushroom butter. I serve the mushrooms with chicken, rabbit, and beef, or on their own as a side dish.

I often make this simple side dish of mushrooms. When we forage, I make it with an array of mushrooms: chanterelles, oysters, and king boletes. It's equally good with trumpet mushrooms, which are easily cultivated and therefore more readily available. If you can't find lemon thyme, consider substituting regular thyme. Unlike porcini, portobello, and other heartier varieties of mushrooms, trumpet mushrooms offer an element of delicacy to the plate. I like to pair them with fish or with Cider-Brined Slow-Roasted Chicken (page 88). SERVES 4

---

4 tablespoons clarified butter (page 59)

8 large king trumpet mushrooms, sliced no thicker than 1/8 inch

2 cloves garlic, minced

Finely grated zest and juice of 1 lemon

1 teaspoon fresh thyme leaves

Finely ground unrefined sea salt

Melt 2 tablespoons of the clarified butter in a large skillet over medium heat. Add the mushrooms and cook for about 1 minute, then turn them over and cook the second sides for another 30 seconds, or until softened slightly and a bit brown at the edges. Transfer the mushrooms to a serving bowl.

Add the remaining 2 tablespoons of butter to the pan, stir in the garlic, and sauté for about 2 minutes, or until softened and fragrant. Stir in the lemon zest and juice and whisk until the mixture forms a uniform sauce. Stir in the thyme leaves, pour the sauce over the mushrooms, sprinkle with salt, and serve warm.

wild mushroom soup

As the afternoon rains of late summer fall in step with the emerging cool-ness of autumn, mushrooms erupt in the forested hills and high alpine valleys that surround our little town. I take my little boy by one hand and a basket in the other, and we walk to where the edge of town meets the little hills that will soon turn into mountains. During good years, when heavy winter snowfalls meet a wet summer, we find plenty of mushrooms, each with their own unique appearance, flavor, and texture. Hawk's wing— a broad, toothed mushroom—tastes of pine, while the creamy-colored oyster mushroom tastes, as you might imagine, faintly of the sea. There's the mild-flavored shaggy mane that grows not only on the forest floor but also in suburban lawns. My favorite are the creamy-colored, cinnamon-capped king boletes, or porcini mushrooms, and the golden chanterelles. Porcini mushrooms taste rich, earthy, and meaty, like a good mushroom should, while chanterelle mushrooms have a more delicate floral and citrusy flavor.

Any mushroom variety works well in this soup, but the key is to use multiple varieties, whether you bought them or gathered them yourself. Each mushroom offers a distinctive flavor and aroma, and, when layered together, the soup develops a rounder and more complex flavor that's enhanced by sherry and thyme. SERVES 6

1 tablespoon unsalted butter

1 shallot, sliced paper thin

1 tablespoon chopped fresh thyme leaves

1 pound mixed mushrooms (such as porcini, shiitake, chanterelle, cremini, and portobello), thinly sliced

2 teaspoons finely ground unrefined sea salt

$^1/_2$ teaspoon finely ground white pepper

2 cups Chicken Bone Broth (page 120)

2 tablespoons sherry

2 cups heavy cream, preferably raw

Melt the butter in a heavy stockpot over medium-high heat. When it froths, turn down the heat to medium-low, stir in the shallot and thyme, and sauté until fragrant, about 3 minutes. Toss the mushrooms into the pot and sprinkle with the salt and white pepper. Cover the pot and sweat the mushrooms until tender, about 10 minutes. Stir in the broth and simmer, uncovered, for 20 minutes. Turn off the heat and puree the soup with an immersion blender until smooth. Stir in the sherry and heavy cream and serve.

pan-fried trout *with* chanterelles *in* cream

In the late summer, the streams and lakes of nearby mountains teem with trout. My husband packs the tackle, I fill a picnic basket with good things to eat, and we both take our little boy out beyond the edge of our little town into the wilds. My husband fishes, my little boy aims to, and I busy myself gathering a few edible plants that lurk nearby. On one particularly lucky trip he landed several trout, and I found a little cache of golden chanterelles. They fit together, the two wild foods. SERVES 4

TROUT

1 tablespoon clarified butter (page 59)

4 (6-ounce) fillets steelhead or rainbow trout

1/2 teaspoon finely ground unrefined sea salt

1 teaspoon freshly ground black pepper

CHANTERELLES

1 tablespoon unsalted butter

1 small shallot, finely minced

4 ounces chanterelle mushrooms, thinly sliced

1/4 cup heavy cream

1 tablespoon chopped fresh flat-leaf parsley

To prepare the trout, melt the clarified butter in a skillet over medium heat. Meanwhile, season the trout fillets with the salt and pepper. Place the trout skin side down in the butter, cover, and cook for about 8 minutes, or until the fish flakes easily when pierced by a fork. Turn off the heat and cover the skillet to keep the fish warm.

To prepare the mushrooms, melt the butter in a separate skillet over medium heat. Stir in the shallot and fry until fragrant and translucent, about 3 minutes. Stir in chanterelles and fry for 3 to 5 minutes, until softened slightly. Pour in the heavy cream and cook, stirring constantly, until the cream is thick and glossy, about 3 minutes. Stir in the parsley and serve over the trout.

dulse *and* potato soup ❧

Traditionally used in both Irish cooking and the cooking of New England, dulse is a mineral-rich sea vegetable with a briny flavor reminiscent of the ocean. You can typically find it in the summer months on long stretches of beach, where it lays stranded by the outgoing tide. Gatherers typically harvest the dulse, then let it dry in the summer sun to preserve it for months to come like any other sea vegetable or herb. You can also purchase dried dulse in most health food stores. Whether you use fresh or dried dulse, take care to look it over carefully, as bits of sand or the little shells of sea creatures may adhere to the dulse's dark, oblong leaves.

I like to serve dulse simply and without fanfare. It's a humble food that doesn't benefit from elaborate preparations. Potatoes and chicken broth allow dulse's delicate, mineral-rich notes to come to the forefront of your palate, where they whisper of the sea. SERVES 6 TO 8

1 ounce dried dulse

1 tablespoon unsalted butter

1 leek, white and light-green parts only, thinly sliced

1 large russet potato, peeled and cubed

1 tablespoon finely ground unrefined sea salt

8 cups Chicken Bone Broth (page 120)

Pick over the dulse, removing any stray bits of sand, shells, or other debris. Place it in a large mixing bowl, cover it with water, and allow it to rehydrate for 10 to 15 minutes. Drain and rinse it well.

Melt the butter in a heavy stockpot over medium heat. When it froths, stir in the leek and sauté until barely softened, about 2 minutes. Stir in the chopped potato, sprinkle in the salt, cover the pot, and allow to cook, undisturbed, for 6 to 8 minutes.

Uncover the pot and stir in the chicken broth. Cover and simmer until the potatoes are tender, about 25 minutes. Puree with an immersion blender until the soup is smooth, then stir in the rehydrated dulse. Continue to simmer, covered, until heated through, about 5 more minutes. Serve hot.

red fruit custard cake 🎗

During wet summers, the folds of the Rocky Mountains hold within them a secret for foragers—wild red fruits. Tiny alpine strawberries line the hills in messy lengths that span across the mountainsides, nourished by mineral-rich soil and afternoon rains and sweetened by the warmth of the summer sun. Ripe red raspberries, fringed by dark green leaves, hang heavy from thorny canes all along the alleys and half-forgotten gardens of the mountain town where I make my home. I take what I can manage, always leaving plenty for the next person who happens by. We eat our fill fresh while they last, but I also enjoy tossing them with red currants from a local farm and into the egg-rich batter of a custard cake that I bake for breakfast, serving it with whipped cream or homemade yogurt. SERVES 6 TO 8

¼ cup fresh red currants

1 cup raspberries

¾ cup fresh strawberries, hulled

½ cup plus 2 tablespoons high-extraction wheat or einkorn flour (see page 157) or unbleached all-purpose flour

6 eggs

1 cup heavy cream

¼ cup unrefined cane sugar

½ teaspoon finely ground unrefined sea salt

Whipped cream or yogurt, to serve

Preheat the oven to 350°F. Butter and flour a 9-inch round cake pan.

Toss the currants, raspberries, and strawberries together in a large mixing bowl with the 2 tablespoons of flour. Spoon them into the prepared cake pan.

Whisk together the eggs and cream in the now-empty mixing bowl until glossy and uniform in color, then beat in the sugar until combined.

In a separate bowl, whisk the remaining ½ cup of flour with the salt. Slowly pour the wet ingredients into the dry ingredients, then stir with a wooden spoon until a smooth, uniform batter forms. Pour the batter over the fruit.

Bake for 45 minutes, or until the outer edges of the cake are set but its interior wobbles slightly when you jostle the pan. Allow the cake to cool until just barely warm, then slice into wedges and serve with whipped cream or yogurt.

Preparing Wild Animals

Wild animals taste of the forests or range where they forage. Their meat tastes strong and lean. Though I haven't yet developed any hunting skills, I enjoy preparing game whenever I can. Many of my friends hunt, and, if we're fortunate, they bring their catch to our little kitchen to share. I try to do their efforts great honor, for I understand the rigorous labor they endure when hunting in the forests surrounding our rural town. Sometimes that labor goes unrewarded, and hunters must wait another year before trying again. If they're fortunate enough to see success, processing an elk or deer in the field can be exhausting, and sometimes dangerous, and they must then begin the journey home, packing out hundreds of pounds of meat and bone on their backs.

Preparing wild meat and fowl requires a set of skills similar to those needed to prepare grass-fed or pasture-raised meats; that is, it benefits from long and slow braising to develop succulence it might otherwise lack, or from a quick sear so that it retains its natural juices.

bacon-wrapped pheasant
with garden herbs

Pheasant is a beautiful little bird, smaller than a chicken, with magnificent, flavorful meat. One of my favorite ways to prepare pheasant seems impossibly simple: just wrap it in bacon, sprinkle it with garden herbs, and roast it. You can follow this same method with any other bird with beautiful results.
SERVES 4 TO 6

1 pheasant (about 3 pounds)

1 yellow onion, quartered

2 tablespoons chopped fresh flat-leaf parsley

2 tablespoons chopped fresh basil

1 teaspoon fresh thyme leaves

8 ounces bacon (about 8 slices)

¼ cup white wine

Preheat the oven to 450°F.

Stuff the cavity of the pheasant with the quartered onion. Tuck the wing tips behind the bird and tie the legs together with 100 percent cotton cooking twine. Sprinkle the bird with the chopped herbs and lay the bacon slices over the top, covering its breast, thighs, and legs. Place the bacon-covered pheasant in a baking dish, pour in the white wine, and roast for 20 minutes, basting the bird after 10 minutes with the juices in the dish.

Reduce the oven temperature to 325°F and continue roasting the pheasant for another 30 to 40 minutes, or until the juices run clear when the tip of a knife is inserted between the breast and thigh.

Remove the dish from the oven, tent the bird with foil or parchment paper, and allow to rest for 10 minutes. Carve and serve with the pan juices.

little sourdough dumplings
with venison ⁂

Inspired by traditional Russian *pelmeni*, I make these little sourdough dumplings in wintertime, when their warm, filling nature seems most needed to combat the cold. After filling the dumplings with spiced meat, I simmer them in a rich bone broth and top them with sour cream and a bit of chopped dill.

SERVES 4 TO 6

DUMPLING

1½ cups soft winter wheat flour, plus more for working the dough

4 egg yolks, beaten

1 teaspoon finely ground unrefined sea salt

½ cup Sourdough Starter (page 160)

FILLING

12 ounces ground venison

1 shallot, minced

½ teaspoon finely ground unrefined salt

½ teaspoon freshly ground black pepper

¼ teaspoon ground allspice

TO SERVE

8 cups Beef Bone Broth (page 117)

Sour cream, to serve

Chopped dill, to serve

To make the dumpling dough, heap the flour into the bowl of a stand mixer so it forms a little mountain, form a well at its center, and pour the egg yolks and salt into the well. Pour in the sourdough starter and mix with the dough hook until a smooth dough forms, about 5 minutes. Cover the bowl with plastic wrap and leave it in a warm spot in your kitchen for 12 to 16 hours.

To prepare the filling, in a bowl, combine the venison, shallot, salt, pepper, and allspice. Knead the mixture by hand to evenly distribute the shallot and spices.

Dust your work surface with flour. Punch down the dough, form it into a ball, and turn it out onto the surface. Using your hands, roll the dough back and forth so that it forms a long snake-like cylinder. Pinch off about 2 teaspoons of dough, roll it into a ball by hand, then flatten it with a rolling pin to a circle about ¹⁄₁₆ inch thick. Spoon about 1 teaspoon of filling onto one half of the circle, then fold the other half of the dough over the filling to form a half moon. Seal by crimping the edges together and place the dumpling on a large plate dusted with flour. Continue forming dumplings until the ingredients are exhausted.

Bring the beef broth to a boil in a stockpot over medium-high heat. Working in batches of four (and no more), slip the dumplings into the bubbling broth and simmer until they rise to the surface on their own, about 4 minutes. Using a slotted spoon, transfer them to a bowl. Divide the dumplings among large individual serving bowls and ladle some of the broth over them. Top with dollops of sour cream, sprinkle with dill, and serve.

rabbit pie *with* bacon *and* chanterelles

Quite mild, rabbit makes a luscious stew, especially when paired with other mild ingredients like leeks and peas. Like most game, rabbit is quite lean and tends toward toughness if not treated with a gentle hand. While I love to braise or stew rabbit on the bone, which infuses it with a lovely richness the mild meat might otherwise lack, my favorite rabbit dish is this rabbit pie. A creamy sauce envelops rabbit, chanterelles, peas, and herbs. I prepare it in late summer with freshly picked chanterelles my little boy and I gather in the neighboring forests. Unlike other mushrooms that can taste of the soil and of the earth, little golden chanterelles sing of sweetness and have a prominent floral citrus note that marries nicely with the other flavors in this simple, old-fashioned pie. If you don't feel comfortable foraging for your own wild mushrooms, you can often find fresh chanterelles at local farmers markets or online, or simply substitute the common button mushroom. SERVES 6

2 tablespoons plus 1 teaspoon unsalted butter

4 ounces bacon, finely chopped

1 pound rabbit loin, chopped into ¹/₂-inch cubes

2 leeks, white and light green parts only, thinly sliced

3 carrots, peeled and chopped into ¹/₄-inch dice

3 small celeriac, peeled and chopped into ¹/₄-inch dice

2 teaspoons finely ground unrefined sea salt

2 tablespoons unbleached all-purpose flour or high-extraction wheat flour (see page 157)

1 cup Chicken Bone Broth (page 120) or Chicken Foot Broth (page 121)

¹/₂ cup heavy cream

8 ounces chanterelle mushrooms, chopped

Preheat the oven to 375°F.

Melt the 1 teaspoon of butter in a 10-inch skillet over medium heat. When it froths, stir in the bacon and fry until crisp, about 6 minutes. Using a slotted spoon, transfer the bacon to a large mixing bowl.

Add the rabbit to the hot fat in the skillet and cook over medium heat, stirring occasionally, until opaque and cooked through, about 8 minutes. Transfer the rabbit to the bowl with the bacon. Toss the leeks, carrots, and celeriac into the skillet. Sprinkle the vegetables with the salt, then cover the skillet and let the vegetables cook undisturbed for 15 minutes, or until softened. Transfer the vegetables to the waiting bowl of bacon and rabbit.

Melt the remaining 2 tablespoons of butter in the skillet over medium-high heat. When it froths, whisk in the flour to form a thickening paste. Continue whisking while slowly pouring in the chicken broth and heavy cream. Bring the mixture to a simmer, whisking, to form a gravy thick enough to coat the back of a spoon. Turn off the heat.

1 pound English peas, shelled,
or 1 cup frozen peas, thawed

1 tablespoon chopped fresh
thyme leaves

$^1/_2$ recipe (1 disk) Simple
Sourdough Pie Crust
(page 178)

Pour the gravy into the bowl with bacon, rabbit, and vegetables. Stir in the chanterelles, peas, and thyme, then pour the filling back into the skillet if the skillet is ovenproof or into a shallow 10-inch round casserole if it isn't.

Roll out the pie dough to an 11-inch round following the directions on page 178. Lay the dough round over the filling, crimp the edges, and cut three or four slits to allow steam to escape. Bake the pie for 1 hour, until golden brown.

Pull it from the oven, let cool about 5 minutes, then spoon the pie into bowls and serve.

coriander-crusted elk backstrap
with spiced plum sauce ᪥

The backstrap is a long, tender cut of meat removed from the outside of the backbone. Like the tenderloin, which sits on the inside of the animal's ribcage, the backstrap lacks fat and can be too easily overcooked. Prepared with a quick sear, elk backstrap retains its succulence and its flavor.

Elk, like most game, tends toward richness. Coriander and other sweet spices help to round out the flavor of elk, while the sweet acidity of a spiced plum sauce provides balance to elk's natural fullness. If you can, take the time to grind the spices just before preparing the elk, because ground spices lose their flavor with prolonged storage. SERVES 6

PLUM SAUCE

2 pounds plums, pitted and chopped

2 tablespoons apple cider vinegar

2 tablespoons honey

1/2 teaspoon ground coriander

1/4 teaspoon ground allspice

1 cinnamon stick

ELK

2 tablespoons ground coriander

1 tablespoon freshly ground black pepper

1 tablespoon finely ground unrefined sea salt

1 tablespoon ground allspice

1 elk backstrap (about 3 pounds)

To make the plum sauce, put the plums in a saucepan. Stir in the cider vinegar, honey, coriander, and allspice. Drop in the cinnamon stick. Bring to a simmer over medium heat, cover, and cook until the plums begin to fall apart when pressed with a fork, about 20 minutes. Turn off the heat, remove the cinnamon stick, and puree the plums with an immersion blender until smooth. Set the sauce aside.

To prepare the elk, combine the coriander, pepper, salt, and allspice in a small bowl. Whisk together until uniformly mixed.

Trim the backstrap of any silver skin or sinew, then rub the seasoning into the meat. Let it rest at room temperature while you warm a large cast-iron skillet over high heat. When the skillet is very hot, sear the backstrap for 4 to 5 minutes on each side, until deeply browned and the spices are fragrant. Leave the meat in the skillet and remove the skillet from the heat. Tent with parchment paper or foil and allow the meat to rest for 10 minutes.

Slice the meat into 1/2-inch-thick medallions and serve with the plum sauce.

chapter seven

from the orchard

IN APRIL AND MAY, fruit trees on Colorado's western slope erupt in snowy white and vivid magenta blossoms, coaxed from their wintertime slumber by the promise of spring's warmth. The aroma of the blossoms perfumes the orchard breeze, enveloping the regimented lines of fruit trees with the faint powdery notes of stone fruit, apples, and pears in full bloom. Bees quickly arrive, lured by the sweet and heady nectar of blossoming fruit. As the blossoms reach their peak, first the cherries and apricots, then the apples and pears, the bees fly from row to row, following the flowers as they emerge, bloom, peak, and fade away. Our high alpine town still rests beneath a blanket of snow while the rest of the state wakens with the emergence of spring, and my husband and I pack the car and leave the valley to visit the orchards that flank our mountains. We take our son by the hand and walk down the rows of trees, where we watch, breathe, and listen. The trees vibrate with the thrum of bees intoxicated by the first flowers of the season.

As spring warms to summer, the flowers fade away. Little fruits replace the blossoms, growing fat in the warm sun and cloudless blue skies of the Colorado Rockies. The orchards yield not only fruit, but honey and nuts, too. We gather the early fruits in June or find them tucked away in the boxes of fresh foods we purchase from farms of neighboring communities. Later, in September and October, once the cold sets in and leads the stone fruit trees to their yearly rest, we pick up bags of fresh nuts—walnuts, almonds, and pecans—pairing them with apples, pears, and quince. At home, I rarely emphasize sweets, preferring instead to serve simple desserts of seasonal fruit and freshly cracked nuts with their smooth and buttery undertones. Yet the produce of the orchard provides an opportunity for the celebration of the feast, and I reserve my more elaborate pies, cakes, and candies for friends and community gatherings marked by collective joy and laughter. In this way, the intense sweetness of dessert retains its appeal without becoming mundane from overindulgence. Until the twentieth century, concentrated sweeteners were both expensive and rare, and, out of necessity, they were reserved for festivities instead of enjoyed every day. While I serve fresh fruit— apricots in spring, meltingly sweet pears in autumn, and nuts and cheese drizzled with the lightest spoonful of honey for desserts at home—I reserve more elaborate cakes for special occasions—birthdays, holidays, and the days that mark the changing of the seasons.

Fruit

In springtime, the first fruits appear—little alpine strawberries, then the sweet and sour cherries, then the larger and more robust stone fruits like peaches and plums, followed by pomaceous fruit, such as apples, quince, and pears—before the dark days return, bringing with them the gift of citrus. My son tends pots of strawberries on our porch, charging himself with their care. Their flowers are the first to appear, five round white petals encircling a sunny yellow center. We watch them patiently, waiting for the petals to fall and for the red or yellow fruit to appear. He chases away the birds that would otherwise avail themselves of our labor, and, eventually, he harvests the little fruits, placing them in a chilled bowl on the dinner table. Later, the cherries come to market, and we eat so many they stain our mouths red.

By the time we sicken of cherries, peaches hang from the trees, and we return to the orchards once more, baskets in hand, to pick our fill. We shield ourselves against August's oppressive heat, finding refuge beneath the shade of the peach trees, reaching up into the dark green leaves to pluck a peach, ripe and still warm from the sun's rays. I take the bandana from my pocket and brush it against the peach's skin to rub away its bitter-tasting fuzz before sinking my teeth into its sweet, syrupy flesh. Peaches taste of summer, as strawberries taste of spring, and apples of autumn. Citrus fruit—oranges and lemons, mandarins, and kumquats—are like little globes of orange and yellow sunlight in the darkest of days. We eat them greedily until spring returns again with blossoms and strawberries that mark the rhythmic beginning of a new cycle.

For the most part, I serve fruit without much fanfare. On its own, a ripe peach speaks volumes and needs little help from me. Its syrupy juices need no sweetening from the jar of honey sitting on my countertop. We eat fruit with joy and with abandon, but very occasionally, and for special moments, I prepare fruit-based desserts: pies and stewed fruit compotes, ice creams and sorbets.

roasted sweet cherry fool

The first few weeks of summer bring much-anticipated sweet cherries to the mountains. Lines weave in and out of the farmers markets as shoppers wait to fill their baskets and bags with the first of summer's fruits. The earliest cherries lack the round and exaggerated sweetness of the later fruits, but we delight in them anyway. Roasting them deepens their flavor and amplifies their sugars. I serve the roasted cherries on their own, or with pillows of whipped raw cream in a simple fruit fool. A lovely combination of fruit and whipped cream, fools come together in just a few minutes for a simple dessert with an old-fashioned charm. SERVES 4 TO 6

2 pounds sweet cherries, such as Bing

1 tablespoon unrefined cane sugar

Pinch of finely ground unrefined sea salt

1 tablespoon kirsch

2 cups heavy cream

2 teaspoons vanilla bean powder or 1 teaspoon vanilla extract

12 Honey Meringues (page 246), coarsely chopped

Preheat the oven to 425°F.

Remove the pits from the cherries, and, as you do, drop the cherries into a mixing bowl. Add the sugar, salt, and kirsch, then toss the cherries until evenly coated. Transfer the cherries to a 9 by 13-inch baking dish and spread them into a single layer. Roast for 10 to 12 minutes, stirring once, until they release their fragrance. Allow the cherries to cool the room temperature, about 20 minutes.

Pour the cream into a bowl and add the vanilla. Whip with a whisk until the cream holds soft peaks. Stir the cherries and their juice into the whipped cream and fold in the chopped meringues. Serve in individual glasses or bowls.

spiced sour cherry compote ⁂

I await sour cherry season all year long, for they enjoy only a very short season. They arrive in August, after we've eaten our fill of sweet cherries. In season for only a fortnight, they disappear for another 50 weeks. I remove their tiny pits and freeze what fruit I can, but the frozen cherries never seem to match the tart complexity of a ripe sour cherry, plucked fresh from the tree and eaten out of hand or made into a dessert right away. A little sugar certainly offsets the cherries' sourness, but sweet spices like vanilla bean, cinnamon, and cloves envelop that natural sourness, adding depth and complexity. Serve the compote in bowls topped with whipped cream, which softens the cherries' assertive sourness, or use them to top pancakes or ice cream. SERVES 4 TO 6

---

³/₄ cup purchased sour cherry juice

¹/₂ cup unrefined cane sugar

2 pounds sour cherries, stemmed and pitted

2 teaspoons ground cinnamon

1 teaspoon vanilla bean powder

¹/₂ teaspoon ground allspice

¹/₂ teaspoon ground cloves

2 tablespoons kirsch

Whipped cream, to serve

Bring the cherry juice to a simmer in a saucepan over medium-high heat. Whisk in the sugar and continue stirring until it dissolves. Decrease the heat to medium-low, then dump the cherries into the pot and stir in the cinnamon, vanilla bean powder, allspice, and cloves. Pour the kirsch into the cherries, cover, and simmer, stirring from time to time, until the cherries are softened and deeply fragrant, about 10 minutes.

Spoon the compote into bowls and serve warm with whipped cream.

honey-poached apricots

Short and fleeting, apricot season begins in mid- to late June in the mountains and lasts only a few weeks. During years with particularly wet and cold springs, the apricots may fail to fruit altogether, and we must wait another year to taste them, our anticipation growing ever more. We often pick them in the wild, near old and abandoned homesteads. The older varieties yield smaller fruit, with more concentrated flavor and a heady sweetness that is unrivaled by the larger modern apricots. While I favor eating most stone fruits, like peaches, plums, and cherries, fresh and out of hand, the apricot yearns for cooking. Its soft and mealy flesh benefits from stewing, allowing its honey-like floral notes to blossom. SERVES 4 TO 6

2 cups sweet white wine, such as a German Riesling

1/2 cup honey

1 vanilla bean, split lengthwise

2 cardamom pods, crushed

12 apricots, halved and pitted

2 tablespoons chopped fresh mint

Whipped cream, to serve

Whisk the wine and honey together in a saucepan. Toss in the vanilla bean and cardamom pods and bring to a slow simmer over medium heat, until the honey dissolves into the wine.

Toss in the apricots, cover, and simmer until just tender but not soft or mushy, about 4 minutes. Using a slotted spoon, transfer the apricots to a serving dish and cover to keep them warm. Bring the poaching liquid to a boil over high heat and let it reduce by half. Strain the syrup through a fine-mesh sieve into a bowl, discard the vanilla and cardamom, and pour the syrup over the apricots. Sprinkle the apricots with the mint and serve warm, topped with spoonfuls of whipped cream.

roasted peaches *with* basil *and* yogurt

Peaches and basil form an unlikely alliance, yet the vibrant licorice-like notes of basil make a beautiful match for peaches' soft, sweet floral undertones. Roasting heightens the peaches' sweetness, as their juices combine with honey and butter to form a fine syrup that blends perfectly into creamy, thick yogurt cheese. It's an example of the beautiful balance of nature that, at the height of summer, both peaches and basil arrive in abundance, their flavors at their peak. SERVES 6

1/4 cup unsalted butter, at room temperature

3 tablespoons honey

1/4 teaspoon finely ground unrefined sea salt

1 vanilla bean

6 peaches, halved and pitted

Yogurt Cheese (page 57), to serve

1/4 cup chopped fresh basil

Preheat the oven to 400°F.

In a mixing bowl, cream together the butter and honey with a wooden spoon until well combined. Add the salt. Split the vanilla bean lengthwise and scrape its seeds into the bowl. Continue beating the mixture until smooth and uniform.

Spoon the honeyed butter into the peaches' cavities, dividing it evenly. Place the peaches cavity side up in a single layer in a 9 by 13-inch baking dish or roasting pan and roast for 20 minutes, until tender and fragrant.

Using a slotted spoon, transfer the peaches to waiting bowls, top with yogurt cheese and the basil, and serve.

roasted plum ice cream

Plums arrive at our market in early September, toward the end of peach season and at the beginning of apple season. They're a gateway fruit of sorts, bridging the seasons of summer and autumn. While the pale, violet-colored and extraordinarily sweet variety called Sugar Plum is my favorite to use in this ice cream, the larger and mellower Italian prune plum works well, too. Unlike classic ice cream, in which eggs and cream are cooked together to form a custard, this recipe uses raw egg yolks, resulting in a flavor and texture that I prefer. MAKES ABOUT 1½ QUARTS

2 cups whole milk

2 cups heavy cream

1 cup honey

¼ teaspoon ground cloves

1 teaspoon finely grated orange zest

2 egg yolks

2 pounds plums

1 tablespoon unrefined cane sugar

Combine the milk, cream, honey, cloves, and orange zest in a saucepan over low heat and whisk until the honey dissolves and the mixture is warm to the touch. Add the egg yolks and whisk until thoroughly combined. Pour the liquid through a fine-mesh strainer set over a bowl to remove any lumps of egg or large bits of orange zest. Cover and refrigerate until the liquid is completely cold, at least 12 hours.

Preheat the oven to 425°F.

Split the plums in half and pluck out their pits. Arrange the plums cut side up in a 9 by 13-inch baking dish and roast for 20 minutes, until they yield to the gentle pressure of a knife. Remove the dish from the oven and let the plums cool completely.

When the plums are cool enough to handle, chop them into bite-sized pieces. Fold the plums and their juice into the chilled liquid.

Churn the mixture in an ice cream maker according to the manufacturer's instructions. Transfer the ice cream to a container, cover, and store in the freezer. It will keep for about 2 weeks.

spiced apple *and* plum sauce

Just as plum season ends in the mountains, apple season begins. The first apples to arrive are small, tart, and green. Later, as the autumn wears on, the apples grow rosier, redder, and larger until they reach the size of a softball. I often purchase several cases of both apples and plums to store away for winter when the local markets close up, and nothing new or green or fresh will arrive for several more months. I make sauces, preserves, and jams this time of year, and this sauce is one of my favorites, for it combines the tartness of green apple with the sweetness of plums. I serve the sauce warm, dropping a pat of butter into each bowl. The butter melts, providing the sauce with an elusive creaminess. MAKES ABOUT 1 QUART

6 large green apples

6 large plums

2 cinnamon sticks

1 (1-inch) knob fresh ginger, peeled and crushed

4 cardamom pods, crushed

2 teaspoons whole cloves

1 cup apple juice

2 tablespoons brandy

Unsalted butter, cut into pats, to serve

Core the apples and chop them into 1-inch pieces. Slice the plums in half, remove their pits, and chop the fruit into 1-inch pieces. Tuck the cinnamon sticks, ginger, cardamom, and cloves into a bit of cheesecloth and tie it closed with 100 percent cotton cooking twine.

Put the fruit and bundle of spices into a heavy saucepan and pour in the apple juice and the brandy. Cover the pan and bring to a boil over medium heat, then decrease the heat to medium-low and simmer for about 30 minutes, stirring occasionally to prevent scorching, or until the fruit falls apart of its own accord.

Remove and discard the spice bundle, then puree the fruit with an immersion blender until smooth. Spoon the warm sauce into small serving bowls, top each with a pat of butter, and serve. The sauce will keep in a tightly sealed jar in the refrigerator for up to 1 week.

quince, apple, *and* pear galette ❦

Quince arrive in the late autumn, along with pears and the last apples of the season. An old-fashioned fruit with a shape like a plump apple and a pale yellow, down-covered skin, quince want a bit of coaxing in the kitchen. Quince's extraordinarily tough flesh is bitter and deeply astringent, but, with a bit of love, sugar, and time, it softens, releasing the fruit's true flavor: floral notes that combine well with vanilla and browned butter.

On its own, the flavor of quince can overpower a dish, so I favor pairing it with other fruits—apple and pear—which temper its floweriness. SERVES ABOUT 6

POACHED FRUIT

2 cups water

1 1/2 cups unrefined cane sugar

1 lemon, halved

2 bay leaves

1 medium quince

3 medium apples

2 medium pears

GALETTE

1/4 cup unsalted butter

1/4 cup unrefined cane sugar

1 tablespoon vanilla bean powder, or 1 1/2 teaspoons vanilla extract

1 tablespoon orange flower water

2 tablespoons arrowroot powder

1/2 recipe (1 disk) Simple Sourdough Pie Crust (page 178)

EGG WASH

1 egg

1 tablespoon honey

2 tablespoons water

To poach the fruit, pour the water into a saucepan. Whisk the sugar into the water, then drop in the lemon halves and bay leaves. Set the pot on the countertop, next to your cutting board.

Peel the quince, quarter it with a sharp knife, and carefully remove the core from each piece with a paring knife. Cut each quarter into 1/4-inch slices, immediately plunging them into the waiting saucepan to prevent discoloration. Place the saucepan over medium-high heat and bring the liquid to a boil. Decrease the heat to medium, cover the pan, and simmer the quince for about 40 minutes, until its color turns slightly rosy and the slices soften slightly. Peel and slice the apples and pears in the same way that you did the quince, then stir the fruits into the saucepan with the quince. Cover, and simmer for another 20 minutes, until the quince takes on a rosy blush and all of the fruits yield easily when pierced with a fork.

Preheat the oven to 375°F.

With a pair of tongs, pluck the lemons and bay leaves from the pot and discard them, then drain the fruit. (Reserve the cooking liquid, if you like. I use it to sweeten teas and to flavor whipped cream.)

To prepare the galette, melt the butter in a skillet over medium heat until it froths, then browns, 3 to 4 minutes. Whisk in the sugar and vanilla bean powder. Stir in the poached fruit and sauté for 3 to 5 minutes, until any juices clinging to them turn syrupy. Transfer the fruit to a mixing bowl along with any drops of browned butter. Stir in the orange flower water and arrowroot powder and set the filling aside.

Roll out the pie dough to a 10-inch round following the directions on page 178. Slide the round on its parchment paper onto a baking sheet. Plop the fruit onto the center of the dough, leaving a border of at least 3 inches all around. Fold the edge of the dough over the filling.

Make an egg wash by cracking the egg into a small mixing bowl and whisking in the honey and water. Brush the egg wash over the dough. Bake for 30 to 35 minutes, until the crust is golden brown. Allow the galette to cool about 10 minutes before slicing and serving.

maple-roasted pears

Maple and pears make a natural match. Roasting the pears in a buttery syrup spiked with nutmeg and cinnamon results in a humble and not overly assertive treat. While these pears make an obvious dessert, they are also excellent served with breakfast or brunch. SERVES 4

1 tablespoon unsalted butter

2 tablespoons Grade B maple syrup

$1/2$ teaspoon freshly grated nutmeg

$1/2$ teaspoon ground cinnamon

$1/4$ teaspoon finely ground unrefined sea salt

4 medium pears, peeled, halved, and cored

Preheat the oven to 375°F.

Melt the butter in an ovenproof skillet over medium heat. When it froths, whisk in the maple syrup, nutmeg, cinnamon, and salt. Remove from the heat and place the pears cut side down in the pan. Spoon a bit of the sauce over the pears and bake for 45 minutes, until tender when pierced with a fork.

Serve warm, drizzled with the pan juices.

mincemeat hand pies ❧

Dried fruit spiked with cinnamon, allspice, and cloves forms the heart
of mincemeat, while beef suet lends a luxuriant richness to the filling.
For these little hand pies, the fruit, suet, and spices marinate in brandy
and orange juice for several days, which helps their unique flavors blend
together. MAKES 6

MINCEMEAT

2 tart green apples, peeled,
cored, and chopped into
1-inch pieces

³/₄ cup dried currants

¹/₂ cup raisins

¹/₄ cup chopped dried figs

¹/₄ cup dried unsweetened
sour cherries

2 ounces beef suet, coarsely
chopped

¹/₂ cup unrefined cane sugar

¹/₂ cup brandy

Finely grated zest and juice
of 1 orange

¹/₂ teaspoon ground cinnamon

¹/₄ teaspoon ground allspice

¹/₄ teaspoon ground cloves

¹/₄ teaspoon freshly grated
nutmeg

TO FINISH

Simple Sourdough Pie Crust
(page 178)

1 egg

1 tablespoon honey

1 tablespoon water

Combine the apples, currants, raisins, figs, dried cherries, suet,
sugar, brandy, orange zest and juice, cinnamon, allspice, cloves,
and nutmeg in a food processor and pulse until very coarsely
chopped, then transfer to a large bowl. Alternatively, mince
the apple, currants, raisins, figs, cherries, and suet very finely;
stir them together in a large mixing bowl; and stir in the sugar,
brandy, orange zest and juice, and the spices. Cover tightly and
let the ingredients marinate in your refrigerator for 3 days,
stirring once a day.

Preheat the oven to 400°F. Line a baking sheet with parchment
paper.

Cut each disk of pie dough into thirds and form each piece into
a ball. Cut six 12-inch squares of parchment paper. Dust one
parchment square with flour and set a dough ball in the center.
Dust the dough and your rolling pin with flour, then roll out
the dough to a 6-inch round about ¹/₈ inch thick; set the round
aside. Roll out the remaining dough balls, using a new square
of parchment for each.

Spoon about ¹/₂ cup of mincemeat onto one half of each dough
round. Fold the other half of the round over the mincemeat
and seal the edges by pressing them together with your fingers
or with the tines of a fork. Pierce the top of the pie with the
fork tines 2 or 3 times, then set the pie on the prepared baking
sheet. Repeat the process using the remaining dough rounds
to form five more hand pies.

In a small bowl whisk together the egg, honey, and water.
Brush the glaze over the pies.

Bake for 10 minutes, then decrease the oven temperature to
350°F and continue baking for another 20 minutes, until the
crusts are golden brown. Allow the pies to cool completely
before serving.

kumquats stewed *with* sweet spices

Of all the citrus, I count the whimsical, oval-shaped kumquat as my favorite. I relish the surprise of biting into the sweet, leathery skin only to be met by the startling sourness of the juice. Available from November through March, kumquats hit their peak in January and February, and, like most citrus fruits, they pair well with the warming sweet spices of cardamom, cinnamon, and clove. While stewed kumquats provide a nice topping for crepes, pancakes, or simple cakes, I like serving them spooned into bowls with a dollop of mascarpone or Yogurt Cheese (page 57). **SERVES 4 TO 6**

1 pound kumquats, thinly sliced and seeded

1 cinnamon stick

6 whole cloves

3 cardamom pods

1 vanilla bean, split lengthwise

¹/₃ cup honey

¹/₂ cup orange juice

¹/₂ cup water

Toss the kumquats into a saucepan, then drop in the cinnamon, cloves, cardamom, and vanilla bean. Pour in the honey, orange juice, and water. Simmer, uncovered, over medium heat for 10 to 15 minutes, or until the kumquats soften and become tender. Serve warm.

Nuts

I keep all sorts of nuts tucked away into glass mason jars in my cupboards: oblong almonds, little hazelnuts, pecans, and walnuts. I buy them in large burlap sacks, still in their shells, and crack them open only as needed. There's a distinct beauty in a freshly cracked nut. The shell of a nut seals its sweet meat, preserving its array of fragile oils that can dissipate or go rancid quickly once that shell is breeched. A nut keeps its buttery sweetness and its aroma only briefly, so cracking them just before you prepare them helps to preserve the integrity of their flavor. Once they have been cracked, storing nuts in the refrigerator or the freezer can help to preserve their flavor longer than leaving them at room temperature.

Nuts, like grains and pulses, offer powerful nutrition—vitamin E and other antioxidants, but, also like grains and pulses, nuts similarly contain an array of antinutrients that can make them difficult to digest or that can prevent you from absorbing the full complement of minerals they contain. Enzyme inhibitors can make them difficult to digest, while food phytates can block your body's ability to absorb their trace minerals. As with most foods, preparing nuts mindfully can help to deactivate these antinutrients, leaving you to fully enjoy not only the flavors, aromas, and textures they contribute to your foods, but also the nutrition they provide your body as well.

Just as the bulk of the antinutrients in grains rest within the bran, antinutrients in nuts largely rest within the papery skin that adheres to the nut's meat. Roasting, blanching, and soaking nuts overnight in water can all help to mitigate the effects of the antinutrients they contain; further, many of these methods also enhance their flavors. Roasting nuts deepens their flavor, helping them to release the volatile oils that account for the striking dark, rich perfume of roasted walnuts or hazelnuts. Blanching nuts in boiling water followed by a plunge in cold water loosens that papery skin, allowing you to remove it without damaging the nut itself. While roasting deepens the flavor of nuts, blanching lightens it. I use both methods frequently, depending on the outcome I wish to create. During the winter, when we lean upon more robust and hearty dishes, I seem to use roasted nuts with greater frequency. In summertime, when we crave lighter foods, I rely more heavily on blanched nuts.

Blanched nuts, and blanched almonds in particular, feature prominently in colonial American confections. Blanched almond flour, rather than white flour, provided the base for many sweets and cakes. Prepared for special occasions and community festivals, confections were not as ubiquitous as they are now, so the expense of nuts, sugars, and dried fruit enhanced their novelty and importance. Later, as white flour became more accessible and more affordable, white flour pastries and cakes often replaced the richer, traditional versions that were made from nuts. I still prefer nuts in my cakes and pastries; I find that their rich assortment of proteins and fats helps to provide satiation as well as flavor, and that nut-based desserts offer a lingering satisfaction thanks, in part, to a more balanced macronutrient profile.

portugal cake ✣

Immensely popular in the eighteenth and early nineteenth centuries, Portugal cake fell from favor as white flour slowly replaced the more luxurious, and expensive, blanched almonds. It's a pity, really. A Portugal cake is an exquisite confection, incomparably rich owing to the inclusion of a pound each of butter, almonds, and sugar. Spiked with sherry and rosewater and dotted with currants, a slice of Portugal cake tastes impossibly moist and rich and is best reserved for special occasions. This recipe makes two 8-inch cakes, and is easily halved to make just one cake. MAKES TWO 8-INCH CAKES, TO SERVE 16

2 cups unsalted butter, at room temperature, plus more for greasing

All-purpose flour, for dusting

2¼ cups unrefined cane sugar

12 eggs, beaten

2 tablespoons sweet sherry

2 tablespoons rosewater

½ teaspoon finely ground unrefined sea salt

4¾ cups blanched almond flour (see page 244)

1 cup dried currants

Powdered sugar, for dusting (optional)

Preheat the oven to 350°F.

Grease and flour two 8-inch cake pans.

Beat the butter and sugar together in a large mixing bowl with a wooden spoon until uniformly combined, then beat in the eggs and continue beating until the batter becomes light and fluffy. Stir in the sherry, rosewater, and salt. Beat in the almond flour ½ cup at a time. Continue beating the batter by hand until you've removed any clumps, then fold in the currants. Pour the batter into the prepared cake pans.

Bake the cakes for 45 minutes, until their tops are a deep mahogany brown but their centers remain a touch wobbly. Let the cakes cool completely in the pans, then invert them onto serving plates. If you like, dust the surfaces with powdered sugar before slicing and serving. Store the cakes in an airtight container for up to 1 week.

sorghum *and* roasted nut pie ❧

The tradition of boiling sorghum, a tiny grain with a grassy, wheat-like flavor, into syrup mirrors that of sugaring maples in New England; both are seasonal and a traditional community-wide endeavor. Sorghum produces a fine amber-colored syrup that offers both the mineral notes of blackstrap molasses and the sweetness of maple syrup. Its overt sweetness balances nicely with the rich meatiness of roasted nuts. **SERVES 6**

¹/₂ cup chopped pecans

¹/₂ cup chopped walnuts

¹/₂ cup chopped almonds

2 tablespoons plus 1 teaspoon melted unsalted butter

4 eggs

¹/₂ cup unrefined cane sugar

1 cup sorghum syrup

¹/₂ recipe (1 disk) Simple Sourdough Pie Crust (page 178)

Preheat the oven to 350°F.

Spread the nuts in a single layer on a rimmed baking sheet and drizzle them with the 1 teaspoon of melted butter. Roast for 10 to 12 minutes, stirring once or twice, until the nuts become deeply fragrant and brown a bit. Remove the baking sheet from the oven and allow the nuts to cool.

Whisk the eggs and sugar in a mixing bowl. Whisk in the sorghum syrup. Slowly drizzle the remaining 2 tablespoons of melted butter into the egg mixture as you whisk continuously. Fold in the roasted nuts.

Roll out the pie dough to a 10-inch round following the directions on page 178. Line a 9-inch pie pan with the dough, then crimp the edges, trimming as needed. Pour the filling into the crust. Bake for 40 minutes, until the crust turns golden brown but the center of the pie remains slightly wobbly when jostled.

Allow the pie to cool completely before slicing and serving.

roasted hazelnut brittle ❧

Hazelnuts are sweet nuts, but their skins are very bitter. Blanching the nuts first then roasting them removes any lingering bitterness, enhancing their buttery sweetness. Unlike cloyingly sweet refined white sugar, whole and unrefined cane sugar tastes more complex, with mineral-like notes that enhance the flavor of roasted nuts. **MAKES ABOUT 1 POUND**

4 cups blanched hazelnuts (see page 244), coarsely chopped

¼ cup plus 1 teaspoon melted unsalted butter

3 cups unrefined cane sugar

¼ cup water

Preheat the oven to 350°F.

Spread the nuts on a rimmed baking sheet and drizzle them with the 1 teaspoon of melted butter. Roast for 10 to 12 minutes, stirring once or twice, until the nuts are deeply fragrant and brown a bit. Remove the baking sheet from the oven and allow the nuts to cool.

Grease a separate rimmed baking sheet with the remaining ¼ cup of melted butter.

Whisk the sugar and water in a large heavy saucepan over medium-high heat and cook until the sugar liquefies and turns light amber in color, about 15 minutes. Turn off the heat, lest you burn the sugar, and stir in the hazelnuts. Pour the contents of the pan onto the buttered baking sheet and allow it to spread. Let cool completely and harden, then break the brittle into bite-sized glassy shards. Store the brittle in an airtight container at room temperature for up to 1 week.

How to Blanch Nuts

The bitter, papery skins that adhere to some types of nuts, including almonds and hazelnuts, contain food phytate, which can bind up minerals, preventing their full absorption. Blanching removes those skins, not only allowing you to be better able to absorb the nuts' nutrients, but also improving flavor and texture. For baking—especially for cake making—I often used blanched almond flour to complement grain-based flours.

4 cups almonds, hazelnuts, or other nuts with tough skins

Bring about 6 cups of water to a boil in a saucepan. Slip the nuts into the boiling water and let them boil for about 3 minutes. While they boil, fill a bowl with very cold water.

Remove the nuts from the saucepan with a slotted spoon and slip them immediately into the cold water. Their skins should pucker and split. Take a nut between your thumb and forefinger and pinch it gently until the skin slips off. Set the skinned nuts in a bowl and use them immediately, or layer them onto a kitchen towel and allow them to dry overnight until crisp.

With an extended period of storage, blanched nuts, like all nuts, will begin to lose their flavor and their fragile oils will turn rancid. So store them in the freezer, or use them within a few days of preparing them.

HOW TO MAKE BLANCHED ALMOND FLOUR

Pour blanched almonds into a food processor and pulse until they form a fine meal the texture of cornmeal. Take care not to over-process the almonds, lest they turn to butter. Use the almond flour immediately, or store in the freezer to prevent rancidity and maintain optimal flavor.

Honey

One of my favorite sweeteners, honey offers multidimensional flavor. It moves beyond the cloying sweetness of sugar to one touched by notes of blossoms, cinnamon, or chocolate. Much as the flavor of milk depends upon the diet of a grazing cow, or the color of an egg yolk depends upon what a hen eats, so do the flavor, color, and texture of honey depend upon where the bees that made it roamed. While the honey we use routinely in my kitchen comes from bees whose hives are nestled between rows of stone fruit trees in the orchards of Colorado's western slope, I also favor single varietal honeys as special treats, treasuring them and dipping into them as opportunity allows; their expense makes them an occasional treat in our home.

Produced by bees feeding predominantly on a single plant, single varietal honeys offer unique and often assertive flavors and colors. These honeys possess distinctive strong notes that differ depending on the nature of the plant upon which the bees feed. While the orchard blossom honey that we pick up at the farmers market rests on my counter, allowing easy access for baking, custards, and other treats. I keep three or four single varietal honeys hidden away in the dark of my cupboards. I treasure their flavors and the richness of their colors, which that range from pale and nearly clear to the dark, rich brown of stout beer or molasses. I use them sparingly, savoring their singular flavors. Star thistle honey tastes of cinnamon, chestnut honey of chocolate, and tamarisk honey of molasses and pine. Orange blossom honey offers a lasting sweetness, soft and floral with faint notes of citrus. Manuka honey, lauded for its health benefits and antibacterial nature, tastes earthy and faintly medicinal. Most are best served on their own, allowing you to savor their unique flavor.

In the recipes I've included here, any local honey that you can access readily and affordably will work, whether mild in flavor or more assertive. I lean on honey more than I do other sweeteners because I can purchase it locally. It doesn't travel far from the orchard, to the bottle, to the market, to my kitchen counter.

Some lingering kitchen lore posits that cooks shouldn't heat honey, lest they destroy all that's good in the sweetener. I don't agree. While I prefer keeping honey raw if the recipe allows, so as to preserve its food enzymes and any heat-sensitive vitamins it might contain, I do not trouble myself over an occasional treat including a small amount of cooked or heated honey.

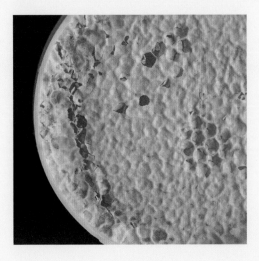

honey meringues ✣

I love the whimsy of homemade meringues, which, in one bite, release both a satisfying crunch and an airy lightness. In making Olive Oil Mayonnaise (page 80) regularly in our home, I find myself with many leftover egg whites that I save in small airtight containers in my refrigerator for these meringues. With so few ingredients to compete for prominence, the variety of the honey you choose can strongly influence the flavor of the meringues. Strongly flavored single varietal honeys like chestnut or tamarisk produce pronounced and distinctive results. **MAKES ABOUT 12 MERINGUES**

2 egg whites

$^1/_2$ cup honey

$^1/_2$ teaspoon vanilla extract

Pinch of finely ground unrefined sea salt

$^1/_4$ teaspoon cream of tartar

1 teaspoon ice water

Preheat the oven to 200°F and line a baking sheet with parchment paper. Place the bowl of a stand mixer in the refrigerator to chill.

Pour about 2 inches of water into a saucepan and bring to a simmer over medium-high heat. While the water heats, whisk the egg whites, honey, and vanilla in a mixing bowl large enough to fit comfortably over the saucepan without slipping in. Fit the mixing bowl over the saucepan and whisk the ingredients by hand continuously for about 4 minutes, until the honey combines smoothly with the egg whites and the mixture is frothy and warm to the touch.

Pull the mixing bowl from the saucepan and pour the egg white mixture into the cold bowl of the stand mixer. Whisk in the salt and cream of tartar until they dissolve. Whisk in the ice water, then whip with the whisk attachment for 4 to 6 minutes, until the meringue is smooth and glossy and holds stiff peaks.

Using a spoon, drop mounds of meringue about 2 inches in diameter and 1$^1/_2$ inches high onto the prepared baking sheet, spacing them about $^1/_2$ inch apart. Alternatively, put the meringue into a pastry bag fitted with a large plain tip and pipe mounds onto the baking sheet. Bake for 1$^1/_2$ hours, or until the meringues are crisp and dry. Turn off the oven and prop open the door just a crack, leaving the meringues in the oven to dry out overnight. The meringues will be ready to eat the next morning, or you can store them in a container with a tight-fitting lid for up to 1 week.

stirred honey custard ❧

Soft and creamy, this stirred custard is faintly sweet and deeply perfumed by the floral notes of vanilla bean and honey. I serve it in the spring, when jars of fresh raw cream begin to appear again after a long winter, when the cows of our local creamery are dry. Eggs, too, are plentiful in the spring. I pour the custard over bowls of just-picked alpine strawberries for a simple springtime dessert. **SERVES 4 TO 6**

1 cup heavy cream

1 vanilla bean, split lengthwise

2 tablespoons honey

6 egg yolks, beaten

Bring about 2 inches of water to a simmer in the bottom of a double boiler or in a saucepan. Pour the cream into the top of the double boiler or into a metal bowl that will fit over the water in the saucepan. Scrape the seeds from the vanilla bean into the cream and set the top of the double boiler or bowl over the simmering water. When the cream is hot to the touch, whisk in the honey until dissolved.

Whisk the egg yolks in a bowl, then spoon a tablespoon or two of the hot cream into the yolks and whisk vigorously to temper them. Pour the tempered yolks into the cream and continue to heat, stirring slowly, until the custard is thick enough to coat the back of a spoon, about 10 minutes. Serve the custard warm or transfer it to a bowl, cover, and refrigerate until chilled.

warm honey-drizzled feta *with* pine nuts, orange, *and* mint 🐝

Honey provides a nice foil for the saltiness of feta cheese. When I'm not in the mood for the cloying sweetness of desserts but still hunger for a little something after dinner, I like to pair cheese with honey. Choose a strongly flavored honey, such as a single varietal or one infused with herbs, because the flavor of the honey will shine through. While you can serve the warm feta and honey smeared onto slices of bread, I prefer to serve it on a plate with a fork, enjoying it on its own. SERVES 4 TO 6

¼ cup pine nuts

1 (8-ounce) block feta cheese

2 tablespoons extra-virgin olive oil

2 tablespoons honey

2 teaspoons chopped mint

1 teaspoon finely grated orange zest

Preheat the oven to 350°F. Line a baking sheet with parchment paper.

Spread the pine nuts on the baking sheet and toast in the oven for 5 to 7 minutes, until toasty brown but not burned, stirring once. Pine nuts can quickly go from a lovely brown color to burned, so be vigilant as you toast them. Remove them from the oven and set them aside. Increase the oven temperature to 400°F.

Brush the block of feta with the olive oil and set it in an attractive baking dish. Bake the cheese for 8 to 10 minutes, or until it softens to the touch. Remove it from the oven and preheat the broiler. Drizzle the feta with the honey and broil it for 5 minutes, or until it browns, taking care lest it burn. Top the feta with the pine nuts, sprinkle it with the mint and orange zest, then serve.

roasted berry panna cotta

I prepare panna cotta, a traditional Italian dessert that combines cream and gelatin, in summer, when I enjoy the luxury of picking up several gallons of sweet raw milk from a local dairy. Cream and berries make a beautiful marriage, and roasting berries enhances their aroma, deepening both their tartness and sweetness, which turns almost candy-like with time. That resonant aroma and flavor combines with the gentleness of raw milk and cream for a simple, light summertime dessert. **SERVES 4 TO 6**

1 cup chopped strawberries

1 cup raspberries

1 cup blueberries

1 tablespoon unrefined cane sugar

1 cup whole milk, preferably raw

2 tablespoons plain gelatin

3 cups heavy cream, preferably raw

½ cup honey

Preheat the oven to 400°F.

Arrange the berries in a single layer a 9 by 13-inch baking dish, sprinkle with the sugar, and roast for 20 to 25 minutes, until the berries release their liquid and the aroma that wafts from the oven perfumes your kitchen with the sweet-tart bouquet of ripe fruit.

Pour the berries and their liquid into a food processor or blender and puree until smooth. Strain through a fine-mesh sieve to remove seeds or bits of skin.

Pour the milk into a small bowl, then sprinkle the gelatin over the milk. Allow the gelatin to soften for 5 minutes.

Transfer the milk and softened gelatin to a saucepan and stir continuously over medium heat for 5 minutes. Do not let the milk boil. Whisk the cream, honey, and berry puree into the milk and continue whisking for 5 to 7 minutes, making sure the gelatin is well incorporated. Pour into four 6-ounce or six 4-ounce individual ramekins or custard dishes, cover, and refrigerate until set, at least 6 hours or up to 1 day.

Serve the panna cotta cold, in the ramekins.

melted blueberries *with* ginger *and* mandarin orange ✤

Tossed into frothy butter scented with ginger, blueberries soften and seem to melt away. I usually use orange blossom honey, as it nicely balances the earthy sweetness of blueberries and the vibrant citrus flavors of mandarin orange. Once the flavors meld together in the heat of the pan, I ladle the blueberries into waiting bowls and serve them with a dollop of whipped cream that melts, ever so slowly, with the residual heat of the berries. SERVES 4

1 teaspoon unsalted butter

1 teaspoon grated fresh ginger

2¹/₂ cups blueberries

1 tablespoon honey

Finely grated zest and juice of 1 mandarin orange

Whipped cream, to serve

Melt the butter in a skillet over medium heat. Stir in the ginger and sauté until it releases its spicy perfume, about 2 minutes. Stir in the blueberries, honey, and mandarin zest and juice. Sauté the berries over medium heat until the berries soften and their juices form a thin syrup, about 6 minutes. Spoon the warm berries into individual bowls and serve topped with a generous spoonful of whipped cream.

strawberries *in* minted honey syrup ⚬

My family grows strawberries in our little patch in the community garden
and in terra cotta pots on our porch. Unlike most fruits that require long,
hot weather, strawberries seem to favor our cool mountain summers. We
often hike along trails near our home, and, on very fortunate days, we find
patches of bright red wild alpine strawberries. Sometimes they are larger
than a dime, and it seems that the smaller they are, the more concentrated
their flavor tends to be. The soft floral flavor of strawberries pairs nicely
with the bright, grassy notes of mint. I like to marinate them in a honey-
based syrup spiked with fresh spearmint or peppermint. We serve them
for breakfast, with a bowl of Slow-Cultured Yogurt (page 56), or for dessert
with whipped cream. SERVES 4

---

1 cup water

1 cup honey

2 pints strawberries

1 small bunch fresh mint
(about 6 sprigs)

Bring the water to a simmer in a saucepan over medium heat.
Pour in the honey and whisk it into the water until it dissolves
fully. Continue simmering over medium heat for 5 minutes.
Remove the pan from the heat and let the syrup cool to room
temperature.

Hull the strawberries, cut them in half, and set them in a bowl.
Pluck the leaves off the stems of mint, tear them with your
hands, and drop them into the bowl with the strawberries. Pour
the cooled honey syrup over the strawberries and mint, then
cover the bowl and transfer it to the fridge. Allow the berries
to marinate for a day, and then serve them with their syrup.

rose petal *and* honey ice cream ❀

Each Saturday from April through November, we drive to a small family farm nestled along the banks of the Uncompahgre River in central Colorado to visit our friends Betsy and Della, who grow some of the most diverse varieties of vegetables, fruits, and herbs on their eight acres. In the early weeks of the year, the farm produces very little—tomato starts, handfuls of young radishes, and bunches of fresh herbs. But those early weeks bring something more, too. Betsy's and Della's mother, Jean, a woman with a broad and joyous smile, occupies her later years by tending flowers: calendula, pinks, pansies, and roses. I take her rose petals, dropping a few into salads, but I reserve most for this ice cream. When I prepare this ice cream, as with others, I use raw milk, raw cream, and raw egg yolks, heating these ingredients only enough to incorporate the honey easily and allow the rose petals to infuse the liquids with their aroma and flavor. MAKES ABOUT 1 QUART

2¹/₂ cups heavy cream

2 cups whole milk

³/₄ cup loosely packed rose petals

1 cup honey

2 egg yolks

Pour the cream and milk into a saucepan, then stir in the rose petals. Warm the mixture over medium heat until the liquid begins to bubble at the edges. Decrease the heat to low, cover the pot, and allow the petals to steep for 10 minutes.

Strain the mixture through a fine-mesh sieve set over a bowl, pressing down on the rose petals with the back of a spoon to extract as much of the liquid as possible. Discard the rose petals and whisk the honey into the liquid until it dissolves.

In a small bowl, whisk the egg yolks to break them up. Pour a spoonful of the warm rose-infused cream into the yolks to temper them and whisk well. Then pour the tempered yolks into the bowl of warm cream and continue whisking until thoroughly combined. Cover the bowl and refrigerate until the ice cream base is cold, at least 12 hours.

Churn the chilled ice cream base in an ice cream maker according to the manufacturer's instructions. Transfer the ice cream to a container, cover, and store in the freezer. The ice cream will keep for up to 2 weeks.

honeyed lemon *and* orange curd ❧

Almost ethereal in texture, this dish combines the vibrant flavors of orange and lemon with the sweet softness of honey. I spread it on toast or biscuits in the morning, or serve it as a dip for fresh berries. **MAKES ABOUT 1 PINT**

¼ cup cold unsalted butter, cut into small pieces

⅓ cup honey

4 egg yolks

2 whole eggs

⅓ cup freshly squeezed orange juice

⅓ cup freshly squeezed lemon juice

2 teaspoons finely grated orange zest

1 teaspoon finely grated lemon zest

Bring 2 inches of water to a simmer in the bottom of a double boiler or in a saucepan. In a bowl (use a heatproof bowl if you're heating the water in a saucepan), cream the butter and honey with a wooden spoon until light and fluffy. Beat in the egg yolks and whole eggs. Whisk in the orange juice and lemon juice, followed by the orange zest and lemon zest, then pour the mixture into the top of the double boiler or set the bowl over the saucepan. Cook, stirring constantly, until the mixture thickens and becomes jellylike, about 5 minutes.

Strain the curd through a fine-mesh sieve set over a bowl to remove bits of egg and citrus zest, then spoon the curd into a jar. Close the lid tightly and transfer the jar to the refrigerator, where the curd will keep for about a week.

concord grape sorbet *with* rosemary *and* black pepper ❧

I look forward to the few weeks of late summer when grapes hang heavy on their vines and arrive at the market in boxes. Of all the table grapes, the Concord grape is the one I cherish most. I buy them by the case in the few weeks they're available, using what I can for jams, sorbets, and pies. The rest I freeze and use throughout the winter.

The flavor of a Concord grape swirls on your tongue, slowly releasing its notes one by one. At first there's a sweetness that lingers before giving way to a faintly bitter inkiness. Rosemary, at once both herbal and floral, elevates the flavor of grape, while black pepper enhances its spiciness. I like them together, with honey, in this sweet and simple sorbet. MAKES ABOUT 1 QUART

2¹⁄₂ pounds Concord grapes, stems removed

¹⁄₂ cup honey

2 large sprigs rosemary

2 tablespoons whole black peppercorns

Toss the grapes into a food processor and process them for 45 to 60 seconds, until they form 3 to 4 cups of a coarse and lumpy, vibrantly purple slurry. If your food processor is small, work in small batches until you've processed all the grapes.

Transfer the puree to a saucepan, pour in the honey, and drop in the rosemary and black peppercorns. Simmer the mixture over medium-low heat for 15 to 20 minutes, until slightly thickened and deeply fragrant.

Set a fine-mesh sieve over a large bowl and pour the puree into the sieve, straining out the grape seeds, rosemary, and peppercorns. Cover the bowl and transfer it to the refrigerator. Allow the puree to chill for at least 12 hours.

Churn the puree in an ice cream maker according to the manufacturer's instructions. Spoon the sorbet into a container, cover tightly, and store it in the freezer. It will keep for up to 2 weeks.

chapter eight

from the larder

GARDENS ARE NOT THINGS OF MODERATION. In my garden, there exists either plenitude or emptiness. After lying dormant all winter long under billows of snow, my garden bursts forth in the spring with an abundance of radishes and herbs—far more than my little family can eat. As spring warms to summer and then summer to fall, the cabbages, beets, and turnips we planted earlier grow ready for the harvest, then my kitchen overflows with vegetables. We eat what we can, we give away bags of vegetables and herbs to neighbors and friends, and the rest we preserve for the cold months, when the garden sleeps until the next spring.

I do my best when the harvest arrives to pack away as much as I can for the cold days, infusing herbs and flower petals in vinegars, oil, or honey to preserve their flavor. I also tend crocks of fermenting vegetables in my kitchen. I fill my old Polish stoneware crocks full of the abundance that arrives in spring, summer, and fall before resting in winter to enjoy what I've put aside. In the spring, when young green shoots appear in the fields, I gather serpentine garlic scapes and pack them into my fermenting crocks, keeping them covered with brine for a few weeks. The crocks sit undisturbed and half-forgotten on my countertop, but within their walls, a transformation occurs as beneficial bacteria pickle and preserve the scapes. Then I transfer the pickled scapes and their brine to glass jars that I store in my refrigerator or root cellar for a year. Later, as spring progresses to summer, stout and bumpy pickling cucumbers take the place of the garlic scapes, and I make traditional sour pickles. Sauerkraut, sauerruben, and fermented beets come later, during the autumn, when cold-hardy vegetables appear at our farmers market.

Less cumbersome than canning, these methods of preserving foods with oil, vinegar, honey, or fermentation provide a rhythmic sense of simplicity to manage an abundant harvest.

Salt, Time, and the Art of Fermentation

Fermentation is a transformative process, yielding complex flavors but requiring so little. Time and salt are all you need to transform a sturdy head of cabbage into a crock of sharp and ripe sauerkraut, or to transform a sweet cucumber into a sour pickle. Fermentation calls to me on a basic and deep level, and as I shred, pound, and salt my way through a case of beets for rossel or turnips for sauerruben, I'm reminded that not too long ago, my great-great-grandmother would have done the same.

In the summer and autumn, I buy vegetables by the case from growers in my area. I buy the ugly, the dirty, the warped, and the vegetables gnawed on and scarred by rodents in the field. These visually unappealing beets and turnips, carrots and cabbages typically cost less, especially when purchased by the case. Once shredded, salted, and packed away into the crocks and jars that line my kitchen counter, all the vegetables look the same, and nothing's gone to waste.

Preserving summer's harvest for winter's use is something best done in the company of friends. A century ago, whole communities of family and friends would glean the fields, then salt their way through bushels of cabbage, packing it into casks and barrels. Then, in the dark and cold days when nothing green comes from the cold earth, they'd open up the barrels and feed themselves until the days grew warm again.

I pick up my own cases of root vegetables and cabbages at the farmers market, carting them home in an overburdened, rusted wagon. Upon arriving home, I sort through them, picking away the stray dirt and straw. I sort anything I plan to pickle whole—like beets, cucumbers, or peppers—by size. Invariably overwhelmed by the task that lies ahead, I call a friend. We open a bottle of wine and begin chopping, shredding, and salting our way through mountains of vegetables. Then we open another bottle of wine. What we put by in our crocks and jars will last all winter long, and can last for years longer in cold storage. With the work done in summer and autumn, making dinner in winter becomes easier.

Like canning, fermentation preserves the harvest, but unlike canning, it also preserves the vegetables' nutrients. Moreover, it enhances them. Fermentation employs the labor of tiny microbes like lactobacillus bacteria, which eat away at the sugar in foods, transforming it into lactic acid that then, in turn, acts as a natural and beneficial preservative. As the beneficial bacteria consume the sugar, they also produce B vitamins, further enhancing the nutritional content of the vegetable, fruit, grain, or milk you're fermenting.

The process of fermentation creates an environment in which beneficial bacteria happily and readily multiply, but in which potentially harmful bacteria are kept at bay, quickly outnumbered by their friendlier cousins. As a result of this process, fermented foods are also extraordinarily rich in probiotics; that is, you not only consume the food, including its existing and enhanced micronutrients, but also the bacteria themselves. These bacteria then help to populate your gut and support your immune system.

How to Ferment Vegetables Safely

There exists a fine line between fermentation and rot; both transform foods through the action of microscopic organisms. One is strategic, and the other is not; one is beneficial, and the other is not. I like to say that I intentionally let foods rot in my kitchen, but this isn't entirely accurate; rather, I nurture the strategic growth of beneficial bacteria in my family's foods through good practices, and in this way I produce traditionally fermented foods with deeply complex flavor that nurture the health of my family rather than threaten it. For this reason, it's critical to approach fermentation with a clear understanding of the process and a mind for good practices; at the same time, you needn't approach fermentation too dogmatically lest you lose the love and artistry of preparing these old-world, time-honored foods. Properly fermented foods do not pose a risk of foodborne illness; rather, the bacteria they contain supports health.

Keep Vegetables Submerged in Brine

To ferment vegetables properly, you must submerge them completely in liquid. The liquid will keep potentially harmful microorganisms at bay while allowing beneficial bacteria to proliferate. If the vegetables creep up over the brine or float in the liquid, mold can begin to grow. If the mold is not dutifully removed, it will create a thickened cap and send stringy shoots down into the vegetables that remain submerged in brine, contaminating them, too. Further, the growth of mold can also change the acidity of the liquid, leaving it open to contamination by potentially harmful bacteria.

You can create a brine for your fermented vegetables in two ways. Ferments of shredded vegetables like cabbage for sauerkraut or turnips for sauerruben will create their own brine. As you shred, salt, and knead them by hand, the shredded vegetables will release their juices. Those juices, in turn, combine with the salt to create a brine. As you pack the salted vegetables into the jar, they'll release more juice, and the juice will eventually submerge the vegetables. By contrast, pickled whole vegetables need a separate brine. To prepare them, place the whole vegetables into a jar or crock with any spices or flavorings that you like. In a separate bowl, whisk together the salt and water called for in the recipe, and pour that liquid over the vegetables.

If your vegetables begin to float and breech the surface of the brine, consider weighing them down. Many crocks and jars sold specifically for fermentation also come with a weight designed to keep vegetables submerged as they ferment. You can also use a sterilized stone or a small ramekin or other dish heavy enough to submerge the vegetables but small enough to fit inside the jar or crock.

Ferment Vegetables at Room Temperature

When just beginning to ferment vegetables, newcomers often feel uncomfortable leaving their jars and crocks full of food out on the counter at room temperature for weeks or months on end. Some make the mistake of attempting to ferment their vegetables inside the refrigerator. Temperature plays an important role in successful fermentation; the beneficial bacteria proliferate best at moderate to warm temperatures. Particularly cold temperatures, like those you find in a root cellar or refrigerator, will inhibit the continued growth and reproduction of beneficial bacteria, leaving you with unpalatable salted vegetables instead of pleasantly sour fermented vegetables. These cold temperatures are better suited to preserving your ferments for storage once they reach a flavor that appeals to you.

In warmer months, vegetables and other foods will typically ferment faster. In cooler months, the fermentation process will be slower. As you grow accustomed to the ranging seasonal temperatures of your kitchen, taste and try your ferments so that you gain better knowledge about not only how long it takes for your fermented vegetables to acquire a sourness that appeals to you, but also how long it takes for your ferments to do so from season to season.

Choosing Equipment

Fermentation relies on the proliferation of beneficial bacteria and an environment that is conducive to their growth but not to the growth of other organisms like molds. For this reason, creating an anaerobic environment for your ferments is important, as it reduces the likelihood that stray microbes or molds will contaminate them. I recommend and use crocks and jars with air locks developed specifically for preparing fermented foods. For anyone seriously interested in fermenting foods at home, these specially designed crocks and jars will become a wise investment. Stoneware fermentation crocks are typically deep and heavy. They come with a set of stoneware weights that weight down the vegetables, ensuring they remain submerged in brine as they ferment. Further, there is a high lip or well at the opening of the crock that you fill with water. As you place a lid over the crock and fill the well, you create an anaerobic environment; that is, you allow the carbon dioxide that builds up during fermentation to escape the crock while preventing oxygen from finding its way in. Similarly, glass jars equipped with a wire clamp and rubber seal will create an airtight environment, although they do not allow the carbon dioxide created during fermentation to escape. However, some suppliers equip these jars with an air lock, which resolves the issue of carbon dioxide buildup.

If fermentation interests you but you cannot afford or do not wish to invest in specialized crocks or bulky glass jars, know that you can ferment in something as simple as a mason jar or an empty pickle jar. These jars will not create the anaerobic environment that is optimal for fermentation; however, they represent a practical alternative to expensive equipment. As we ferment vegetables, we encourage the growth of myriad beneficial bacteria, but predominantly the lactobacillus variety. Lactobacillus will proliferate in both anaerobic and aerobic environments. The critical component of fermenting in a jar or crock where airflow might occur is to keep your vegetables completely submerged beneath the brine. You can do this by weighing them down with a purchased glass weight, a sterilized stone, or a plate or other heavy item small enough to fit inside your jar or open crock. These inexpensive methods can produce successful ferments, but due to the exchange of oxygen, they are more likely to become contaminated by stray microbes and molds, necessitating a closer watch than if you were to ferment in a traditional air locked crock. Cover the ferment, watch it closely, and lift off any film that might appear.

Signs of Contamination

Open fermentation systems are more prone to contamination than are fermentation crocks or jars with air locks; however, contamination by stray microbes occurs only very rarely—especially in properly fermented vegetables. If the liquid in your ferment takes on a viscous or slimy texture, if it takes on a pinkish hue (and your vegetables are not pink or red in color), if it smells of mold, or if a cap of mold develops on the vegetables, consider throwing them away. If your vegetables are floating in the brine or otherwise exposed to air and exhibit signs of contamination, consider throwing them away. If a thin film develops on the surface of your brine, simply lift it off with a spoon. A thin film or "bloom" does not typically threaten the health of your ferment nor the health of those that consume it accidentally; however, you should remove it promptly lest it continue to grow.

Ferments sometimes become fizzy or will foam when opened. This typically occurs when you ferment your vegetables in an airtight device that does not allow the carbon dioxide that builds up during fermentation to escape. Fizziness does not pose a risk; however, it can build up over time, compromising the stability and structural integrity of your jar. Burping the jar and immediately resealing it can help to prevent this issue.

Storing Your Ferments

Fermented vegetables will last for several months and can last for a year or longer. You can keep fermented vegetables at room temperature indefinitely; however, they will continue to ferment, growing more and more sour with time. Eventually the texture or flavor will suffer. I allow my vegetables to ferment for several weeks to several months, and once they acquire a strength and sourness that I like, I transfer them to the refrigerator. You can also transfer your ferments to a root cellar, cool basement, or garage where the temperature remains cold without freezing.

spiced sour pickles *with* garlic *and* dill ❦

Real pickles do not acquire their sourness from vinegar; rather, they acquire it with time and the action of beneficial bacteria, which convert sugars naturally present in cucumbers into lactic and acetic acids.

In this dish, cucumbers slowly ferment with flowering dill, bulbs of fragrant garlic, mustard seed, allspice, cloves, and sweet bay to produce a truly traditional sour pickle. Horseradish leaf, rich in tannins, ensures that the pickles remain crisp. If you can't find horseradish leaf at your farmers market and can't grow it, both grape and oak leaves will also work. MAKES ABOUT 1 GALLON

---

4 quarts unwaxed pickling cucumbers (about 4 pounds)

2 heads flowering dill

3 bulbs garlic, cloves peeled and crushed

3 tablespoons Hot Pickling Spice (page 277)

2 bay leaves

1 horseradish leaf

8 cups water

¼ cup finely ground unrefined sea salt

Fill a sink with cold water, plunge the cucumbers into the water, and let soak for 30 minutes.

Remove the cucumbers and gently rub them dry with a kitchen towel, taking care not to bruise the tender fruits. Trim the cucumbers of any bits of blossom or vine that might cling to their ends, because these can lend a bitter flavor to your pickles.

Put the cucumbers, flowering dill, garlic cloves, pickling spice, bay leaves, and horseradish leaf into a gallon-size glass jar or fermentation crock.

Heat the water in a saucepan until it feels neither hot nor cold (98° to 100°F) and pour it into a clean pitcher. Stir the salt into the warm water until it dissolves. Pour this brine over the cucumbers and spices. If any cucumbers float, weigh them down with a small plate or other weight.

Seal the crock or jar and allow the cucumbers to ferment at room temperature for 3 to 4 weeks. Check the crock every few days to ensure that the cucumbers remain submerged in brine. Remove any film that might accumulate on the surface with a spoon and continue to ferment.

Once the pickles have achieved a sourness that appeals to you, usually after 3 to 4 weeks of fermentation, transfer them to the refrigerator, root cellar, or other area of cold storage where they will keep for 6 months or longer.

brine-pickled garlic scapes ⚜

In the spring, the serpentine buds of the garlic plant shoot up beyond its leaves, threatening to flower as they reach for the sun. Farmers typically remove these buds—the garlic scapes—young, so that the plant can send its energy down to its growing bulb instead of skyward. As a result of trimming these buds, farmers and gardeners can produce bulbs of garlic with larger cloves and still have a bit of something to sell until the bulbs come in.

The flavor of a scape is milder, softer, and greener than the robust sharpness of mature garlic cloves, which is why I favor them in this simple pickle. I serve brine-pickled garlic scapes as an appetizer with olives, crackers, and cheeses. MAKES ABOUT 1 QUART

1 pound young garlic scapes, trimmed of any tough or dried-out stems

4 cups water, plus more if needed

2 tablespoons finely ground unrefined sea salt

Pack the garlic scapes tightly into a quart-sized mason jar, taking care not to bruise the tender young flowers.

Create a brine by warming the water in a saucepan until it reaches blood temperature (98° to 100°F), so it feels neither hot nor cold when you touch it. Whisk in the salt until it dissolves and pour the brine over the garlic scapes, taking care to submerge all the scapes. If the scapes are not completely submerged, simply pour in additional water to cover. Weigh down the scapes with a glass weight, sterilized stone, or lid to prevent them from floating in the brine and close the crock, leaving at least 1 inch of headspace to prevent overflow.

Ferment at room temperature for 10 to 14 days, then taste the scapes to see if they've acquired the level of sourness you like. If you prefer a sourer or more complex flavor, continue fermenting—testing every 3 to 5 days—until done to your liking. Transfer to cold storage such as a refrigerator, cool basement, or root cellar and use within 1 year.

brine-pickled swiss chard stems ✿

I use every bit of every vegetable when I can. Instead of throwing away Swiss chard stems, which can be tough, I prefer to pickle them. Mild on their own, the chard stems take on the flavor of the spices you add to your brine. I serve them as a side dish, as you would a cucumber pickle, or I finely chop them to make a relish. MAKES ABOUT 1 QUART

1 pound Swiss chard stems

4 cups water

2 tablespoons finely ground unrefined sea salt

¼ cup Hot Pickling Spice (page 277)

2 bay leaves

Trim the stems of any bits of leaf still clinging to them. Cut the stems to a length to match the depth of your fermentation jar or crock, then arrange them tightly inside.

Heat the water in a saucepan until it reaches blood temperature (98° to 100°F), so it feels neither hot nor cold when you touch it. Whisk the salt into the warm water until it dissolves, then stir in the pickling spice and bay leaves. Pour the liquid over your chard stems so that the stems are completely submerged in the brine. If the stems float, weigh them down with a glass weight or a sterilized stone.

Close the crock and allow the Swiss chard stems to ferment for 3 to 4 weeks. Taste them from time to time, and when they become sour enough for your liking, transfer them to the refrigerator where they should keep 6 months or longer.

brine-pickled radishes *with* mustard seed *and* allspice ❧

Vegetables from my garden seem to be ready all at once. They seem to spring from seed to sprout, and sprout to harvest in an instant, and that's especially true of radishes, which can grow their plump, spicy bulbs in just 3 weeks' time. When vegetables arrive in abundance, I invariably turn to fermentation—pickling them in a spice-filled brine.

Choose tender-skinned, young radishes for pickling. Their vibrant colors will bleed into the brine, coloring it a very faint pink that children always seem to enjoy. MAKES ABOUT 2 QUARTS

2 pounds mixed radishes, such as French Breakfast, Icicle, or Cherry Belle

3 tablespoons Sweet Pickling Spice (page 277)

1 teaspoon allspice berries

1 teaspoon mustard seed

2 bay leaves

About 6 cups water, plus more if needed

2 tablespoons finely ground unrefined sea salt

Trim the radishes by removing their root tips and any greens. Chop the radishes into bite-sized pieces about 1/2 inch thick if they're large, and leave them whole if they're not. Put the radishes in a 2-quart fermentation crock. Pour the pickling spice, allspice, and mustard seed over the radishes, and drop in the bay leaves.

Heat the water in a saucepan until it reaches blood temperature (98° to 100°F), so it feels neither hot nor cold when you touch it. Whisk the salt into the warm water until it dissolves, then pour the brine over the radishes and spices.

Weigh the radishes down if they float and close your fermentation crock, taking care to leave at least 1 inch of headspace. Ferment at room temperature for at least 10 and up to 14 days before tasting. If you prefer sourer pickles, continue fermenting the radishes for another week or two. Once they've acquired a flavor to your liking, transfer them to cold storage and eat within about 6 months.

sour collards

Uniquely American, fermented collard greens represent an amalgamation of several cultural influences. Collard greens, related to the cabbage, arrived to the southern United States from Africa during the slave trade. It grew well, providing food in autumn and winter when little else grew. Later, German and Austrian immigrants began to arrive, and many of them found new homes in the South. Collard greens, unlike the cabbages of their homeland, grew rapidly and easily in the warmth of the South. Eventually, the immigrants, hungry for the foods of their homeland, replaced cabbage with collards in traditional sauerkraut, giving birth to this dish of slow-fermented collard greens. MAKES ABOUT 1 QUART

---

5 bunches (about 2 pounds) collard greens

2 tablespoons finely ground unrefined sea salt

Trim the collards of any tough stems or veins, then stack them one on top of another. Roll them together like a cigar and slice them crosswise into strips about 1/8 inch thick.

Toss the collards in a large mixing bowl and sprinkle them with the salt. Let them rest in the salt for about 5 minutes, then begin kneading the greens and salt together by hand to break down the cell walls of the greens. Continue kneading and squeezing the greens for about 5 minutes, until the shreds of collards soften and go limp in your fingertips. Spoon them into a quart-sized jar or fermentation crock. Layer by layer, tightly pack the collards into the jar so that any air bubbles escape and the greens begin to release their juice.

When you've packed all the collards into the jar, press them down firmly so that all of their juice rises to the top and the collards are completely submerged. Weigh them down with a glass weight or sterilized stone to prevent them from floating, then seal the crock and ferment the greens at room temperature for at least 6 weeks.

After 6 weeks, taste the collards; if they've achieved the level of sourness you like, transfer them to the fridge. If they're not quite sour enough for your liking, continue fermenting them at room temperature, testing every week until you like their flavor. Store the fermented collards in the fridge for up to 6 months.

horseradish, apple, *and* beetroot relish

When summer turns to autumn, I harvest the beets and horseradish from my garden, plucking them from the earth, shaking off the soil, and readying them for this relish that combines the sweetness of apples and beets with horseradish's bite. This apple and beetroot relish pairs well with meats like Coriander-Crusted Elk Backstrap (page 221). As with all fermented foods, the relish should not be exposed to air during the fermentation process. Keep the relish submerged beneath the brine to ensure that beneficial bacteria proliferate while opportunistic microorganisms are kept at bay. A good-quality fermentation jar or crock, equipped with a weight, helps to ensure proper fermentation takes place. MAKES ABOUT 1 QUART

2 pounds apples, cored and cut into large chunks

2¹/₂ pounds beets, peeled and cut into large chunks

1 pound horseradish, peeled and cut into large chunks

2 tablespoons finely ground unrefined sea salt, plus more as needed

Working in batches, shred the apples, beets, and horseradish in a food processor fitted with the shredding disk. The volatile oils in horseradish can irritate your eyes and lungs, so take care to open the food processor in a well-ventilated area. Transfer the shreds to a large mixing bowl, stir in the salt, and knead for about 3 minutes to break up the fruit and roots.

Cup by cup, transfer the mixture to a quart-size crock and pound it down with a wooden dowel or spoon until it releases its juice. The juice, once released, combines with the sea salt to create a brine. Continue packing the crock until the roots and apple mixture are exhausted and the brine created by the juice and salt completely submerges the relish. Seal the crock and place it in a warm spot in your kitchen where it will ferment. Check the crock periodically to ensure that the relish remains submerged in brine. If it does not remain submerged, whisk 1 teaspoon of unrefined sea salt into 1 cup of water and pour this over your relish.

After about 10 days, taste the relish. If you prefer a sourer flavor, let it ferment 5 to 7 days further. Transfer the relish to the refrigerator or other cold storage when it has reached a flavor to your liking. The relish should keep for 6 months or longer.

fennel, kohlrabi, *and* green apple relish ✳

In August, apples make their first appearance in the mountains. It's about this time that the year's first kohlrabi are ready for picking, while the last of the summer's fennel still lingers in the field. I like all three together, fermented into a sauerkraut-like relish with a subtle hint of apple and a potent licorice-like kick of fennel. I typically use tiny green apples—about the size of a golf ball—from the mystery tree in my farmer's front yard, but any green apple will do nicely. MAKES ABOUT 1 QUART

6 kohlrabi

6 fennel bulbs with fronds

2 small green apples (about 8 ounces), cored and finely chopped

3¹/₂ teaspoons finely ground unrefined sea salt

Trim the kohlrabi of their leaves and stems, then peel them. Slice them thinly into matchsticks about 2 inches long by ¹/₈ inch thick. Place them in a large mixing bowl.

Remove and discard the long stalks of the fennel bulbs, but reserve about ¹/₂ cup of loosely packed fronds. Chop the fronds finely, and then slice the fennel bulbs no thicker than ¹/₈ inch. Add the sliced bulbs and chopped fronds to the bowl with the kohlrabi.

Toss the apples and salt into the bowl and knead the ingredients with your hands until they release their juice. Layer the mixture into a quart-sized fermentation crock, 1 cup at a time. Pack it tightly into the crock so that any air escapes and the ingredients release more of their juice. Continue packing and layering until you've added the entire contents of the mixing bowl to the crock. Pack down the ingredients once more to ensure that they are completely submerged in the brine and that the brine rests below the lip of the crock by at least 1 inch.

Close the crock and ferment at room temerature for 10 to 14 days before tasting. If you prefer a stronger or sourer flavor, continue fermenting until done to your liking, testing every 3 to 5 days. Transfer to the refrigerator, root cellar, or other place of cold storage once the relish achieves the level of sourness you prefer and use within 6 months.

sauerkraut

I make sauerkraut several times a year, as cabbages grow readily in the high and cold mountains. In warmer climates, cabbages are a cool-weather crop; but in my area, all months are cool-weather months, and some are downright frigid. We plant a few heads of cabbage in our community garden and have successfully planted a few dwarf varieties in large clay pots on our patios. They grow all summer long, enjoying the cool mountain air. I also buy cabbages by the case and implore friends to visit my home for sauerkraut making parties. We shred, salt, and pack our way through 50 pounds of cabbage in an hour or two, and it gives us an opportunity to connect, learn from one another, and enjoy each other's companionship.

While it does not matter what kind of cabbage you use to make sauerkraut (red cabbage, Napa cabbage, green cabbage, and other varieties all work well), the freshness of the cabbage you choose matters a great deal. Fresh cabbage is juicier than cabbage stored for a long time, and that juice is critical in making the brine that helps to create optimal conditions for fermenting cabbage. Similarly, do not begin cutting and slicing into your cabbage, then leave it in the refrigerator with the intention of returning to it later, because those cuts will seal up, the cabbage will dry out, and it will not produce the ample brine needed for proper fermentation.

MAKES ABOUT 2 QUARTS

---

5 pounds cabbage

2 tablespoons finely ground unrefined sea salt

Remove the tough outer leaves of the cabbage. Slice each cabbage into quarters and cut out the tough core that can reach from the cabbage's base to its center. Slice the cabbage quarters into ribbons about $1/16$ inch thick. The thinner you slice the cabbage, the more readily it will ferment.

Toss the sliced cabbage and salt in a large mixing bowl. Leave the cabbage to macerate for 5 minutes, or until it softens and begins to release its juice. Knead the salt into the cabbage for 5 minutes to break down the cell walls of the cabbage and allow it to further release its juice.

Layer the salted cabbage about 1 cup at a time into your fermentation crock, taking care to pack it very tightly as you add more. As you pack the cabbage, the juice it releases should rise up and cover it. Pour any juice remaining in your mixing bowl into the crock and weigh down the cabbage with a glass weight or a sterilized stone to prevent any shreds from floating at the surface of the brine.

Seal your crock tightly and allow it to ferment at room temperature for at least 6 weeks before opening the crock to taste the sauerkraut. If you prefer a stronger sourness, like I do, allow the cabbage to continue fermenting until it reaches a sourness you prefer. Test it every week or so until done to your liking. For me, this means leaving my cabbage to ferment for at least 3 months and often longer, until it acquires the potent sourness that appeals to me. Once your sauerkraut achieves the flavor you like, transfer it to smaller jars and store them in the refrigerator or root cellar for up to 9 months.

sauerruben *with* caraway

The first turnips of the season arrive in spring, tied in little bundles like you might find radishes. They're little, pale salad turnips—a mild Japanese variety well loved by specialty growers at farmers markets. Later in the season, the larger old-fashioned purple-topped turnips arrive.

Early in the year, I implore my CSA farmers and the growers at our farmers market to grow a patch of turnips just for me. They wait for the first frost, which sweetens the turnips' bracing bitterness, and bring them to my doorstep in large cardboard boxes. I enlist my husband, my son, and my friends to help me chop, shred, and salt my way through the boxes, and in a few months, we share the sauerruben. It is a forthright food, strong and assertive, pairing well with roasted meats and hearty whole grain breads. MAKES ABOUT 2 QUARTS

---

5 pounds turnips

2 tablespoons caraway seeds

2 tablespoons finely ground unrefined sea salt

Cut away the leaves and root tip from each turnip. Rub the turnips vigorously with a kitchen towel to remove any dirt that might cling to their skin, then shred them coarsely, either with a box grater or in a food processor fitted with the shredding disk.

Toss the shredded turnips, caraway, and salt in a large mixing bowl. Let the mixture rest for 5 minutes to allow the salt to begin its work of extracting the juice from the turnips. Knead the ingredients by hand until the turnips are juicy and limp, 3 to 5 minutes. Working with about 1 cup at a time, layer the turnips in your fermentation crock, packing them tightly so that the brine created by the juice and salt completely covers the shreds. Weigh down the turnips with a glass weight or sterilized stone to prevent any bits from floating to the surface, seal, and ferment at room temperature for at least 6 weeks before tasting.

If you prefer a stronger sourness, allow the turnips to continue fermenting, tasting them every week or so, until done to your liking. I like to ferment my turnips for 3 months, which increases their acidity and reduces their bitterness. Transfer the sauerruben to the refrigerator or root cellar, where it should keep for 9 months.

sweet pickling spice ❧

You can find pickling spice in the spice section of most well-stocked grocery stores, but I prefer to make my own, adjusting the spices to better suit the flavors in the recipe. Radishes, turnips, and beets benefit from sweet spices, while cucumbers and kohlrabi often benefit from hotter flavors.

MAKES ABOUT 1/2 CUP

2 tablespoons mustard seeds

2 tablespoons allspice berries

2 tablespoons coriander seeds

2 tablespoons whole black peppercorns

2 teaspoons whole cloves

1 teaspoon ground ginger

2 cinnamon sticks, broken up into small pieces

2 dried bay leaves, crumbled

Spoon all the spices into a small mixing bowl, stir to combine, and store in an airtight container for up to 1 year.

Variation

Hot Pickling Spice: Make the Sweet Pickling Spice, then stir in 1 tablespoon crushed red pepper flakes. Store in an airtight container for up to 1 year.

preserved lemons ❦

Fermentation tempers the distinct sourness of lemons and infuses them with a pleasant saltiness. As the lemons ferment, the rinds soften and become edible. Meyer lemons, with their thin rind, are particularly well suited to fermentation. MAKES ABOUT 2 QUARTS

5 pounds Meyer lemons

Finely ground unrefined sea salt

Slice the nubs off the ends of each lemon, then slice the lemon lengthwise as if to quarter it, but leave one end intact. Let the lemon open in the palm of your hand like a flower and sprinkle $^1/_8$ teaspoon of salt into its center. Place the lemon in a 2-quart jar or fermentation crock, then continue slicing and salting more lemons until you've placed enough in your crock to cover the bottom with a single layer.

Take a wooden spoon or masher and press the lemons down to pack them tightly, then continue slicing, salting, layering, and packing lemons until no more remain. Pack the lemons tightly once more, making sure that they are completely submerged in their brine, weighing them down with a glass weight or sterilized stone if necessary. Seal the crock, place it out of direct sunlight, and allow the lemons to ferment at room temperature for 8 weeks.

After 8 weeks, open up the crock and taste a lemon. Properly preserved lemons taste salty and softly sour without the abrupt tartness of fresh lemons, with no residual bitterness in the rind. If the rind is still bitter, reseal the crock and continue fermenting them for another week or two before tasting them again. When fermented to your liking, transfer the lemons to the fridge. They'll keep for 2 years.

Herb Oil and Herb Vinegar

In the summer, I like to make herb oil by steeping fresh herbs in extra-virgin olive oil. Herbs arrive in huge bunches from my family's favorite growers, and I always buy as many fresh herbs as I can to preserve for long storage by drying or by making herbal oils and vinegars.

Herbs release their volatile oils and their flavors into the oil or vinegar, and in that way you can preserve the flavor of spring's chive blossoms or summer's flowering oregano long past the close of the season. Use them as you would any oil or vinegar, as a seasoning for salads or as a finishing touch for side dishes and main courses.

herb-infused oil ❄

I preserve spring and summer's bounty of fresh herbs by making a variety of herb-infused oils. Sturdy herbs such as thyme and rosemary work best, but even more delicate, leafy herbs like basil and mint do well for infusing into olive oil. Later in the year, when herbs have abandoned the garden, pull out a bottle of herb-infused oil to add fresh herbal flavor and aroma to salads and all types of dishes. MAKES ABOUT 2 CUPS

Handful of fresh herbs

2 cups extra-virgin olive oil

Rinse the herbs well, removing any dried out, bruised, or wilted leaves and stems. Pat them dry and stuff them into a pint-sized jar. Cover them with the olive oil and set the jar in a window. Every day for 4 to 6 weeks, shake the jar and return it to the windowsill. The longer the herbs steep in the oil, the stronger the herbal flavor will become. Taste the oil after 4 weeks, and if you prefer a stronger flavor, allow the herbs to continue steeping in the oil for 2 weeks longer.

After 4 to 6 weeks, line a fine-mesh sieve with a piece of cheesecloth and set it over a bowl. Open the jar and pour the herbs and oil into the sieve. Discard the herbs and pour the oil into a clean jar. Store the jar in a cool, dark place and use the oil within 9 months.

herbal vinegar ❧

Vinegar, like oil, absorbs the flavor of fresh herbs with time. Herbal vinegars, like herb-infused oil, help to preserve the vibrant flavor of springtime herbs. Use herbal vinegar as a replacement for apple cider vinegar or wine vinegar in your salads, where they can impart not only their acidity but also the distinct flavor of the herbs you used in the preparation. Thyme, chive blossoms, and rosemary work well. MAKES ABOUT 2 CUPS

Handful of fresh herbs

2 cups apple cider vinegar or red or white wine vinegar

Rinse the herbs well, removing any bruised or wilted leaves and stems. Pat them dry and stuff them into a pint-sized jar. Pour in the vinegar, tighten the jar's cap, and set it in a window. Every day for 2 to 4 weeks, shake the jar and return it to the windowsill. After 2 weeks, taste the vinegar, and if you prefer a stronger herbal flavor, allow it to continue sitting on your windowsill a week or two longer, or until it develops the strength of flavor that appeals to you.

Line a fine-mesh sieve with a piece of cheesecloth and set it over a bowl. Open the jar and pour the herbs and vinegar into the sieve. Discard the herbs and pour the flavored vinegar into a clean jar. Store the jar in a cool, dark place and use the vinegar within 6 months.

garden blossom honey

Spring brings the sweetest and softest scents to our valley, of lilacs blooming in good years, of violets and lavender in little pots, of chamomile and mint in gardens, and of wildflowers along the mountainside. While their fleeting aroma may be difficult to notice when the doldrums and routine of life distract the mind, it exists for those who take the time to step outside, venture into a garden or park, and breathe deep. I capture that light and lovely perfume of spring by gathering edible flowers into a little jar and covering them with honey's sticky sweetness. Steeped for a few weeks, the flowers release their aroma and flavor into the honey, preserving the perfume of spring indefinitely.

While I prefer rose, violet, chamomile, and lavender for my blossom-infused honeys, any edible flower works well, so use what blooms in your garden. Lilac releases a lovely citrus note to honey, while borage tastes of cucumber and nasturtium infuses the honey with the spicy notes of black pepper. Take care to choose only unsprayed flowers, and make sure they're completely dry before placing them in honey, as wet petals may leave the honey prone to mold. MAKES ABOUT 2 CUPS

1 tablespoon rose petals

1 tablespoon violets

1 tablespoon chamomile flowers

1 tablespoon lavender flowers

2 cups mild-flavored honey, such as clover honey

Put the flowers in a pint-size glass jar with a tight-fitting lid. Pour the honey over them and tighten the lid. Set the jar in a sunny window and leave it there for 2 weeks, turning the jar every few days as the flowers tend to float to the top of the honey.

After 2 weeks, transfer the honey to your cupboard and use in any recipe that calls for honey. You may leave the flowers in the honey or you may strain the honey to remove the petals if you prefer a smoother consistency.

Fermented Beverages and Tonics

Beyond naturally fermented relishes and pickles exists a world of naturally fermented beverages, homemade sodas, and tonics. Blessedly easy to prepare, fermented drinks and tonics typically require little more effort than making sweetened teas or herbal infusions and letting them sit until the beneficial bacteria and naturally occurring yeasts do their work. In the span of a few days to a few weeks, the fermentation transforms the original drink into something decidedly more complex.

These drinks and tonics balance a natural sweetness with the characteristic tartness acquired through fermentation as beneficial microorganisms break down the sugars present in the sweetened drinks and transform them into various acids. Fermented drinks, like other fermented foods, are also rich in beneficial bacteria as well as B vitamins. They may contain a small amount of alcohol, typically less than 1 percent, which is a byproduct of fermentation. If you're new to fermented foods and fermented drinks, it's best to begin consuming only small amounts at first, as they may upset your stomach if you're unaccustomed to foods rich in beneficial bacteria.

When I prepare fermented beverages for my family, I use filtered water, as the chemicals added to municipal water may adversely affect the proliferation of beneficial microorganisms or adversely affect the flavor of the tonics. If you live in rural area, spring or well water also works well.

water kefir

Water kefir is a light lemon-flavored fermented tonic that can serve as the base for other fermented drinks. It offers a mild sweetness coupled with a pleasant but light sourness owing both to the lemon it contains and to the fermentation process itself. Its mild flavor is particularly well liked by young children, and they often enjoy the brewing process itself, as the tiny translucent, gelatinous grains rise and fall as they release carbon dioxide during the fermentation. You can find water kefir grains online, or see the Resources section on page 300. MAKES ABOUT 1 QUART

4 cups water, preferably filtered

¼ cup unrefined cane sugar

¼ cup water kefir grains

1 lemon, halved

2 unsulphured dried Mission or Calimyrna figs, halved

Bring the water to a boil. Pour the boiling water into a pitcher and stir in the sugar until it dissolves. Let the sugar water cool on the countertop until it reaches room temperature, 68° to 72°F.

Spoon the water kefir grains into a 2-quart mason jar or glass canister. Pour the sweetened water over them and then drop in the lemon halves and halved figs. Cover and allow to ferment for 2 to 3 days. The water kefir will ferment faster in warm kitchens and more slowly in cool kitchens. You'll know your brew is finished when the dried figs rise to the top of the jar and float with the lemons.

Strain the water kefir through a fine-mesh sieve and into another pitcher, reserving the water kefir grains for future batches but discarding the lemon and figs. You can enjoy the water kefir right away or transfer it to bottles and store it in the refrigerator for up to 3 weeks. After this initial fermentation, the water kefir will taste mildly sweet and tart and will be flat. To develop a fizzy water kefir, flavor it and follow the instructions on page 288.

(The grains are ready to immediately brew another batch of water kefir, or they may be stored in about ½ cup of water in the refrigerator for up to 1 week. Take care to prepare another batch of water kefir at least once a week to maintain the health and vibrancy of your water kefir grains, because the act of brewing water kefir supports the health and growth of the microorganisms that make up the grains.)

kombucha

At once both sour and sweet, with a delightful fizz, kombucha is an enigmatic tonic. It relies upon the action of a complex matrix of bacteria and yeasts that exist together in one gelatinous, somewhat stringy disc. Most accurately, the disc is described as a SCOBY—a symbiotic colony of bacteria and yeasts. However, fermentation lovers and kombucha brewers also refer to it as a mushroom, which it most decidedly is not, or a "mother." I prefer the term "mother," which is less clinical but still fitting, as the kombucha starter will produce miniature versions of itself over time. These kombucha "babies" can then be passed onto friends or neighbors so that they, too, can begin preparing the medicinal tonic.

Kombucha relies on the fermentation of strong, sweet tea. While most brewers favor black tea and white sugar, all varieties of the *Camellia sinensis* plant work well, including green tea, white tea, and oolong tea. Herbal teas, by contrast, do not support the health of the kombucha mother over the long term. MAKES ABOUT 1 QUART

4 cups water, preferably filtered

2 tablespoons loose-leaf Darjeeling or other tea (not herbal tea)

¼ cup white granulated sugar

¼ cup kombucha tea with live active cultures, brewed from a previous batch or purchased

1 kombucha mother

Bring the water to a boil if using black tea, to 180°F for oolong, to 175°F for green tea, or to 165°F for white tea. Drop the tea and sugar into a pitcher. Pour the hot water over the tea leaves and sugar, stirring until the sugar dissolves; let steep for 3 minutes if using black tea, 2 minutes for green tea, or 1 minute for white tea. Pour the sweetened tea through a fine-mesh sieve and into a large mason jar or glass canister and discard the spent tea leaves.

Allow the tea to cool to room temperature, 68° to 72°F. Stir in the brewed kombucha tea and drop the kombucha mother into the jar. Cover the jar loosely with a piece of cheesecloth and secure it to the jar with a length of kitchen twine. Allow the tea to ferment for 7 days at room temperature. Kombucha completes its brewing cycle when a new layer develops above and separates from the kombucha mother. Taste the kombucha, and if you prefer a sourer brew, continue fermenting, tasting every few days, until it achieves the flavor you like.

Once the kombucha acquires the flavor and strength that suits you, gently lift the mother from the jar and set it in a bowl with ¼ cup of the finished tea. Pour the remaining finished kombucha tea into jars or bottles. You can enjoy the kombucha right away. After this initial fermentation, the kombucha will be flat. To develop a fizzy or flavored kombucha, follow the instructions on page 288.

Now that your first batch of kombucha is finished, you can prepare a second batch using the reserved mother and the reserved kombucha tea. If you're not ready to prepare another batch of kombucha quite yet, place the reserved kombucha mother into a clean quart-size glass jar, add brewed kombucha tea to cover, and place a lid loosely on top. The mother will store for 30 days or longer at room temperature, and you can remove it from the jar at any time to brew another batch of kombucha tea.

How to Flavor Kombucha and Water Kefir

While I often enjoy both water kefir and kombucha after an initial fermentation, they both benefit from a secondary fermentation, a process that can infuse them with flavor and develop the bubbles and fizz so desirable in fermented tonics and homemade sodas. In their initial period of fermentation, water kefir and kombucha are brewed in a large jar with the kefir grains or kombucha mother. By contrast, the optional secondary fermentation process ferments the strained water kefir or kombucha once more, this time with the intention of increasing its flavor and developing carbon dioxide so that the tonic fizzes when opened. For a successful secondary fermentation, a new source of sugar must be added in the form of fruit juice, sugar, honey, or other natural sweetener. The carbohydrates support continued fermentation and the proliferation of microorganisms in the final brew. MAKES ABOUT 1 QUART

> Scant 4 cups Water Kefir (page 285) or Kombucha (page 286)
>
> ¼ cup fruit juice or 1 tablespoon natural sweetener
>
> Spices, as desired

Pour the freshly prepared water kefir or kombucha into a pitcher. Stir in the fruit juice or sugar, then pour the mixture into pint-size flip-top bottles, leaving at least 1 inch of headspace. Drop in any spices that suit you, close tightly, and allow to ferment at room temperature. Let water kefir ferment for up to 18 hours; allow kombucha to ferment for 3 days. Transfer to the refrigerator and chill completely to set the carbonation.

Open your bottles carefully over the sink, as the contents of the bottles are under pressure, and they may fizz and foam when you break the bottle's seal. Serve over ice.

APPLE SPICE KOMBUCHA

> 4 cups kombucha
>
> ¼ cup apple juice
>
> 2 cinnamon sticks
>
> 1 teaspoon whole cloves
>
> 1 teaspoon allspice berries

POMEGRANATE KOMBUCHA

> 4 cups kombucha
>
> ¼ cup pomegranate juice

GRAPE WATER KEFIR

> 4 cups water kefir
>
> ¼ cup Concord grape juice

SOUR CHERRY WATER KEFIR

> 4 cups water kefir
>
> ¼ cup sour cherry juice

wild yeast *and* ginger starter *for* homemade sodas ❦

Traditional fermented sodas need a starter—beneficial bacteria and wild yeasts that help to convert sugars into acids and, more importantly, generate the carbon dioxide that gives these sodas their natural bubbles. Much like I keep a jar of sourdough starter, feeding it weekly and dipping into it as I need, I also keep a pint-sized jar of a yeasty ginger brew fermenting on my kitchen counter for our homemade sodas and herbal tonics. The combination of ginger and sugar provides a happy home to wild strains of yeasts and lactobacillus bacteria that begin to proliferate, bubble, and foam within a few days' time. I add the brew to sweetened herbal infusions, and, about 3 days later, the wild yeasts and native bacteria in the starter will have eaten most of the sugar in the herbal infusion, leaving it less sweet and somewhat tart, with a delightful fizz. **MAKES ABOUT 1³/₄ CUPS**

Fresh ginger

Unrefined cane sugar

Water, preferably filtered

Break off a knob of ginger that's about 2 inches long and ¹/₂ inch thick. Peel away its skin and grate it until you have 2 heaping tablespoons. Place the grated ginger in a pint-size jar and whisk in 2 tablespoons of unrefined cane sugar and 2 tablespoons of water. Cover the jar with a small square of butter muslin or cheesecloth and secure it tightly to the jar's rim with a length of kitchen twine or a large rubber band. Place the covered jar in a warm spot in your kitchen, a bit out of the way so it won't disturb your normal cooking routine, to ferment.

Every day for at least 5 days, mix an additional 2 tablespoons of grated ginger, 2 tablespoons of sugar, and 2 tablespoons of filtered water into your jar. The ginger will begin to foam and bubble at its top and will develop the yeasty aroma of beer. After 5 days, it should be ready to use as a starter culture for homemade sodas and probiotic herbal tonics; however, if you see no signs of fermentation—no bubbles, no foam, or no yeasty and faintly sour aroma—continue feeding it until it develops these characteristics.

continued

wild yeast and ginger starter for homemade sodas, *continued*

To store the wild yeast and ginger starter for long-term use, tightly cover the jar and transfer it to the refrigerator. Take care to feed the starter weekly by first removing it from the refrigerator, then mixing in 2 tablespoons of grated ginger, 2 tablespoons of unrefined sugar, and 2 tablespoons of water. Let it sit on the counter for 1 to 2 hours after a feeding, then return it to the refrigerator.

When using the wild yeast and ginger starter to prepare homemade sodas and probiotic tonics, remember to replace the amount of starter you remove with an equal amount of fresh ginger and sugar slurry; that is, if you remove ¼ cup starter to prepare a homemade soda or tonic, whisk together enough grated ginger, sugar, and water to replace the amount you removed.

Well kept and routinely fed, your ginger bug will last indefinitely.

vanilla mint soda

I enjoy an irrational love of mint, growing five or six varieties each summer in worn and cracked terra-cotta pots on the deck outside my bedroom. I grow the well-known mints, of course, spearmint and peppermint, but I favor the lesser known and more unusual mints—apple mint with its large, serrated leaves; chocolate mint; dotted mint; and soft-leafed mountain mint with its strikingly medicinal notes.

Vanilla's sweet and floral perfume softens mint's assertiveness without subduing it, and I often pair the two together. In this homemade soda, a third flavor—ginger—punches through with a bit of its soapy heat and gives the soda a little natural fizz and foam. Because the microbes in the wild yeast and ginger starter can proliferate quickly, take care to use flip-top glass bottles that will pop their tops rather than explode if the pressure created by the buildup of carbon dioxide proves too great. MAKES 2 PINT-SIZE BOTTLES

4 cups water, preferably filtered

¼ cup chopped fresh mint

¼ cup white granulated sugar

¼ cup strained Wild Yeast and Ginger Starter for Homemade Sodas (page 289)

2 vanilla beans, split lengthwise

Bring the water to a boil. Put the mint into a 1½-quart pitcher. Pour the boiling water over the mint and add the sugar. Stir until the sugar completely dissolves. Let the infusion cool until it is comfortable to handle, about 100°F.

Strain the cooled infusion through a fine-mesh sieve and into a second pitcher or jar, then stir in the strained starter.

Drop two vanilla bean halves into each of two pint-size flip-top glass bottles, then pour in enough of the mint infusion to fill the bottles within an inch of their tops, taking care not to over-fill them. Close the bottles and set them aside in a warm spot in your kitchen out of direct sunlight. Allow to ferment at room temperature for 3 to 5 days. The longer the tonic ferments, the less sugar will remain in the final brew. If your kitchen is cool, allow it to ferment longer. Transfer the bottles to the refrigerator and let chill for at least 3 days to allow the cold to help set the bubbles.

Open and serve at your leisure. The soda may fizz and foam when opened, so take care to open it over a sink. It will keep in the fridge for at least 6 months.

spiced ginger beer ❧

Tart and faintly hot, this spiced ginger beer lacks the cloying sweetness of store-bought ginger ales and instead brings an old-world charm as the flavors of ginger, star anise, clove, and allspice hit the palate first, with sweetness a mere afterthought.

Whereas I lean upon herbal infusions and homemade fermented sodas in spring and summer, I rely upon ginger beer in the colder months, when the heat and warmth of its spice can help to brace us against winter's bite. I also drink ginger beer for its medicinal notes. Ginger soothes the belly against upset, nursing away motion sickness and stomach bugs.

MAKES 2 PINT-SIZE BOTTLES

4 cups water, preferably filtered

4 star anise pods

1 teaspoon whole cloves

1 cinnamon stick (about 4 inches)

$1/2$ teaspoon whole white peppercorns

$1/2$ teaspoon allspice berries

1 hand-size piece fresh ginger, peeled and grated

$1/4$ cup unrefined cane sugar

$1/4$ cup strained Wild Yeast and Ginger Starter for Homemade Sodas (page 289)

Combine the water, star anise, cloves, cinnamon, peppercorns, allspice, and grated ginger in a saucepan and bring to a boil. As soon as the water comes to a rolling boil, remove from the heat, cover, and allow the spices to steep for 10 minutes. Strain the spice infusion through a fine-mesh sieve and into a pitcher. Discard the spices and stir the sugar into the infusion until it dissolves entirely. Let the infusion cool on the kitchen counter until it is comfortable to handle, about 100°F. (A cooler temperature will lengthen the fermentation time slightly.)

Stir in the strained starter and pour the mixture into two pint-size flip-top bottles, leaving about 1 inch of headspace in each. Ferment at room temperature, out of direct sunlight, for 3 to 5 days. If you prefer a tarter brew, ferment the ginger beer for up to 1 week. Keep in mind that cool temperatures can slow down fermentation and warm temperatures accelerate them, so you may need to adjust your fermentation time accordingly. After 3 to 5 days, or up to a week if you prefer a stronger ferment, transfer the bottles to the refrigerator for at least 3 days; the cold will set the ginger beer's bubbles. Take care when opening because home-fermented sodas tend to fizz and foam. Serve cold, over ice.

red berry kvass

A traditional fermented tonic of Russian origin, *kvass* tastes both sweet and sour at once, and, like many traditional foods, it varies from season to season, because the makers used bread and grain in winter, apples in autumn, and red berries in summer.

While eating berries out of hand or plunking them into lofty pillows of whipped cream might call to you, if you find an abundance in your kitchen garden or at your farmers market in summertime, take the time to try this simple, old-fashioned berry *kvass*. I prepare it at the peak of summer's heat, when red fruit hangs heavy against the thorny canes of raspberry bushes in our community garden and everbearing strawberry plants that began bursting with berries in spring continue to produce their little red gems until early autumn. The *kvass*'s mild sweetness coupled with a pleasant tartness quenches the thirst after long days in the hot summer sun.

MAKES ABOUT 6 CUPS

8 cups water

1 cup stale sourdough bread crumbs

8 ounces raspberries

8 ounces strawberries

2 tablespoons unrefined cane sugar

1/4 cup strained Wild Yeast and Ginger Starter for Homemade Sodas (page 289)

Bring the water to a boil. Dump the bread crumbs into a large mixing bowl. When the water reaches a boil, pour it over the bread crumbs. Let them soak in the hot water for 4 to 5 hours, until the water cools to room temperature and acquires the flavor and aroma of bread.

Dump the berries into a separate mixing bowl and toss them with the sugar and strained starter. Mash the berries with a fork to break up their structure ever so slightly.

Line a sieve with cheesecloth and set it over a jar or fermentation crock with a wide opening. Strain the water into the crock, pressing on the hydrated bread crumbs with a spoon to release as much liquid as possible. Pour the berries into the crock with the strained liquid, close it tightly, and allow the mixture to ferment for 2 to 3 days in a dark corner of your kitchen, until it acquires a flavor you like. Strain the *kvass* through a fine-mesh sieve lined with cheesecloth or with butter muslin into a pitcher, then pour it into pint-size flip-top bottles. Seal the bottles, transfer to the refrigerator, and consume within 3 months.

beet kvass *with* ginger *and* mandarin ✣

Beet *kvass* tastes of the earth, faintly reminiscent of mineral-rich soil with a mild sweetness that fades to sour as the tonic ferments and ages. Like many traditional foods, beet *kvass*, which is nothing more than the juice of fermented beets, can overwhelm the palate of those unaccustomed to the strong flavors of the Old World. Yet, with time, many people find that they develop a yen for the robust earthiness and sour-sweet flavor of the tonic.

My interest in other homemade sodas and herbal tonics waxes and wanes, but my love of beet *kvass* remains constant. I like to serve it over ice, diluted with sparkling or still mineral water. While I often prepare plain beet *kvass*, I also find that ginger and mandarin oranges temper its earthiness, providing a nice variation. The beet's betacyanin content not only gives beets and this *kvass* their characteristic color, but it also provides potent antioxidants. MAKES ABOUT 6 CUPS

---

¹/₄ cup strained Ginger and Wild Yeast Starter for Homemade Sodas (page 289)

2 teaspoons finely ground unrefined sea salt

6 cups water, plus more as needed

3 pounds beets, peeled and chopped into ¹/₂-inch pieces

2 mandarin oranges (with the skin on), sliced into ¹/₄-inch-thick rounds

2 tablespoons peeled and freshly grated ginger

Pour the strained starter into a large pitcher, then whisk in the salt and water.

Put the beets, mandarins, and ginger in a 1-gallon fermentation crock. Pour in the liquid until the crock is full within 1 inch of its lip and the beets are completely submerged, adding additional water as necessary. Weigh the beets down with a sterilized stone, a glass or stoneware weight, or other utensil small enough to fit within your crock but heavy enough to act as a weight. Seal the crock and allow the *kvass* to ferment at room temperature for at least 7 days. Taste the *kvass*, and if you prefer a stronger or sourer flavor, continue fermenting for another week.

Strain the *kvass* and funnel it into pint-size flip-top bottles. Discard the mandarins, but reserve the beets, if you like, and serve them as you would a pickle or other fermented vegetable. Store the *kvass* in the refrigerator for up to 1 year, noting that it may thicken slightly as it ages.

glossary

All Natural / Naturally Grown: As it relates to growing practices, as opposed to animal husbandry, the terms "All Natural" and "Naturally Grown" are unregulated.

Artisan: Artisan refers to time-honored, traditional techniques of producing food. Artisan foods are produced by hand in very small quantities.

Beyond Organic: Beyond Organic is a term used by growers and ranchers to describe farming methods that not only meet the standards of the National Organic Program but exceed them; however, the term is not otherwise regulated.

Biodynamic: Biodynamic farming refers to a method of farming put forth by Rudolf Steiner of Waldorf and anthroposophy fame. Biodynamic farming regards the farm holistically, as one living organism rather than as a combination of isolated crops. While biodynamic farming includes organic farming methods, it also relies on the use of special composts and field preparations, as well as astronomical sowing, planting, and harvesting schedules.

Certified Farmers Market: A handful of states, including California, Texas, and Nevada, certify farmers markets. The certification process ensures that vendors at certified farmers markets actually produce what they sell and thus minimize peddling or brokering.

Certified Naturally Grown: Certified Naturally Grown (CNG) is a grassroots third-party certification program that offers small-scale farmers an alternative to the hefty fees and paperwork associated with Organic Certification. Farmers who are Certified Naturally Grown grow in accordance with organic methods and quite often exceed organic methods required by the National Organic Program. Farms are inspected by neighboring farmers, inspection reports are made available to the public, and all farms are subject to random testing for pesticide residue. Certified Naturally Grown is inexpensive for small-scale farmers and provides a comforting third-party reassurance to consumers.

Certified Organic / Organically Grown: Certified Organic is a USDA term that denotes foods and products that have been grown and processed in accordance with the standards of the National Organic Program (NOP). Such requirements require avoidance of synthetic inputs, including, but not limited to, synthetic fertilizers, synthetic pesticides, and food additives. Moreover, it disallows genetically modified organisms (GMOs) from being considered organic. Fields must be chemical-free for three or more years before qualifying as organic. This period is called "transitional." Organic certification also requires record keeping, field inspection, and considerable fees. Growers who sell $5,000 or less per year may call themselves "organic" and refer to their produce as "organically grown," but they may not refer to themselves as "Certified Organic."

Closed Herd: A closed herd means that all livestock are bred from the original herd, with no animals being purchased and introduced. Closed-herd operations offer a way to protect animals from potential pathogens introduced by purchased or leased animals.

Community Supported Agriculture (CSA): CSAs are a system by which consumers pay the farmer in advance for a portion of the year's produce. This system allows farmers to receive income when expenses for seeds and equipment are high prior to the start of the growing season, and few other avenues for income exist. CSAs also provide customers with a consistent amount of seasonal produce delivered by the farm each week for the duration of the growing season.

Conventional: Conventional, in reference to meats and animal foods, means that the animals were raised according to the standard practice in the industry. This standard of practice often includes the use of feed lots, battery cages, antibiotics, hormones, and a grain-based diet. In reference to produce, conventional refers to the practice of using chemical-based fertilizers, pesticides, and other inputs in growing crops.

Dry-Farmed: Dry farming techniques include the use of special tilling that reduces or eliminates the need for irrigation.

Farmstead Products: Farmstead refers to value-added products like wine, cider, cheese, jellies, and jams produced on the farm. The majority of ingredients used in farmstead products are produced on the farm.

Free Range: While similar to "pastured" or "meadow-raised," free range refers to animals that are not confined; however, this customarily means that animals are given access to the outdoors for an unspecified amount of time each day.

Genetically Modified / GE / GMO / GM: Genetically modified refers to crops whose gene structure has been altered through biotechnology. In this way, plants are altered through manipulation of their genes to have traits they would not naturally have (for example, resistance to certain pests). When genes from one species that exhibits a desired trait are inserted into the genetic code of another species, the resulting produce is considered genetically engineered. GM crops are permitted in conventional farming but disallowed in organic farming. Currently, ingredients sourced from genetically engineered crops do not require labeling in the United States, though a strong movement of activists seeks to push labeling nationally.

Grass Fed / Grass Finished: Grass fed refers to ruminant animals such as lamb, cows, bison, and elk that are fed a natural diet of fresh grass during growing season and hay or grass silage during winter months. They are fed this natural diet until slaughter. The term is not regulated.

Heirloom: Heirloom refers to plant varietals that are a minimum of 50 years old and that have been developed by farmers for their special traits, such as color, flavor, appearance, or suitability to microclimates. They are most often sold through direct marketing at farmstands and farmers markets but are increasingly available in health food stores and national chain grocery stores.

Herd Share: Similar to a CSA, a herd share allows consumers to purchase an interest or share in a herd of dairy cows or goats and then pay monthly boarding fees to the operator of the dairy. With meaningful legal ownership of a share of the herd, the consumer is then permitted to receive a portion of the raw milk the herd produces. Herd share arrangements are popular among raw milk consumers in states where the retail sale of raw milk is illegal; however, not all states recognize the legality of the herd share arrangement.

Heritage Breed: Heritage breeds refer to animals that have been bred over a long period of time and are well adapted to the local environment and often resistant to disease. These animals retain historical characteristics that are absent from breeds customarily used in conventional farming.

Holistic Management: Holistic management eschews systemic use of antibiotics and hormones while encouraging the prevention of disease through natural methods. Holistic management views animals, the land they graze, and the farm as a whole. With emphasis on proper and sustainable grazing techniques, holistically managed herds may actually reverse desertification and improve soil ecology. While the term is not regulated, discussing livestock management with your local rancher or cattle farmer may help to illuminate his or her practices.

Integrated Pest Management / IPM: Integrated Pest Management is a pest-control system in which a variety of techniques are used that strategically complement one another. Integrated Pest Management relies first upon prevention techniques, followed by close observation, and finally by intervention if necessary. Pesticides are used as a last resort, with other pest management techniques being implemented first.

Non-GMO / GMO-Free: Non-GMO and GMO-free are terms to describe foods that are not sourced from genetically engineered or biotech crops. While most foods are GMO-free, this term is usually applied only to those foods that are customarily produced from genetically modified seed.

Pastured / Pasture Fed / Meadow Raised: Pastured refers to omnivorous animals, such as poultry and hogs, that are raised on meadows and pastures instead of on conventional farms. Pastured and meadow-raised animals will graze on bugs and vegetable matter and are usually supplemented with a small amount of grain. While given access to shelter, pastured and meadow-raised animals are generally unconfined and fed a natural diet. The term is not regulated.

Producer-Only / Grower-Only Market: A producer-only farmers market is a market that disallows resell, peddling, and brokering. In short, all produce and goods sold at the market are represented by the people who produce them.

Raw: Raw refers to foods that have not been pasteurized by being heated to a minimum of 145°F for 30 minutes. Foods that are customarily pasteurized include milk and dairy products, fermented foods, and almonds. Some states prohibit the sale of these raw foods directly to the public.

Reseller / Broker / Peddler: A reseller is a vendor at a farmers market who sells product that he or she did not produce. The reseller purchases from the farmer or from a wholesaler and then sells purchased goods to consumers.

Transitional: Transitional refers to farms that are seeking Organic Certification, which requires that fields be free of synthetic fertilizers and pesticides for a minimum of 3 years. These years and the produce grown during these years are referred to as transitional.

#2 Produce / Seconds: The term seconds refers to produce that is visually unattractive or marred in some way and not ideal for sale at regular prices. Seconds may be misshapen, slightly scarred, overripe, underripe, blemished, too large, or too small. Seconds are often sold in bulk at a steep discount.

resources

Beans and Lentils

Adobe Milling
www.anasazibeans.com
Heirloom beans, including anasazi,
bolita, pinto, and turtle beans.

Purcell Mountain Farms
www.purcellmountainfarms.com
Heirloom beans and lentils, including
marrow, appaloosa, cannellini, cranberry
beans, Swedish brown beans, and others.

Cheesemaking Supplies

New England Cheesemaking Supply
www.cheesemaking.com
Supplier of cheese cultures, rennet,
cheesecloth, and butter muslin.

Fermented Food Starters

Cultures for Health
www.culturesforhealth.com
Thermophilic and mesophilic yogurt
starters, kefir grains, water kefir grains,
sourdough starters, and other fermentation supplies.

Kombucha Kamp
www.kombuchakamp.com
Kombucha mothers and water kefir grains.

Siggi's
www.siggis.com
Producer of traditional Icelandic skyr,
available in the dairy case at many
well-stocked health foods stores.

Fruits and Vegetables

Chaffin Family Orchards
www.chaffinfamilyorchards.com
Fifth-generation biodiverse family farm
selling mandarins, oranges, olives, and
olive oil.

La Vigne Organics
www.lavignefruits.com
Organic citrus fruits, including Meyer
lemons, blood oranges, oranges, and
kumquats.

Local Harvest
www.localhavest.org
Connections to local farms, farmers
markets, and CSAs.

Grains and Flours

Bluebird Grain Farms
www.bluebirdgrainfarms.com
Hard white wheat berries, hard red
wheat berries, emmer berries, rye
berries, and their flours.

Jovial Foods
www.jovialfoods.com
Einkorn wheat berries and
high-extraction einkorn flour.

King Arthur Flour
www.kingarthurflour.com
A wide variety of flours.

Shiloh Farms
www.shilohfarms.com
Sprouted whole grain flours and
other sprouted foods.

Sunrise Flour Mill
www.sunriseflourmill.com
Heirloom wheat and flour.

To Your Health Sprouted Flour
www.organicsproutedflour.net
Sprouted whole grain flours and
sprouted whole grains.

Grass-Fed Dairy

Ancient Organics
www.ancientorganics.com
Ghee from organic, grass-fed cows.

Campaign for Real Milk
www.realmilk.com
Listings of raw, grass-fed dairies.

James Ranch
www.jamesranch.net
Aged raw milk cheeses from grass-fed
Jersey cows.

Pure Indian Foods
www.pureindianfoods.com
Ghee from organic, grass-fed cows.

Grass-Fed and Pasture-Raised Meats

Eat Wild
www.eatwild.com
A listing of grass-fed and pasture-raised
meat producers.

Grass Roots Meats
www.grassrootsmeats.com
Grass-fed beef and lamb. Free-range
chicken.

Kol Foods
www.kolfoods.com
Grass-fed beef and lamb. Pasture-raised
chicken, turkey, and duck. Bones for broth
and fat to render.

Schlitz Foods
www.schlitzfoods.com
Goose, duck, pheasant, and capons,
as well as duck liver, goose liver, and
fatty goose liver.

US Wellness Meats
www.grasslandbeef.com
Grass-fed beef, certified humane pork,
chicken, and rabbit. Many varieties of
offal, bones for broth, chicken feet, and
beef suet.

Oils

Chaffin Family Orchards
www.chaffinfamilyorchards.com
Fifth-generation biodiverse family farm
selling a variety of mild olive oils, as
well as citrus fruits.

Euphoria Olive Oil
www.euphoriaoliveoil.com
Assertive and fruity Greek olive oils.

Flora
www.florahealth.com
Cold-pressed sunflower seed, pumpkin
seed, walnut, and other oils.

Green Pasture
www.greenpasture.org
Fermented cod liver oil, fermented skate
liver oil, and high-vitamin butter oil.

Jovial Foods
www.jovialfoods.com
Heirloom Italian olive oil.

Spices and Dried Herbs

Mountain Rose Herbs
www.mountainroseherbs.com
Organic and wild-crafted dried herbs,
teas, and spices.

Savory Spice Shop
www.savoryspiceshop.com
Wide variety of spices and dried herbs.

Sustainable Seafood

I Love Blue Sea
www.ilovebluesea.com
Sustainable seafood choices, including
wild-caught Alaskan salmon and halibut,
as well as oysters, clams, mussels, and
other shellfish.

Vital Choice
www.vitalchoice.com
Wild-caught Alaskan salmon, Oregon pink
shrimp, and other sustainable seafood
choices.

Sweeteners

Bee Raw Honey
www.beeraw.com
Raw single varietal honeys.

Grampa's Honey
www.grampashoney.com
Raw single varietal honeys.

Pure Indian Foods
www.pureindianfoods.com
Organic jaggery.

Rapunzel
www.rapunzel.de
Unrefined cane sugar and other whole
sweeteners.

Really Raw Honey
www.reallyrawhoney.com
Raw unfiltered honey and pollen.

real food advocacy groups

Farm-to-Consumer Legal Defense Fund
www.farmtoconsumer.org
Defending the rights of family farms and artisan food producers, while also defending consumers' right to access raw milk and other foods of their choice.

Marine Stewardship Council
www.msc.org
The Marine Stewardship Council maintains labeling standards for sustainably caught fish and seafoods and also certifies fisheries so that consumers can be better informed about the source of the seafoods they purchase.

Nourishing Our Children
www.nourishingourchildren.org
An educational initiative of the Weston A. Price Foundation, Nourishing Our Children is dedicated to teaching parents about the nutritional risks of the standard American diet, and to restoring the place of nutrient-dense, traditional foods that are crucial to the health of children.

Price-Pottenger Nutrition Foundation
www.ppnf.org
A not-for-profit educational organization dedicated to teaching the value of traditional diets for achieving health in the modern world.

Savory Institute
www.savoryinstitute.com
Dedicated to restoring the world's grasslands through holistic management and properly managed livestock.

Seafood Watch
www.seafoodwatch.org
A program of the Monterey Bay Aquarium that helps consumers make choices for healthy oceans by categorizing seafoods as "Best Choice," "Good Alternative," or "Avoid."

Slow Food USA
www.slowfoodusa.org
Slow Food is an educational organization devoted to reviving heritage breeds and heirloom seeds and cultivating the joy of food and the connection among farms, communities, and the environment.

Weston A. Price Foundation
www.westonaprice.org
The Weston A. Price Foundation is a not-for-profit organization dedicated to restoring nutrient-dense, traditional foods through public education, research, and activism.

measurement conversion charts

Volume

U.S.	IMPERIAL	METRIC
1 tablespoon	1/2 fl oz	15 ml
2 tablespoons	1 fl oz	30 ml
1/4 cup	2 fl oz	60 ml
1/3 cup	3 fl oz	90 ml
1/2 cup	4 fl oz	120 ml
2/3 cup	5 fl oz (1/4 pint)	150 ml
3/4 cup	6 fl oz	180 ml
1 cup	8 fl oz (1/3 pint)	240 ml
1 1/4 cups	10 fl oz (1/2 pint)	300 ml
2 cups (1 pint)	16 fl oz (2/3 pint)	480 ml
2 1/2 cups	20 fl oz (1 pint)	600 ml
1 quart	32 fl oz (1 2/3 pints)	1 l

Temperature

FAHRENHEIT	CELSIUS/GAS MARK
250°F	120°C/gas mark 1/2
275°F	135°C/gas mark 1
300°F	150°C/gas mark 2
325°F	160°C/gas mark 3
350°F	180 or 175°C/gas mark 4
375°F	190°C/gas mark 5
400°F	200°C/gas mark 6
425°F	220°C/gas mark 7
450°F	230°C/gas mark 8
475°F	245°C/gas mark 9
500°F	260°C

Length

INCH	METRIC
1/4 inch	6 mm
1/2 inch	1.25 cm
3/4 inch	2 cm
1 inch	2.5 cm
6 inches (1/2 foot)	15 cm
12 inches (1 foot)	30 cm

Weight

U.S./IMPERIAL	METRIC
1/2 oz	15 g
1 oz	30 g
2 oz	60 g
1/4 lb	115 g
1/3 lb	150 g
1/2 lb	225 g
3/4 lb	350 g
1 lb	450 g

acknowledgments

After countless hours spent researching and writing this cookbook, I find myself humbled by the grace and generosity of spirit of the many people who provided me with unwavering support during the last several years.

I wish to thank my husband for his warmth, his kindness, and his willingness to wipe up spills, sweep away crumbs, and wash dish after dish without complaint. I wish to thank my son who dutifully helped to style photographs and who took his job as a taste tester with fierce seriousness.

I wish to thank the many friends who provided support both in the kitchen and beyond it. I am thankful to Robin who drove to my kitchen on snowy mornings to test and retest recipes. And I am thankful to Justin and his family. When deadlines loomed, I knew I could count on him to connect me with farmers willing to open their fields to my camera lens.

I wish to thank the farmers and ranchers whose tireless work and commitment to restoring the Western landscape through sustainable methods has provided my family with food. I can only hope that my work is a tribute to theirs, if even in a small way. Thank you to Bill and Kelli of Parker Pastures and to Betsy, Jean, and Della of Circle A Gardens for feeding us these many years. Thank you to the countless other farmers who welcomed me into their homes, gardens, orchards, and fields.

I wish to thank the team at Ten Speed Press who saw opportunity in my work and *The Nourished Kitchen*. I am thankful, in particular, to my editors for their valuable and unique insight and wisdom, as well as for the patience and kindness they showed me. And I am thankful to Dianne Jacob for her guidance, and to Sally Ekus for her support throughout the project.

I wish to thank the Weston A. Price Foundation for its work in supporting and advocating for a return to traditional pathways in food, farming, and the healing arts. Thank you, too, to the Farm-to-Consumer Legal Defense Fund, an organization that works tirelessly to support the rights of both small farms and the consumers who wish to support them.

about the author

Jennifer McGruther is a food educator and the author and creator of the award-winning traditional foods website, Nourished Kitchen (www.nourishedkitchen.com). She teaches workshops on traditional foods, fermentation, and food activism. Jennifer lives with her husband and son in the central mountains of Colorado where she and her husband started and managed a farmers market for seven years. Her work emphasizes traditional, from-scratch cooking with a focus on farm-to-table recipes.

index

To my husband and my son,
whom I love very deeply.

Text and photographs copyright © 2014
by Jennifer McGruther

Published in the United States by Ten Speed Press, an imprint
of the Crown Publishing Group, a division of Random House LLC,
a Penguin Random House Company, New York.
www.crownpublishing.com
www.tenspeed.com

Ten Speed Press and the Ten Speed Press colophon are registered
trademarks of Random House LLC

Library of Congress Cataloging-in-Publication Data is on file
with the publisher.

Trade Paperback ISBN: 978-1-60774-468-9
eBook ISBN: 978-1-60774-469-6

Printed in China

Design by Chloe Rawlins

10 9 8 7 6 5 4 3 2 1

First Edition